LEARNING TO SMOKE

Jason Hughes

LEARNING TO
SMOKE

TOBACCO USE IN THE WEST

The University of Chicago Press / Chicago and London

Jason Hughes is lecturer in the Centre for Labour
Market Studies at the University of Leicester.

The University of Chicago Press, Chicago 60637
The University of Chicago Press, Ltd., London
© 2003 by The University of Chicago
All rights reserved. Published 2003
Printed in the United States of America

12 11 10 09 08 07 06 05 04 03   1 2 3 4 5
ISBN: 0-226-35910-7 (cloth)

Library of Congress Cataloging-in-Publication Data

Hughes, Jason.
    Learning to smoke : tobacco use in the West/Jason
Hughes.
        p. cm.
    Includes bibliographical references and index.
    ISBN 0-226-35910-7 (hardcover : alk. paper)
    1. Tobacco habit—History.   2. Smoking—His-
tory.   I. Title.
    HV5730.H84 2003
    613.85′09—dc21

                                    2002005315

For my parents, Allan and Elisabeth Hughes,
and for my sisters, Kahryn, Colette, and Jo-Ann.

Contents

Preface

There is a story behind my interest in tobacco use. As a twenty-one-year-old sociology major at Leicester University, I needed to come up with a topic for my undergraduate dissertation. I sat in the students' café, drinking a coffee and smoking a cigarette—as I frequently did between lectures. "I know," I thought (exhaling tobacco smoke). "I'm going to do something on artists and their art . . . on how an artist's background is reflected by his or her work of art . . . on how class, gender, ethnicity, and so on can be inferred from *reading* art." I remember punctuating my thinking with drags on my cigarette and sips of my coffee. Then I changed my mind. "No, it's probably been done . . . no, there's a whole subject area—the history of art, perhaps—that must look into precisely those kinds of questions." And then I considered what I was doing at that moment. I held up the cigarette and thought, "What about this? Can a sociologist research smoking? *Have* sociologists researched smoking?" To find out, I conducted a computer-based literature search of holdings in the university library, using the search term "smoking sociology." Very little came up on the screen: a few studies that examined the relationship between the levels of smoking and social class; some diagnostic research on the incidence of cigarette smoking among children in different geographical regions; political/legal discussions; that kind of thing. Next I changed the parameters of the search, this time to just one word—*smoking*. Of course, I got thousands of hits, but these query results lay mostly in the fields of clinical psychology and medicine. I was not surprised by this outcome, but it became more intriguing when I started to think about smoking *sociologically*. There were literally *masses* of sources pursuing highly specific topics: "Do smokers of lower tar cigarettes consume lower amounts of smoke components?"; "Smoking and pulmonary function in five Solomon Island populations"; "Development and psychometric evaluation of the primary appraisal of smoking cessation inventory"; and so on. I wondered how I could possibly contribute to this already vast body of literature.

At about this time, I was introduced to the work of Norbert Elias by my sociological theory lecturer, Eric Dunning. To illustrate one of Elias's key concepts, lengthening chains of interdependence, Eric described the breakfast he'd had that morning: coffee from Colombia, orange juice from Florida, butter from New Zealand. He was making the point that even something as routine as breakfast required a lengthy network of mutual dependence: just as he was dependent on transporters, growers, grocers, shelf stackers, and others for his breakfast, so were they, to varying degrees, on his purchasing and consuming their products. Consequently, a thought occurred to me: what better example of these chains of interdependence was there than cigarettes? As with Eric's breakfast, smoking involves a vast chain of interdependence, in this case among tobacco producers, cigarette manufacturers and transporters, and the regulators of those industries and the consumption of tobacco. Thus it was no accident that my Marlboros contained a specific amount of nicotine and tar that was clearly listed, along with the warning that "Smoking Kills," on the pack. On the basis of my preliminary understanding of the history of tobacco use, the packaging, design, and form of the cigarettes in front of me were all apparently related, at least in part, to a long-term shift in the power relations among governments, tobacco producers, tobacco consumers, and the medical profession.

These findings led me to ask myself why I felt the "need" to smoke, particularly when thinking or concentrating—was this simply a biological urge? Or were there also more social or psychological reasons for my behavior? As a sociologist, I was immediately suspicious of the distinctions to which I was subscribing. For me, the exciting thing about Elias's sociology was that it tried to move beyond these kinds of divisions; beyond thinking of the biological, the social, and the psychological as separate entities. So it was at this point that I had found both my question for research and my approach toward it: Why do people smoke?, to be investigated at not just the biological level but also the social and psychological ones, among others—and at the *hinge* between these (Elias 2000).

Why do people smoke? was a *weighty* question, but, I soon realized, not a very good one, particularly for a ten-thousand-word undergraduate dissertation—it needed refining. I told a friend about my dissertation plans, for I knew she would provide me with useful feedback. "Why do you want to research smoking?" she challenged. "That's a bit anemic—uncontroversial."

I'd already been thinking and reading about the topic for some time, so I'd gathered enough material to muster a defense. Taking the moral high ground, I mentioned that it was the leading cause of preventable disease in Europe, that it was the ultimate in commodity fetishism, a "false need"; she was a little more convinced. When I told her the question I would be pursuing, her response was, "That's not a question for a sociologist." I knew she had a point; the question definitely needed reformulating for it to suit my purposes (I will discuss *how* in the introduction to this book). However, through further discussion with my friend it emerged that her objection was based on the assumption that the answer to my question could not be obtained through sociological inquiry, that surely it was a question for the clinical sciences. My feeling, however, was that sociology—perhaps better, a sociology that aimed to move beyond treating biopharmacological and social-psychological levels of tobacco use as separate entities—might indeed have something to offer. My intention was not to take on the clinical sciences in learning why people smoke but rather to explore what an interdisciplinary, developmental approach to the subject might be able to contribute to the existing knowledge in this area. The undergraduate dissertation through which I first pursued this area of interest eventually formed the basis for a doctoral thesis (completed in 1997), which, in turn, eventually formed the basis for this book.

When I tell people how I became interested in researching smoking, I very often get asked whether I have subsequently stopped using tobacco. I know this question is posed partly as a joke, as if to test the integrity of my research and ideas. I *have* stopped. I used to smoke nearly forty cigarettes a day. I stopped from one day to the next. At the time of this writing, I have not had a puff for ten years, partly as a result of the research that I conducted for the undergraduate dissertation. For that project I reviewed the stop-smoking literature. One book in particular—Allen Carr's *The Easy Way to Stop Smoking*—was excellent; it helped me to approach smoking cessation in a way very different from the methods discussed in many of the other self-help books that were then available. The book's emphasis on stopping without the use of nicotine patches or other such devices, and on thinking about smoking differently, reinforced for me the importance of also taking seriously the social-psychological aspect of tobacco use. Perhaps, therefore, my having stopped smoking is more of a testimony to Carr's book than it is to my own research. Nonetheless, I do very much hope that the arguments presented herein will contribute to our understanding of tobacco use by indicating new directions for research into the subject area, more successful policy interventions, and, indeed, more effective smoking cessation strategies.

For the reader who wishes to begin with a quick sense of my arguments, I would suggest reading the introduction—particularly the synopsis I present at the end of it; the overall conclusion to the first three chapters of the book that I present toward the end of chapter 3; and the conclusion to the book as a whole.

Acknowledgments

First and foremost I would like to thank Professor Eric Dunning. Since my years as an undergraduate at the University of Leicester, Eric has been a source of academic inspiration, motivation, critical discussion, and very good quality red wine. He has had an enormous influence on my thinking as a sociologist and the development of my academic career. Eric is a truly great teacher and academic, and an excellent friend. I owe him at least a thousand fish meals!

I would also like to acknowledge the fantastic support that I received from everyone at the Centre for Labour Market Studies, University of Leicester. In particular, I thank Johnny Sung, David Ashton, John Goodwin, Katharine Hills, Patrick Baughan, Sally Walters, and Henrietta O'Connor.

I extend my gratitude to my family for all of their support and encouragement. In particular, I am indebted to my sister Kahryn Hughes for her direct help with writing the book, for stimulating my thinking, and for pointing me in directions that I would not have otherwise pursued.

Many thanks also to Howard Becker, Stephen Mennell, Ivan Waddington, Cas Wouters, Anne Murcott, Joe Gusfield, Sandy Hazel, and Nick Jewson, for their guidance and advice on writing this book.

Finally, thanks to everyone whose friendship, support, motivation, help, and other contributions have made this book possible, especially Helen Riley, Jane Riley, Fiona Harris, Stephen Joy, Simon Masters, Beata Michaluk, Simon Fox, Astrid Buhrow, John Goodacre, Joanne Harmer, Robert Ash, Lucy Dobey, Nikki Vallings, Louise Rigby, Arwen Raddon, Anne Colling, and all of the people who participated in the research.

Introduction

Why People Smoke:

A Question for Sociologists?

Why do people smoke? This is at once an interesting and a flawed question. It is a question that has been pursued extensively by clinicians but not by sociologists. As we shall see, this might simply be indicative of the dominance in present-day Western[1] thinking of medical understandings of tobacco use. According to such understandings, the "answer" to this question is understood to be already available: people smoke primarily because they are addicted to nicotine. Alternatively, perhaps this circumstance relates to the question's flaw: it almost begs for a "totalizing" answer—as though there might exist an essential, generic explanation that merely awaits discovery.

The sociologist, characteristically, would be suspicious of any question that needs an essential explanation that is blind to the differences between people. Instead, sociologists have historically tended to use this question about smoking as an issue around which particular understandings of social difference can be illustrated, such as the relationship between smoking, social class, and women's lives (Graham 1992). In effect, sociological studies have tended to reformulate the question Why do people smoke? so that it might variously read, Why are women more likely to smoke than men?; Why are members of social class X more likely to smoke than those of social class Y?; and so forth. However, in so doing, many of these studies have effectively sidestepped addressing the question directly, and leave unchallenged dominant understandings of smoking. For example, part of Graham's (1992) thesis involves linking smoking to class through the issue of stress (to over-

1. Throughout this book I have used the terms *Western* and *West*. These terms refer less to geographical location than to the sociocultural "type" of a society.

simplify somewhat): since smoking is in the present-day West widely understood to be a stress reliever, and since disadvantaged lives are more stressful, it follows that people from disadvantaged backgrounds are more likely to smoke.

With this book, I intend to depart from existing sociological studies in this area by attempting to tackle head-on the historical emergence of dominant understandings of the "why people smoke" question, including the more recent ones in which smoking is considered an inherently stress-relieving activity. My central aim is to reframe both this question and its "answers" partly through an investigation of the long-term development of tobacco use in the West. In this connection, the main questions to be pursued are as follows:

- How and to what extent have understandings of tobacco use changed over time and in different cultures?
- How and to what extent have these understandings mediated experiences of tobacco use and of being a tobacco user?
- How and to what extent have tobacco and patterns of its use changed over time and in different cultures?
- How and to what extent are these processes of change linked to broader long-term social processes?
- How and to what extent can an analysis of the long-term development of tobacco use inform our understandings of the practice, and, ultimately, point toward more successful intervention strategies?

This book contains two main sections. The first (chapters 1–3) involves an analysis, based on extensive documentary research, of the long-term development of tobacco use in the West and elsewhere by considering the practice among Native American peoples before and after their initial contact with European colonizers. I trace transformations in understandings of tobacco use: from its role as a hallucinogen in shamanistic ritual among Native American peoples, and its widespread status as a panacea in much of sixteenth- and early-seventeenth century Europe, to its current popular status as a pandemic—an addictive disease that spans the globe. My aim is to build an understanding of these long-term paradigmatic shifts by considering their relationship to broader-scale social processes.

The second section of the book (chapter 4) examines tobacco use at the level of individuals. Through a discussion of research in which a number of tobacco users' biographies were collected, I consider the processes involved in becoming a smoker. Central themes explored include the relationship between understandings and experiences of tobacco use and personal identity, life changes, and the broader processes of change discussed in the first three chapters of the book.

As I am a sociologist, it follows that reference is made throughout this book to sociology: both sociological approaches, and questions that have been formulated sociologically. However, my intention in writing this book has not been to reach solely a sociological audience. I have tried to presume no previous knowledge of sociology on the part of the reader, and I have tried not to dwell too extensively on points of sociological debate and general theoretical discussion. Where I have used sociological concepts, I have explicated these. Thus my intention, quite consciously, has been to write a book that has appeal beyond a narrow academic specialty. Indeed, a central aim of the book is to escape the confines of disciplinary boundaries, and to explore the merits of an open, interdisciplinary approach to the subject of smoking.

My intention is to promote a holistic understanding of tobacco use: one that focuses on the dynamic interplay of processes occurring at what we currently label as social-psychological and bio-pharmacological levels, which, I shall argue, together constitute the experience of tobacco use. I aim both to be critical of, and to draw upon, clinical understandings of the practice. It is this interdisciplinary, holistic approach to the topic that, I hope, will constitute the distinctive contribution of this book.

An astounding number of texts on tobacco use have been produced. Most have a clinical-psychological or medical orientation to the subject matter, such as pharmacological analyses and epidemiological studies.[2] Others focus on tobacco use within broader social contexts: in this I would include a number of social-historical studies, and texts that concentrate on the political and legal debates over the advertising, consumption, and marketing of tobacco products. In what follows, I shall briefly discuss some of the key texts that have informed and influenced this book, and outline how I intend to build upon these.

Starting Points for This Book

One of the most important and comprehensive historical texts on tobacco use is Jordan Goodman's *Tobacco in History: The Cultures of Dependence* (1993). Goodman provides a rich, coherent, and detailed account of tobacco: its emergence as a commodity, and a social history of its use (upon which I draw extensively, particularly in chapters 1 and 2 of this book). The

---

2. It is interesting to note that both the activity of smoking and smoking-related diseases have come to be understood and labeled as an epidemic.

central objectives of Goodman's research are to explore and to understand the processes underlying the current ubiquity of tobacco use in so many societies across the globe. Where many texts adopt a present-centered standpoint, Goodman's position (and mine) is that the tobacco phenomenon has a "profoundly historical dimension that is much more than simply a background to contemporary issues" (Goodman 1993: 24). Goodman (quoting here from the work of Goodin [1989: 574, 587]) points toward some important shifts in understandings of tobacco use:

> [T]he identification of nicotine as an addictive drug has led to a change in the image of the smoker and the appropriation of a lexicon typically reserved for addicts of hard drugs. Moreover, it has also led to a restoration of the concept of tobacco use as a disease in itself, partly by a change of language, introducing for example, words such as "nicotinism" and "tobacconism." In other words nicotine addicts are seen as needing help to quit (as most smokers attempt to do more than once in their smoking life); and the act of smoking is no longer portrayed as a 'private-regarding vice' but rather as a serious addiction. ". . . [O]nce you have become addicted to nicotine, your subsequent smoking cannot be taken as indicating your consent to the risks." (Goodman 1993: 243)

Considering the above passage in isolation, it would appear that Goodman may wish to keep a critical distance from contemporary conceptions of smoking as an addiction. However, this is not the case. In fact, he consistently subscribes to the present-day "addict lexicon." Indeed, Goodman's central argument is that tobacco generates a culture of *dependence* among all who are associated with it. He writes, "[T]he history of tobacco is full of conflict, compromise, coercion and co-operation. It is through this historical process that tobacco has become a universal addiction for consumers, for growers and for governments" (Goodman 1993: 14).

It is not Goodman's intention to explore further the significance of these statements, in which he discusses a change in the smoker's image, the restoration of the concept of smoking as a "disease," the move toward understanding tobacco use as a "serious addiction," and so on. However, in this book I will explore how the changes that he indicates have emerged in relation to other long-term processes, such as civilization and medicalization (more on these terms later). Moreover, a central theme in this book is the examination of how such changing understandings profoundly mediate the experience of tobacco use itself. This endeavor involves a break with conventional explanations of the practice, which stress only its biological dimensions. Goodman's analysis remains underpinned by such an explanation. Indeed, this is something about which he is explicit:

> There are two facts about nicotine which are now irrefutable but which, until recently, were not confirmed. They are: first, that people consume tobacco in whatever form in order to administer nicotine to themselves; and second, that "tobacco use is regular and compulsive, and a withdrawal syndrome usually accompanies tobacco abstinence." (Goodman 1993: 5)

Looking beyond solely the biological level in accounting for why people smoke opens up a range of possibilities for how understandings of tobacco use might be developed. An excellent model in this connection is provided by Howard Becker in his classic 1963 essay, "Becoming a Marijuana User."

In this essay, Becker depicts the "career" of a marijuana user. The first stage of this career involves learning the smoking technique. Novices do not usually get high on their first smoke; several attempts are normally necessary. They first need to learn the most effective techniques from other members of their social group. Through direct teaching by others, or through indirect learning (such as observing and mimicking other users), novices learn how to hold the smoke in their lungs for as long as possible. Without this technique, Becker suggests, marijuana produces minimal effects, making it unlikely that users would progress to further stages of their "careers."

The next stage involves learning to perceive the drug's effects, which are initially somewhat ambiguous. For a high to be achieved, two elements are required: the presence of effects from marijuana consumption and the interpretation and recognition of these by the user. Users must be able to identify the results upon themselves and consciously connect these with having smoked marijuana, before a state of "high" can be achieved. New users respond to cues from other members of the group in order to ascertain what they are supposed to experience. In every case of continued use in Becker's study, users had acquired the necessary cues with which to express to themselves that they were experiencing new sensations induced by the drug.

Continued marijuana use, Becker proposes, is further dependent on users learning to perceive the drug's effects as pleasurable. The taste for marijuana is a socially learned one, and not greatly different from the acquired taste for dry martinis or oysters. It is equally possible to perceive the drug's effects as extremely uncomfortable. As Becker states, "The user often feels dizzy or thirsty; his [sic] scalp tingles; he misjudges time and distances. Are these things [inherently] pleasurable?" (1963: 53)

Many comparisons can be drawn between the "career" of a marijuana user and that of a tobacco user. The cigarette smoker goes through a similar process: first, a good deal of effort is required to learn how to smoke.[3] Novices must learn to inhale the smoke without coughing, they often feel dizzy and nauseated, they learn the socially "correct" way to hold the cigarette[4] and to exhale the smoke, and so on. Second, the "effects" of the cigarette, like those of marijuana, are open to interpretation (in this connection, I shall shortly be examining the debate over the "biphasic"[5] action of nicotine). In particular instances the cigarette is said by many present-day Western smokers to pick them up; in others, to calm them down.

Moreover, as novices start to become smokers they draw upon contemporary understandings of smoking. Characteristically, smokers learn to use tobacco as a psychological tool. They may draw upon associations with the bohemian academic woman who, half starved, smoking large quantities of tobacco, produces beautiful work from the chaos of her life. They may begin to use tobacco as a reward, to punctuate their speech, to aid concentration, or, perhaps, to articulate their distress. Or, they may associate with the single mother who, surrounded by screaming children, carves out areas of the day in which she can relax: the cigarette calms her down, rewards her patience, helps to control her mood.

Smokers may switch between drawing upon these and a multitude of other images and associations from prevailing understandings of tobacco use. What is important to recognize is the crucial role that smokers have in the *construction* and *maintenance* of what is variously understood to be their dependence or addiction—that smokers are not simply receiving cues at a biological level. In chapter 4 of this book I draw upon Becker's model as part of the discussion of "Becoming a Smoker." He focused primarily on the influence of group-level understandings on experiences of marijuana use. The discussion presented in the present text goes a step further by considering the influence of much broader-scale social processes on experiences of tobacco use. What I also aim to show is how the patterns of use described above—tobacco as a psychological tool, as a stress reliever, as a boredom breaker—are most characteristic of present-day cigarette smokers; such patterns contrast quite starkly with those of early European tobacco consumers, and even more dramatically with those of traditional Native American users.

3. For the purposes of this example I shall concentrate only on cigarette smoking; different patterns of behavior are associated with different media of consumption.

4. There are many variants. For example, the Russian technique involves gripping the cigarette between the thumb and forefinger, whereas in the West it is more common to grip the cigarette between the first and index fingers.

5. In one instance nicotine is said to act as a sedative; in others, as a stimulant. These apparently contradictory effects are clinically described as *biphasic*.

Such observations are used to show how understandings of tobacco use as, essentially, a generic set of processes related to nicotine dependency are oversimplistic and too static.

My intention in this book is not to challenge clinical models of tobacco use on, for instance, the importance of nicotine as a pharmacological agent, but rather to explore how such models might be developed. We might, for example, define human consciousness itself as fundamentally a particular form of electrochemical activity. However, this would give us very little insight into consciousness and the specific kind of awareness to which this term refers. Proceeding from this definition, investigations seeking to understand consciousness, while not fruitless, would be limited. They would inevitably search for the nature of this electrochemical activity—its essential characteristics and dynamics. In the same way, to reduce the experience of tobacco use simply to processes occurring at a biological level is to have a somewhat partial and limited account of the practice. It is not so much that prevailing clinical accounts of tobacco use ignore social-psychological dimensions to the practice; rather, it is that these dimensions are not properly incorporated into their explanatory models. Such is the case with another key text that has informed this book: Heather Ashton and Rob Stepney's *Smoking Psychology and Pharmacology* (1982).

Ashton and Stepney begin their study with a brief historical analysis, which, they propose, contextualizes contemporary patterns of smoking. Their main focus is on the pharmacological properties of tobacco and the physiological effects that are seen to be "induced" by consuming it. Their secondary focus is on psychological and, to a much lesser degree, social aspects of smoking. They examine, for example, relationships between smoking behavior and personality. The text provides a useful overview of debates relating to understanding smoking, and examines in some detail the various current explanations of the activity.

Ashton and Stepney's model of tobacco use is remarkably similar to that contained within the previously cited extract from Goodman:

> It is . . . our thesis that the use of cigarettes can best be understood when viewed as a means of nicotine self-administration. In this way, the unique role of tobacco and the prevalence of inhalation can be explained, together with the fact that smokers habitually take into their bodies quantities of the drug sufficient to have important effects on the brain and behaviour. (Ashton and Stepney 1982: ix)

As can be observed from this extract, in Ashton and Stepney's analysis tobacco is more or less equated with nicotine. This starting point informs the rest of their analysis: tobacco use is stylistically reduced to, essentially, the action of nicotine on "the body." [6] But tobacco itself should not be considered a "given" in terms of its effects on "the body"; as we shall see, the range of psychoactive alkaloids present in consumed tobacco, and the proportional yield of these, varies a great deal historically. For example, there are significant differences in this respect between the species and varieties commonly used by Native American peoples prior to their contact with Europeans and those widely used in the present-day West. The average cigarette smoked today yields, relative to earlier forms of tobacco/modes of consumption, much lower quantities of nicotine. A central theme in this book is to show how shifts in the form of tobacco and popular modes of its consumption relate to a range of long-term social processes, not simply to concerns about the ill-health effects of tobacco use. Moreover, while nicotine self-administration is, of course, a crucially important aspect of tobacco use, an examination of the changing social patterns of "administration"—how much nicotine is consumed, in conjunction with which other psychoactive alkaloids, how frequently, and so forth—has profound implications for our understandings of why people smoke.

Furthermore, a central problem with the nicotine self-administration model is that it reduces social-psychological dimensions of tobacco use to, at best, a secondary level—as though they were not really an essential part of the practice. The limitations associated with this tendency are most apparent in Ashton and Stepney's discussion of the biphasic properties of nicotine. To elaborate: if you were to ask a present-day cigarette smoker to describe the effects of smoking, he or she might have difficulty articulating these to you. Instead, a range of feelings, such as relaxation, stimulation, and enhanced concentration, might be given. For the clinical researcher, the question emerges of how to account for this range of seemingly contradictory effects from what is understood to be essentially one main psychoactive agent: nicotine. The term *biphasic* literally refers to its two-phase action: in one instance it acts as a depressant; in another, a stimulant. Ashton and Stepney's proposal is that the overall effect of nicotine is dependent on the dose administered:

> The initial combination of nicotine with the ACh[7] receptor at first stimu-
> lates an ACh-like response, but the fixity of the drug/receptor combina-

6. I place this term within quotation marks because I wish to distance myself from the idea of a universal, generic human body.

7. ACh (acetylcholine) is a chemical neurotransmitter. It conveys information from one nerve cell to another. Nicotine has a molecular structure that is similar to acetylcholine and thus behaves in a similar way to a neurotransmitter (Ashton and Stepney 1982: 36).

tion then blocks any further response to ACh (or to more nicotine). The degree of stimulation versus block depends on the amount of nicotine present relative to the number of available ACh receptors: in general small doses of nicotine produce a predominantly stimulant effect at synapses,[8] larger doses produce a mainly depressant effect, while the effect of a lethal dose is to block nervous transmission altogether. . . . Depending on factors such as the size of the puff, the depth of inhalation and the individual sensitivity of the subject's receptors, a smoker can get a predominantly inhibitory or a predominantly excitatory effect—or indeed a mixture of both effects—from one cigarette. The ease with which nicotine can produce rapid, reversible, biphasic effects over a small dose range is a . . . remarkable characteristic which singles it out from most other drugs. (Ashton and Stepney 1982: 38–39)

To clarify: nicotine has a similar molecular structure to acetylcholine (ACh)—one of the human "body's" main neurotransmitters. On reaching a gap between nerve cells (a synapse), nicotine (like ACh) bridges the synapse by combining with the next cell's ACh receptor, initially generating a stimulant effect. Depending on the size of the dose, nicotine combines with the ACh receptor with proportionately greater strength than its ACh counterpart, reaching a point where it partially blocks full response to more ACh or nicotine, thus generating a depressant effect. Depending on the size and frequency of the dose, the effects of the drug can come on and wear off between puffs.

While I do not wish to take issue with Ashton and Stepney's account of how nicotine acts on the central nervous system, this analysis—chosen precisely because it is characteristic of clinical models of tobacco use—is inadequate in that it completely lacks a social-psychological dimension. The smoker is objectified in this account, almost as though the processes of feeling and experience in relation to smoking begin and end at a purely biological level. Such a model ignores how smokers themselves have an active and crucial role in shaping the experience of smoking. While Ashton and Stepney examine social and psychological factors in tobacco use more extensively than many of their counterparts, the dynamic interplay between these and bio-pharmacological levels is neglected. Indeed, quite often,

8. A synapse is an infinitesimal gap between the end of one nerve fiber and the next nerve cell. When a nerve is excited, the initial response takes the form of an electrical impulse, which carries the message to the end of the nerve fiber. When the electrical impulse reaches the "synaptic cleft," the neurotransmitter (normally acetylcholine) bridges this gap and causes a chemical reaction with the next cell's ACh receptor, thus serving as a messenger to pass on information carried in the nerves (Ashton and Stepney 1982: 36).

social-psychological factors are simply reduced to biological processes. Furthermore, these factors are not studied developmentally: the processes to which Ashton and Stepney refer are assumed to be generic, universal to the history of tobacco. As shall be seen, a central theme in this book is that Ashton and Stepney's observations regarding the effect of nicotine at the physiological level can be viewed as characteristic of a relatively recent stage of the development of tobacco use in the West. I aim to show how, over time, there has been a *gradual* move toward the pattern of tobacco use that Ashton and Stepney assume as given in their models of the practice—a pattern involving the frequent administration of nicotine over a small dose range—which, in turn, relates to long-term shifts in the purpose for which tobacco is being used. I also aim to explore the implications of this observation for our understanding of smoking behavior.

To demonstrate how I intend to build upon the work of Ashton and Stepney, and to provide an example of the interplay between the bio-pharmacological and social-psychological levels of tobacco use to which I refer above (rather statically, for the moment), I would like briefly to explore one of the models of smoking dependence they identify—they label it the addiction model. According to this example, the nicotine contained within an average cigarette is fully metabolized very rapidly, after approximately thirty minutes (which suggests why most smokers consume approximately twenty cigarettes per day). After all the nicotine from a cigarette is metabolized, the smoker normally experiences withdrawal symptoms—feelings that may be experienced as tension, insecurity, emptiness, and general discomfort. Consequently, these symptoms usually serve as a cue for the smoker to have the next cigarette.

However, withdrawal syndrome is not merely a biological "trigger"; it must be recognized by the smoker as being associated with tobacco abstinence. The biological cues thus combine with the smoker's own perception that she should be smoking—for use as a psychological tool, for reward, or for whatever reason. This scenario is not as unproblematic as it might initially appear. It is possible, for instance, to confuse these cues with hunger pangs or emotional arousal. Furthermore, as we shall see, if the smoker finds that he is out of cigarettes or in an area where smoking is prohibited, the cues commonly intensify. The conscious recognition of cues, then, is a crucial part of the process of withdrawal. A simple observation can be used to support this line of argument. It would be most unusual for a smoker to awaken at thirty-minute intervals in order to smoke a cigarette. Or, for another example, ex-smokers who have not consumed tobacco for ten years or more—the residual nicotine having completely left their bodies—will still sometimes feel withdrawal symptoms after meals or on social occasions such as weddings.

After the smoker experiences withdrawal symptoms, the addiction model maintains, a new intake of nicotine will relieve the tension, insecurity, and other negative feelings brought on by abstinence. However, it is this experience of relief that is ambiguous. It can be interpreted in a number of ways, as a "pick me up" or a "calm me down"—as a stimulant or a sedative. This duality may be related to the function that the cigarette is being used to serve, which is in turn related to the prevailing understandings of tobacco use. As we shall see in chapter 4, present-day Western smokers adopt a range of strategies to manipulate the effects of tobacco consumption. For example, smokers may vary the dose by inhaling more deeply and taking more puffs at times of stress, thereby influencing the effects generated. Alternatively, she may purposely prolong abstinence from smoking in order to experience greater feelings of relief on smoking the next cigarette. The point I am making is that smokers and the larger groups in which they are involved play a very important role in producing and reproducing the experience of using tobacco.[9] In this way, the human body is not simply a biological surface upon which nicotine can act: the effects of tobacco consumption are interpreted, shaped, and mediated through a broader set of social-psychological processes. In short, a great deal is missing from our understandings of the "why people smoke" question if the experience of tobacco use is explained solely in terms of the pharmacological action of nicotine.

Thus, conceptually speaking, the distinctive starting points for this book can be summarized as follows:

- a shift from focusing solely on nicotine and nicotine administration to a broader investigation of tobacco and tobacco use and of how both change over time;
- a move away from an exclusive emphasis on bio-pharmacological processes to an examination of the dynamic interplay between these and social-psychological processes;
- a move away from a focus on effects toward a preoccupation with experiences of tobacco use, and an analysis of the extent and manner in which shifting understandings mediate these; and
- a departure from static models, which attempt to explain, universally, why people smoke toward a dynamic model of tobacco use

9. However, this does not lead me to conclude that smokers smoke simply out of free choice. That smokers play an active role in the construction and maintenance of their addiction does not make this addiction any the less compelling.

that reframes the question as I have outlined at the beginning of this chapter.

Outline of the Book and Synopsis of Main Arguments

This book is divided into four chapters. The premise for chapter 1, "Tobacco Use among Native American Peoples," is that it would be misleading to consider the development of tobacco use in the West as having an absolute starting point, as though it began with the introduction of tobacco seeds and leaves in Europe in the sixteenth century. This part of the book thus examines tobacco use among indigenous Americans before and after contact with European colonizers. My aim is to demonstrate how an understanding of tobacco use among Native American peoples is, in turn, crucial to understanding the development of tobacco use in the West. In this connection, I use this chapter to trace a number of processes that are of central importance to my arguments throughout. I show how tobacco use among Native American peoples involved the use of much stronger strains of tobacco than those used widely in the present-day West. I aim to illustrate that such consumption was, in turn, intrinsically linked to Native American understandings of tobacco, in which the plant was seen to be sacred, central to communication with the spirit world, and an important symbol of masculine strength. I describe how tobacco was used by Native Americans in ways fundamentally different from present-day Western cigarette smokers—in ways frequently involving a loss of control, acute intoxication, even hallucinogenic trances. I explore how these users experienced tobacco use and being a tobacco user, and how their experiences, in turn, were mediated by their understandings of, and shaped via rituals relating to, the practice. Finally, I explore how tobacco-using practices, understandings, and experiences changed after Native American contact with Europeans. I aim to elucidate an overall direction to these changes, and to propose that this is in fact characteristic of the long-term development of tobacco use in the West.

Chapter 2, "Tobacco Use and Humoral Bodies," further explores this direction of change in the long-term development of tobacco use. It traces developments of the practice, from the introduction of tobacco into Europe during the sixteenth century through to the emergence of cigarette smoking in the early twentieth century. I begin the chapter by considering how it was possible for tobacco to be transferred successfully between sharply contrasting sociocultural environments. A central theme I explore is how the understandings, uses, and experiences of tobacco were influenced by prevailing humoral conceptions of health and of "the body." I trace a number of broad shifts in tobacco use: from its initial use as primarily a medicinal remedy, to the pipe-sharing characteristic of a smoking *Gemeinschaft,* through to snuff taking, then cigar smoking, and, finally, early cigarette smoking. At the simplest level, I argue that the development of tobacco use in this period is characterized by increasing levels of regulation. I account for this increased regulation and many of the other processes observed by exploring their relationship to broader scale social processes of "civilization" in the sense that Elias (2000) used this term.

In this connection, I explore the further move away from the use of tobacco to lose control and the move toward its use in more controlled, differentiated, and individualized ways. I examine the rise of tobacco as an instrument of self-control and, in relation to this, changes in the form of tobacco, the mode of its consumption, and the function of its use. I suggest that while the tobacco widely used in early European societies was considerably milder than that used in traditional Native American practices, it was significantly stronger than present-day species and varieties. I show how tobacco was initially compared to alcohol through terms such as *dry drunks* and *tobacco drinkers*. I argue that this comparison was made not simply because no other model for the practice existed at the time, but because the tobacco used then, particularly given the mode of its consumption, actually was capable of intoxicating users to a degree more closely approximating that of alcohol than present-day equivalents. Furthermore, I show, particularly in relation to the rise of the cigarette, that the development of tobacco use in the West has over the long term been characterized by the increasing consumption of milder, less potent strains and forms of tobacco, and an associated move toward modes of consumption that yield less of the psychoactive alkaloids that they contain. I propose that these changes in the form and use of tobacco were intimately related to the function that tobacco was used to serve. That is to say, this overall decrease in the potency of consumed tobacco resulted in a corresponding increase in the ambiguity, vagueness, and malleability of experiences of tobacco use: it broadened the scope for greater function individualization by users. So, over the long term, the development of tobacco use has been characterized by a move away from the use of tobacco to *escape* normality and toward its implementation as a tool to *return to* normality through the individualized countering or augmentation of feelings, moods, emotional arousal or underarousal, and the like.

Chapter 3, "Tobacco Use and Clinical Bodies," considers the practice in the twentieth-century West. Just as in chapter 2 I explore how the prevailing humoral conception of the body profoundly influenced understandings, methods, and experiences of tobacco use, so in chapter 3 I analyze the significance of the prevailing clinical conception of the body. The relationships between changes in tobacco use and processes of informalization, mass consumerization, and medicalization are considered. Debates surrounding smoking by women and young people, and the idea of "passive" smoking, are also explored within this context. This part of the book concludes with a critical analysis of prevailing understandings of the "why people smoke" question by placing these within the context of the long-term development of tobacco use in the West.

Thus, in chapter 3 I trace a number of the processes and changes that ultimately undergird dominant present-day Western understandings of tobacco use, and the patterns and character of consumption relating to these. In particular, I explore the shift away from focusing on the short-term, immediate, visible effects of tobacco use that characterized late nineteenth and early twentieth-century understandings of the practice, toward the focus on long-term hidden effects. I propose that this shift corresponds with a broader set of changes relating to the rise of the "clinical gaze." It is in this connection that I discuss the work of Michel Foucault—his account of the rise of clinical medicine, and of the particular form of simultaneously "seeing" and "saying" that accompanied this.

I propose that clinical medical discourse is instrumental in a kind of "discursive reductionism" of tobacco: a dissection of the commodity into its constituent parts—most notably, nicotine—and of the practice of tobacco use itself. In other words, such discourse promotes the search for the set of generic bio-pharmacological processes that explain the mechanism of why people smoke. I argue that the increasing medicalization of tobacco use (of which this discursive reductionism forms part) is interrelated to the rise of relatively recent debates about smoking and individual freedom; I suggest that this tendency is most evident in relation to the issue of "passive" smoking. I explore the emergence of a defiant community of opposition, one characterized by a nihilist cynicism, a backlash against the anti-tobacco movement, in which smokers, particularly younger ones, smoke precisely because tobacco use is understood to be risky. Furthermore, I continue the examination of processes and themes begun in chapters 1 and 2. Specifically, I explore how the individualization of tobacco use is extended even further, such that the practice has increasingly become a means of individual self-expression. I propose that tobacco use has come to play an ever more important role in identity building; in part, I suggest, this phenomenon links to the mass consumerization of tobacco, particularly the associated rise of package "branding" and processes of "informalization" (Wouters 1976, 1977, 1986, 1987),[10] which in turn are linked to civilizing processes.

In chapter 4, "Becoming a Smoker," my focus shifts to the development of tobacco use at the "micro" level of individuals. Through discussion of the previously cited work of Becker, the chapter depicts some of the processes involved in becoming a tobacco user. A range of experiences surrounding different stages in the career of the contemporary Western smoker are explored: for example, how the meaning, utility, and experience of smoking for the teenage boy in the very early stages of his activity differ fundamentally from those of the adult woman who sees herself as a helpless addict. The relationships between social identity, emotions, life changes, and tobacco use are a central concern in this part of the book. My main line of argument is that, most interestingly, the development of tobacco use at the level of individuals parallels, in many important ways, the overall direction of the historical development of tobacco use at the societal level. I explore how, for example, "lose control" experiences of tobacco are very much confined to early "stages" of users' careers, and how, over time, the use of tobacco as a means of self-control becomes increasingly important. Corresponding to this shift, I examine how tobacco consumption as a marker to others, initially very important during early stages of users' careers, begins to decline as these careers progress, and the role of tobacco use as a marker *to* oneself and *of* oneself begins to take on central importance. I explore how dominant present-day understandings of tobacco use as a clinical addiction, and ultimately as a pandemic, inform experiences of smoking and of stopping smoking.

In the conclusion I attempt to bring together the main arguments presented throughout. My central objective here is to explore why the development of tobacco use at the level of individuals (outlined in chapter 4) follows a similar trajectory to that of the long-term development at the societal level. I consider a range of possible explanations in this regard. Part of the answer might reside in Elias's arguments that processes of civilization extend both to individuals in their short-term histories, and to the much longer-term development of society as a whole. Another possible explanation considered is that participants in the research I undertook (discussed in chapter 4) have progressed through their smoking careers in a period of *increased*

10. I will explain this term. But put briefly, informalization refers to a change in codes of etiquette and manners, the increasing permissiveness of society, and a shift in the character of self-control.

opposition to tobacco use. Finally, I explore individual processes of nicotine habituation as a parallel to the long-term shift toward the use of progressively milder forms of tobacco and modes of consuming these. I suggest that each of these possibilities is mutually supporting, and should be taken together as an explanation for the observed link between the two levels studied. I then go on to consider the implications of the arguments I present in the book for current debates on smoking as a social problem. For example, the implications of *Learning to Smoke* for policy interventions aimed at reducing levels of smoking among all, or specific, social groups are considered, as are the implications for approaches to smoking cessation; debates over whether smoking can best be understood as an act of free will or as succumbing to an addiction over which the individual is powerless; and proscriptions on smoking in public places. The conclusion points toward new directions for research, particularly that which adopts an interdisciplinary and developmental approach.

1

Tobacco Use among Native American Peoples

Unlike many other long-term social processes, tobacco use in Europe would appear to have a very definite starting point: what is conventionally known in the West as the discovery of the New World in the late fifteenth century. However, it would be misleading to begin examining the process at that point. Indeed, an understanding of tobacco use among Native American[1] peoples reveals a great deal about the practice in contemporary Western societies.

In this chapter, I focus upon the development of tobacco use among Native Americans before and after their contact with Europeans. From examining processually the uses and experiences of tobacco among these peoples, it is possible to trace the beginnings of an overall *direction* of change that characterizes the long-term development of tobacco use in the West up to the present day. The changes that I will highlight are as follows: a move away from using tobacco as a means of losing control; a move away from the use of highly potent strains of tobacco; a departure from highly ritualized tobacco use; the increasing prevalence of tobacco use by women; a move away

One of the main problems with the bulk of ethnographic data on Native American tobacco use is that they are collected through Western eyes. Where possible, I have focused on studies that include direct translations of Native American accounts of tobacco use. I have also attempted to highlight the incidence and character of Western evaluations in the other accounts that I draw upon. However, I do not claim to have in any way fully escaped the cultural relativism of these, nor indeed my own, interpretations of Native American tobacco use.

1. Throughout this book I shall use the term *Native American* to refer to the indigenous peoples of the Americas. It is difficult to talk with any degree of meaning of Native American peoples, as these cannot be considered to constitute a homogeneous group. However, in selecting anthropological data for this chapter I have tried to concentrate on examples which, to the best of my knowledge, are characteristic of traditional Native American practices.

from a pattern of smoking involving the relatively infrequent consumption of high-yield doses of tobacco; and an increasing movement toward the recreational use of tobacco.

I shall begin to outline these processes of change by pursuing three central areas of concern. First, how was tobacco understood, used, and experienced by Native American peoples? Second, why did they use tobacco more extensively than any other psychoactive plant? Third, how did their tobacco use change as the Americas were colonized by European nations? While there is considerable overlap among these areas of concern, they are artificially separated here for practical reasons.

Native American Tobacco Beliefs

As a psychoactive plant, tobacco lay at the heart of many Native American belief systems.[2] Indigenous societies made use of seven to eight times more narcotic plants than the Old World, and a large number of these had been in more or less continual use since the earliest habitation of the Americas (Goodman 1993: 20). Characteristic of Native American understandings of social reality was the belief that hallucinogenic plants joined the natural and supernatural worlds. These plants were sacred; they were understood to house spiritual beings and to facilitate altered states of consciousness essential to communication with the spirit world (22).

Along with the supernatural powers ascribed to tobacco, the plant was understood to have supernatural origins. In fact, a remarkable recurrence of theme is found in various Native American origin myths concerning the tobacco plant (Goodman 1993: 26). Typical in such myths is the notion that tobacco was given to humans as a resource that could be exchanged with the spirits. Spirits were understood to have an endless longing for tobacco, which went beyond a mere attraction to its aroma and taste: more fundamentally, these beings were seen to need tobacco for their sustenance and survival (Wilbert 1987: 173). Since they could not grow tobacco for themselves, spirits were understood to be dependent on humans to supply them (Goodman 1993: 26; Wilbert 1987: 177). Thus it was understood that humans and spirits were locked into a fundamental interdependence that hinged on the use of tobacco.

The "hunger" for tobacco experienced by Native American tobacco users was perceived as the hunger and longing of the spirits (Wilbert 1987:

---

2. I have written this chapter in the "ethnographic past." I have used the past tense to convey the sense that the practices considered are dynamic, and to facilitate an engagement with long-term processes throughout.

177). Tobacco was used to appease the spiritual hunger, thereby gaining favors and good fortune. This was achieved not only through the direct consumption of tobacco, such as smoking or chewing, but also through ritual tobacco offerings and invocations. The following account taken from an ethnography of seventeenth-century Huron peoples typifies traditional Native American understandings of the spiritual role of tobacco:

> The Huron believed that animate spirits resided in the earth, the rivers, lakes, certain rocks, and the sky and had control over journeying, trading, war, feasts, disease, and other matters. To appease and obtain the favor of these spirits, tobacco was thrown into the fire and a prayer said. If, for example, the offering was to implore health, they would say, *taenguiaens,* "Heal me." . . . Tobacco frequently was used in ritual contexts and offered to the spirits with a prayer. In addition to those occasions . . . , it was thrown into the water of a great lake in order to calm it and to appease a spirit *(Iannoa)* who, in despair, once cast himself into a lake and who caused . . . storms. Before going to sleep a man might throw some tobacco on the fire and pray to the spirits to take care of his house. It was offered to some rocks that the Huron passed when going to Quebec to trade. One of these was called *hihihouray,* 'a rock where the owl makes its nest' . . . they stopped and put tobacco into one of the clefts saying, *oki ca ichikhon condayee aenwaen ondayee d'aonstaancwas,* etc., "spirit who dwellest in this place, here is some tobacco which I present you; help us, guard us from shipwreck, defend us from our enemies, and cause that after having made good trades we may return safe and sound to our villages." (Tooker 1964: 80–82)

Tobacco had such symbolic value and significance that, among some Native American peoples, those who merely planted and nurtured tobacco attained high prestige and honor. The Crow Nation are a particularly good example in this respect. Despite the fact that the Crow were "roving peoples," since their very earliest times they had cultivated tobacco (Denig 1953: 59). They had carefully maintained a consistent strain by preserving the seed from one crop to the next, in keeping with what they believed were their ancestors' wishes. It was understood by the Crow that without the seed, leaf, and blossom of their particular tobacco, their nation would "pass away from the face of the earth" (ibid.). Those who continued this tobacco-planting tradition were said to be endowed with a wide range of supernatural powers: "bring rain, avert pestilence, control the wind, conquer disease, make the buffalo come near their camp, and increase the number of all kinds of game; . . . in fact bring about any event not dependent upon ordinary human possibility" (ibid.). The few people who were involved with the tradition were keen to hold on to their superior power, status, and standing and the considerable resources the position afforded. Indeed, there was an extensive ordeal involved with attaining the right to join their elite ranks:

> Sometimes, with a view to acquiring property, one of them will sell his right or powers to some aspiring individual. In this case the candidate gives everything he has in the world—all his horses, dresses, arms, even his lodge and household utensils—to pay for the great medicine and honor to become a Tobacco Planter. On an occasion of this kind the applicant is adopted with great ceremonies into the band of Planters. His flesh is cut and burned in large and deep furrows around the breast and along his arms, leaving for a long time dangerous and disgusting wounds difficult to heal. He is also obliged to go several days without food or water. After passing through this ordeal, he is furnished with some tobacco seed in exchange for everything he possesses. In this way the rite is perpetuated, and never has received the least check or interruption. On the contrary, it appears to become more honorable from being more ancient and from the difficulties attendant on becoming a conductor of the ceremony. (59–60)

When explorers from the Old World initially encountered tobacco among Native American peoples, they understood very little of the complex systems of beliefs that mediated and governed its use (Goodman 1993: 37). To the earliest European travelers, and those who settled in subsequent centuries, the sight of Amerindians offering tobacco to the spirits was confusing, perhaps even comical. As Higler recounts:

> An old Mille Lacs informant noted: "Some white men drowned here in the lake, and that did not happen for nothing. Some things are sacred to Indians and white people who make fun of it can expect to be punished. Whites have laughed at Indians putting tobacco in the lake. We put tobacco into the lake whenever we go swimming, or when we want to cross the lake. One time, long ago, we were crossing the lake in a steamboat called 'Queen Anne.' Many Indians were on the boat. We were coming from Waukon and going to the Point. The waves were so high that we thought we were going to drown. My great-grandfather threw three or four sacks of tobacco into the water and soon the waves took us back to Waukon. We were all saved." (Higler 1951: 62)

Thus tobacco was of great significance to Native American peoples, playing a fundamental role in religious and medical practice. Their understandings of the plant led to ways of using it that were remarkably different from those characterizing present-day Western cigarette smokers and also early-European users. Indeed, Europeans encountering Native American peoples had little understanding of the plant's sacred status in their cosmology.

Native American Tobacco Use

Of the sixty-four species of *Nicotiana* that have been identified in the Americas (Wilbert 1987: 1), two were used far more extensively than any others: *Nicotiana rustica,* predominantly among Amerindians north of Mexico; and *Nicotiana tabacum,* mainly used within and south of Mexico (Goodman 1993: 25). The nicotine yield of these tobaccos, particularly of the *Nicotiana rustica* strains, was substantially higher than today's commercial species and varieties; a wealth of evidence attests that they were fully capable of producing hallucinations (Haberman 1984; Adams 1990; Wilbert 1987: 134–36; von Gernet 1992: 20–21; Goodman 1993: 25). In addition, there is a strong possibility that psychoactive alkaloids other than nicotine were present in the varieties consumed by Native Americans. These may have merely contributed to the hallucinogenic properties (especially when mixed with high levels of nicotine), or may *themselves* have been the primary hallucinogenic agents (Goodman 1993: 25).

A wide range of tobacco-consumption practices had been developed by Native American peoples long before the first Europeans made contact. Tobacco was snuffed as a dry powder; chewed; drunk by ingesting the juice of the tobacco plant; licked by rubbing a syrupy tobacco extract along the gums and teeth; absorbed locally as an analgesic by applying the leaves or leaf extracts to cuts, bites, stings, and other wounds; absorbed ocularly by applying tobacco leaf or leaf extracts to the surface of the eye; and injected anally as an enema (Wilbert 1987: 19–144). However, by far the most popular mode of tobacco consumption was smoking (64). There are several reasons for this. First, tobacco *smoking* was the most effective means of nicotine absorption (Goodman 1993: 33). If we accept—for the moment, at least—the primacy of nicotine as a pharmacological agent in tobacco and as a factor in generating the experience of tobacco use, it follows that smoking would prevail as a mode of tobacco consumption.[3] Second, tobacco smoke had a high degree of symbolic potency: the rising smoke was believed to symbolize an ascending petition to the spirits (ibid.; Morgan 1901: 155). Symbolic associations with fire and heat may have also been significant. The indigenous peoples of North America generally smoked through pipes (Goodman 1993: 34), while those of South America favored cigars and an

---

3. However, this argument alone cannot explain the prevalence of smoking as a mode of tobacco consumption. Indeed, it cannot explain long-term changes in the development of tobacco use, in which, for example, dipping snuff became widespread in Europe in the eighteenth century, and chewing, for a period, was the most popular mode of consumption in the United States.

early form of cigarettes, dried tobacco leaves in a corn-husk wrapper (Koskowski 1955: 26, 57).[4]

Native American Tobacco Experiences

As I have argued in the introduction, the *experience* of tobacco using cannot be adequately understood simply by examining the body's responses to pharmacological stimuli. How users experience tobacco, the feelings that are brought on by its socially indexed consumption, depend upon a large number of processes that combine and interplay with the pharmacological action of the plant's psychoactive substances. There are relatively few first-hand accounts of Native American experiences of tobacco; as previously discussed, we are essentially limited to studying European perceptions of these practices. There is, however, a somewhat limited amount of source material, from which we can begin to develop an understanding of the experiential aspects of Native American tobacco use.

The following passage is taken from a direct translation of a twentieth-century Native American account of traditional forms of tobacco use among the Karuk Indians of California:

> Sometimes he takes out the coal just with his fingers, they had such tough fingers! He uses no stick. He holds his pipe low when he puts the coal in with his fingers, so he can put it in more easily. He feels kind of smart. . . . Most of the time he takes it out with his fingers, but burns his fingers, whereupon he puts it into his palm. He knows how to handle it. For a moment he rocks it, the fire, in his palm, so it will not burn him. Then he holds the pipe underneath, the tobacco in it. Then he drops there the coal into the pipe. Then he smacks in. . . . He smacks in a few times with the pipe still in his mouth. About three times it is that he smacks in. He fills his mouth with the tobacco smoke. Then he takes the pipe out of his mouth slowly. Then he takes the smoke into his lungs. He sucks in, makes a funny

---

4. Another, somewhat underestimated, means of tobacco smoke inhalation was through the practice of smoke blowing. Wilbert (1987: 76–77) cites this account from Wafer (1934) in this connection:

> Their way of Smoking when they are in Company together is thus: a Boy lights one end of a Roll and burns it to a Coal, wetting the part next it to keep it from wasting too fast. The End so lighted he puts into his Mouth, and blows the Smoak through the whole length of the Roll into the Face of everyone of the Company or Council, tho' there be 2 or 300 of them. Then they, sitting in their usual Posture upon Forms, make, with their Hands held hollow together, a kind of Funnel round their Mouths and Noses. Into this they receive the Smoak as 'tis blown upon them, snuffing it up greedily and strongly as long as they are able to hold their Breath, and seeming to bless themselves, as it were, with the refreshment it gives them.

sound, he goes this way: "* . . ." Then quickly he shuts his mouth. For a moment he holds the smoke inside his mouth. He wants it to go in. For a moment he remains motionless holding his pipe. He shakes, he feels like he is going to faint, holding his mouth shut. It is as if he could not get enough. It is just as if "I want more in, that tobacco smoke." That is the way he feels. Then tobacco smoke comes out from his nose, but his mouth is closed tight. It comes out of his nose before he opens his mouth, he breathes out the tobacco smoke. . . . He shuts his eyes, he looks kind of sleepy-like. His hand trembles, as he puts the pipe to his mouth again. Then again he smacks in. He smokes again like he smoked before. A few or maybe four times he takes the pipe from his mouth. Then, behold, he knows he has smoked up the tobacco, there is no more inside [the pipe]. As he smokes he knows when there are only ashes inside. He just fills up the pipe once, that is enough, one pipeful. He rests every once in a while when smoking. The[n] he puffs again. He does not have the pipe in his mouth long, but it takes him a long time to smoke.

Then after he gets through with smoking he inhales with spitty sound for a long time. Sometimes he lies down, making the spitty inhaling sound yet. It [sounds] like he is still tasting in his mouth the tobacco smoke yet. . . . He feels good over all his meat when he takes it into his lungs. Sometimes he rolls up his eyes. And sometimes he falls over backward. He puts his pipe quickly on the ground, then he falls over. Then they laugh at him, they all laugh at him. Nobody takes heed, when one faints from smoking. . . . That is the way they used to do in the old times. They used to like the tobacco so well. They used to like the tobacco strong. Whenever they faint from tobacco, they always get ashamed. They used to do it that way, get stunned. Sometimes one fellow will have so strong tobacco that nobody can stand it without fainting, it is so strong. He feels proud of his strong tobacco. (Harrington 1932: 188–195)

On examining the above account, it becomes immediately apparent that the experience of tobacco using by the Karuk was intimately bound up with the understandings and practices that were, for them, connected to tobacco. In smoking, they sought the effect of what we might currently recognize as nicotine intoxication; the tobacco user exerted a great deal of effort to hold the smoke in his[5] lungs for as long as possible (Harrington 1932: 183). The Karuk cultivated no plant other than tobacco, and despite the fact that to-

5. It was almost exclusively men, or women doing a "man's job," who used tobacco (Harrington 1932: 12). I also use the male gender here to emphasize the central importance of masculinity in tobacco use among the Karuk. I do not wish to make women invisible in this analysis; on the contrary, the rise of tobacco use among women in the contemporary West will constitute a central theme in later chapters. Rather, I wish to convey accurately the gender-specific character of tobacco use among the Karuk.

bacco grew wild throughout Karuk country, it was cultivated nonetheless, "solely for the purpose of making it 'ikpíhan,' strong" (9).

Tobacco use among the Karuk was almost exclusively a male pursuit; only the women who were doctors would smoke. The various practices and rituals associated with the activity were, indeed, an articulation and expression of "warrior masculinity." The Karuk tobacco user displayed stoicism, tolerance, and strength at various stages of the process: from rolling the hot coal in his palm, through holding the smoke in his lungs, to attempting to remain conscious after "smacking in." Indeed, smokers who fainted after "smacking in" would be slightly ashamed and embarrassed. Moreover, the strength[6] of the consumed tobacco was at once a physical and symbolic metaphor for masculine strength. Even the language depicting tobacco use among the Karuk (provided the English translation is reliable)—"smacking in,"—indicates the pursuit of altogether more pronounced, *stronger,* rougher experiences of the practice than those of tobacco users in present-day Western societies. For the Karuk, tobacco use was also very much an *adult* pursuit. It was a *rite de passage* to mark the transition to manhood: "The young boys did not smoke. They played smoke, that was all. When a small boy smoked he used to get sick. They do not smoke until their throats get husky. Then they think: 'We are already big boys'" (Harrington 1932: 214–15).

Tobacco was smoked at specific points throughout the day, particularly after the evening meal (Harrington 1932: 11). The act of smoking symbolized friendship and "was regarded the same as a friendly embrace" (ibid.). When two Karuk men, or women doctors, met "on the trail," they would smoke together before continuing on their journey. Once again, this practice was strongly related to expressing and reinforcing masculine strength, and the bond between men:

> When a man is traveling on the trails, and has strong tobacco with him, he thinks so much he is a man, he feels high up. . . . Whenever he meets a man, he has to smoke before he travels. He thinks: "I am going to treat him before we travel." He thinks: "I am a man" when he does that. When two men first meet on the trail, then one of the men always says: "Let's sit down." Then they always sit down, they rest. Then one of them takes out his pipe. "Friend, let's smoke," he says. Then the other answers him and says: "Friend, let's smoke." Then he lights his pipe. Then he smokes, he himself smokes first. All do that way, smoke first before they pass it. Then he passes it to that one he has met. Then he smokes in turn, he is being treated. He

6. Throughout this book I use the terms *strong* and *weak* to refer to *degrees of pharmacological involvement.* I discuss this particular phrasing in the conclusion to chapter 3.

smokes in turn the same pipe. Then they finish smoking. Then the other one in turn takes out his pipe. He treats him back, the one who has treated him. He says to him in turn: "You would better smoke my tobacco." He says: "Friend, I am going to treat you back." Then he smokes it himself first. He does the same way, smokes first. Then he gives it in turn to the one that has treated him first. Then he says: "Well, friend, your tobacco is strong." Then the other says: "Well, friend, no." He denies it. He kind of smiles as he says: "Well, friend, no." Then they are through smoking. He gives back the other fellow's pipe. He can hardly put it back in the sack, his hand trembles. His tobacco is so strong. He is tasting it yet in his mouth.

It takes them a long while to smoke. It takes them a long time to finish. Then they say: "All right, let's travel, and I am going to travel, too. Then, friend, good-bye." (207–8)

There may be some significance to the practice of smoking one's own pipe first—a practice that would seem to run counter to contemporary Western patterns of smoking etiquette. Perhaps it signified that the tobacco was safe, of a good quality, and, furthermore, it may have been a way of saying, "I can handle this tobacco with no difficulty. You will see how strong I am when you come to smoke it." Indeed, there was definitely an element of friendly competition involved in this ritual.

Tobacco was also used by the Karuk as a poultice and an analgesic on wounds and other painful areas. It was also used as a sedative to aid sleeping (Harrington 1932: 11). The Karuk believed that it was bad luck to smoke standing up, probably because smokers commonly fainted after using strong tobacco. They also believed that it was bad luck to smoke when defecating, and that one should not laugh when smoking, as it may crack the pipe (214). These beliefs may again have been related to practical considerations; they serve here to demonstrate that, for the Karuk, smoking was a relatively serious activity. Harrington summarizes tobacco use among the Karuk as follows:

> The tube in which tobacco is burned is to the Karuk mind an escapement from the boredom of life and the entrance to a world of medicine, ceremony, myth—an entrance reaching out in various ways into the unknown. Tobacco was never smoked for pleasure, but always for some definite purpose, if only that of filling out the daily routine prescribed by the Ikxareyavs[7] and followed by the ancestors. . . . Only its strength was

7. The "Ikxareyavs" referred to here were ancient people who occupied the Karuk country before the Karuk Indians and who were believed to have turned into various spiritual objects. According to Harrington, "These Ikxareyavs were old-time people, who [were believed to have] turned into animals, plants, rocks, mountains, plots of ground, and even parts of the

sought; and it was used only in the way to produce the most acute poisoning. Custom and superstition entirely guided its use. There was no question as to whether it was good or bad to smoke tobacco, whether one
should or should not smoke, if one were a man, or a woman doctor. Practically all men smoked, and smoked at the same times and in exactly the
same way. Women doctors smoked only because they were doing a man's
job and must do as men did. Women who were not doctors never smoked.
Smoking by youths was frowned upon. If prescribed custom made its use
a habit, there was never any talk of its being a habit and there was little individual variation. (12–13)

The above extract reveals as much about tobacco use in twentieth-
century Western societies as it does about tobacco use among the Karuk Indians. Harrington appears, to some degree, to have been engaged in a comparative analysis. That is to say, he was providing an account of Karuk tobacco
use *in opposition to* his implicit observations and understanding of tobacco
use within white-centered, industrialized, and *civilized* America. His statements, particularly "Tobacco was never smoked for pleasure, but always for
some definite purpose," and "If prescribed custom made its use a habit,
there was never any talk of its being a habit and there was little individual
variation," serve to contrast implicitly the *ritualized* use of tobacco among
the Karuk with the more *individualized*[8] use by Western Americans. The
custom and superstition, or perhaps better, the religious and spiritual meanings of tobacco, strictly framed, contextualized, and *mediated* its use among
the Karuk: "Practically all men smoked at the same times and in exactly the
same way." Harrington's statements also implicitly contrast smoking as a
moral concern among his contemporary Americans ("whether it was good
or bad to smoke tobacco,") with the Karuk's understanding (in which these
concerns were not considered to be an issue).

When the Karuk tobacco user smoked, he experienced a "smack of
strength"; the strength of the tobacco he consumed reinforced the strength
of the masculinity he was expressing. He felt male, he felt good, he felt
fulfilled. In bio-pharmacological terms, he had consumed enough nicotine
to partially block nerve message transmission at nerve cell receptor sites in

---

house, dances, and abstractions when the Karuk came to the country, remaining with the Karuk
only long enough to state and start all customs, telling them in every instance, 'Human will do
the same'" (1932: 8).

8. This is not to imply that tobacco is not smoked for a *purpose* by members of white, industrialized, and civilized America, but that the purpose of smoking for the Karuk was governed much more by ritual and ascribed belief than more individually based understandings
and *rationalizations*.

his body, generating a highly sedative effect (Ashton and Stepney 1982: 38–39). The large dose of ingested nicotine may have also spurred the release of various "neurohormones"—such as serotonin and dopamine (Wilbert 1987: 148)—in the Karuk tobacco user's body, adding to the initial "smack" of nicotine and the good feelings experienced shortly after. However, this only partly accounts for his experience. It is highly unlikely that cigarette smokers in contemporary Western societies would feel at all good after consuming tobacco of the Karuk variety in the Karuk mannner. Thus, there was clearly a *learned* component in obtaining such enjoyment. Harrington's text includes an account of "How the white men tried at first to smoke Indian tobacco": "When the White men first came in, some of them tried to smoke the Indian tobacco. They thought: 'We can smoke it.' They took it into their lungs just once, they thought 'We will do like Indians do.' Then they were sick for a week. The Indian tobacco is so strong. They never tried to smoke it again" (Harrington 1932: 277–78).

The Karuk method of smoking required the user to undergo an extensive process of tobacco *habituation*. That is to say, he needed to invest a good deal of time and effort into accustoming his body to the large amounts of nicotine and other active substances that were consumed when using tobacco according to Karuk ritual and practice. More fundamentally, the experience of nicotine poisoning was by no means inherently pleasurable.[9] The Karuk tobacco user had to learn to enjoy—to perceive as good—the convulsions, hand trembling, and occasional fainting that accompanied the smoking experience. The Karuk actively pursued these effects: they learned the most effective technique of nicotine consumption; they went to great lengths to cultivate the most potent tobacco possible. Thus, the *experience* of tobacco use for the Karuk comprised the complex *interplay* between the expectations, understandings, rituals, narratives, practices, perceptions, and bio-pharmacological action of tobacco use.

That the use of tobacco by the Karuk was governed by ritual, ascribed belief, custom, and collective will can also be seen when one examines their *abstention* from tobacco:

> Many Indians in primitive times would get a strong craving and impatience for tobacco, which had become a habit with them. But the old-time Indians never smoked but the merest fraction of the day, disapproved even of the smoking of men as old as in their twenties, and regarded the modern boy and girl cigarette fiend with disgust, as they do many White man ex-

9. I refer to Becker's model of becoming a marijuana user discussed in the introduction to this book.

27

cesses. The early Karuk could deny themselves smoking or quit smoking altogether with much more fortitude than the average white man can. Their daily life schooled them to all kinds of self-denial and hardship. (Harrington 1932: 216)

Harrington explains the relative success of the Karuk in denying or quitting smoking compared to the average white man, by proposing that the Karuk were more used to self-denial. While this may have been the case, it is also possible that they *experienced* and *acted on* the withdrawal syndrome that accompanied tobacco abstention in a substantially *different* way. Just as I have argued that the experience of tobacco use by the Karuk involved a complex interplay of processes, it shall be contended that this was also the case for tobacco *abstention* and *cessation*. Ethnographic evidence certainly points toward there being significant variation in how tobacco withdrawal had been experienced. The following twentieth-century ethnographer's account refers to the Klamath Indians, who lived a short distance up river from the Karuk:

> The Klamath people have the same kind of tobacco that grows over a large part of the United States, which, when it grows up has small leaves. . . . It becomes very strong and often makes the oldest smokers sick, which they pass over lightly, saying that it is a good quality of tobacco. The women doctors all smoke but the other women never do. . . . They hold the pipe upwards if sitting or standing and it is only when lying on the back that one seems to enjoy the smoke with perfect ease; however they can handle the pipe to take a smoke in any position. Some of these pipes are small, not holding any more than a thimble-full of tobacco. My people never let the tobacco habit get the better of them as they can go all day without smoking or quit smoking for several days at a time and never complain in the least. The men, after supper, on going into the sweat-house take their pipes and smoke and some take two or three smokes before they go to bed. The old women doctors will smoke through the day and always take a smoke before lying down to sleep. All inhale the smoke, letting it pass out of the lungs through the nose. (Thompson 1916: 37)[10]

In the above account Thompson expresses how the Klamath peoples—who used tobacco in a manner very similar to that of the Karuk—were able to abstain from smoking for considerable periods of time without "complain[ing] in the least." By contrast to Harrington's statements that in ab-

---

10. This passage was also quoted in Harrington (1932: 32). Harrington explicitly states (p. 216) that Thompson's statements in no way apply to the Karuk Indians.

staining from tobacco use the Karuk were practicing a form of "self-denial," Thompson appears to imply that the Klamath found it relatively easy to undergo lengthy periods of abstention. Once again, the contrast between the above two quotations may be magnified by the fact that both these accounts are given through Western eyes, rather than being first-hand accounts by Karuk and Klamath Indians.

Tobacco Use in Shamanism

As I have aimed to show, tobacco use was of crucial significance and importance to many Native American peoples. However, the question remains of why it was tobacco, rather than any other psychoactive plant, that was used most extensively by Native American peoples. A consideration of tobacco in Native American shamanistic ritual provides much insight.

Since tobacco and other psychoactive plants were believed to facilitate communication with the spirit world, they were crucial to many indigenous American cultures. Shamans were thought to have access to more spirits than any other members of their social groups, and would, over time, come to be recognized as having traveled widely through the spirit world (Goodman 1993: 22). Accordingly, they would use ecstatic performances in their attempts to heal people. Native American belief systems typically held that illness and disease were caused by spiritual forces, which could act in two main ways. First, they could perpetrate an intrusion, in which a magical physical object or the essence of a malevolent spirit would cause sickness by entering the body (23). In the following account, a Camayurá Indian described how he was cured of an intrusion:

> I went fishing one morning and while I was busy fishing I suddenly felt a sting or bite in my side. When the sun was in the middle of the sky I began to shiver and I sent for Kantú, the Iwalapetí shaman. That night Kantú and six other shamans went into the woods and brought back a mama'é [spirit]. They smoked and sang and the Iwalapetí shaman sucked out the moan [intruding object, in this case a small piece of burnt wood]. . . . When I saw the moan I knew that it was the mama'é called yarúp which had caused it to enter my body and I also knew that this mama'é belonged to the Cuicúru. I paid the Iwalapetí shaman a necklace for curing me. (Oberg 1946: 61)

Second, it was believed that spiritual forces could cause "soul loss." In the case of illness or disease brought on in this manner, the affected person's soul was said to have been drawn into the supernatural world. Curing the illness therefore involved bringing the sick person's soul back to the natural world, a task belonging to the shaman. Through the use of hallucinogenic plants, he could access the supernatural world and retrieve the victim's soul, thus restoring the sick person's health (Goodman 1993: 23). A range of plants were used for various cures and for different strains of potency, but, the one plant used more than any other by Native American peoples was tobacco (24).

The use of tobacco in shamanistic ritual usually involved consumption on a much larger scale than for recreational use (Wilbert 1987: xvi). The shaman would typically inhale large quantities of tobacco smoke, causing nausea, then vomiting, then convulsions, and finally a deathlike trance (157). As Wilbert has observed, it is this pattern of "death" and "restoration" that forms the center of Native American theories of healing. The underlying belief is that only "he who overcomes death by healing himself is capable of curing and revitalizing others" (156). Furthermore, Wilbert proposes,

> Because catatonic states near death are so essential to the proper conduct of shamanism, it is not surprising to find evidence throughout the ethnographic literature of the existence among South American Indians of a tendency toward acute nicotine poisoning. I am referring not so much to instances where tobacco appears to have been used to produce deathlike states in victims marked for execution (Yupa) or live burial (Muisca), but to cases where shamanic masters take their apprentices after months or even years of progressive nicotine habituation to the very brink of death. . . . When a Warao shaman was initiated, his death was announced in a loud voice. The old shamans of the Tupinamba congregated to instruct the candidate and make him dance until he fell down unconscious. Forcing his mouth open, they inserted a funnel and made him swallow a cup of tobacco juice. This made the novice swoon and vomit blood, and the ordeal lasted for days. (157–58)

Once again, Wilbert's observations also serve to illustrate the extensive degree of habituation that was involved with tobacco use in shamanistic ritual. He shows that the model of revival from near-death was not purely a symbolic one. Wilbert concludes that the reason tobacco was used in shamanistic medicine more than any other drug was as follows:

> [N]icotine, the biphasic drug in tobacco, is exceptionally well suited to manifest the continuum of dying, which begins with initial nausea, heavy breathing, vomiting, and prostration (illness); continues with tremors, convulsion, or seizure (agony); and ends with peripheral paralysis of the respiratory muscle (death). Progressive blockade of impule transmission at autonomic ganglia and central stimulation are the primary pharmacological

conditions of this journey toward death whence, if appropriately dosed, the shaman is granted safe return thanks to the prompt biotransformation of nicotine in the body. (1997: 157)

In this way the physiological action of tobacco served as a natural model that both paralleled and reinforced shamanistic belief systems. Furthermore, unlike many other psychoactive substances used by Native American peoples, tobacco had a relatively mild and short-term effect. These properties allowed it to have a "vast functional repertoire" among Native American peoples (Goodman 1993: 24). It is predominantly for these reasons that tobacco was used more extensively than any other drug in pre-Columbian America (ibid.).

It may initially seem paradoxical that the success of tobacco was related to the fact that the effects of its consumption were "weak" relative to other drugs.[11] However, as will be shown, it is this aspect of tobacco that continued to be significant, and increasingly so, when it was introduced into the West. The relative ambiguity, in turn related to the comparative mildness of tobacco, has allowed the plant, its use, and its effects to be adapted to fit into a wide range of sociocultural environments, and has been a key factor in its current ubiquity. In other words, one of the most significant characteristics of tobacco is that, compared with many other drugs, the effects of its consumption are easy to control, and that the experience of these effects is malleable, or open to interpretation and manipulation.

Postcontact Native American Tobacco Use

Since most accounts of Native American tobacco use have been collected since Amerindians' contact with the West, it is difficult to assess the extent of the white man's impact on these practices. However, the relatively strong sense of tradition among many indigenous Americans has lent a retrospective narrative structure to a number of these narratives. While most refer to a period that was still some time after initial contact with the West, they do provide some indication of the general *direction* in which practices appear to have changed.

The experience of the Karuk is, once again, a useful one to draw upon. After contact with Western travelers, they began to smoke much more frequently and recreationally. They also began to smoke "White Man's tobacco," which was generally much milder than the traditional Karuk variety.

---

11. By this I mean that the short-term effects of tobacco consumption were relatively controllable, and, generally, were not seriously damaging in a readily apparent way.

One of the respondents in Harrington's study provided the following account:

> After the White men came in it was no time at all before all the Indians were smoking their tobacco, the White man tobacco. The old-time Indians, as soon as they see a White man, they ask for tobacco, they say: "Give me some tobacco." . . . Axvahitc Va'ara was a married woman, but she used to go around bumming tobacco and food from the Whites. She was a doctress. Once she asked Andy Merle for tobacco. She kept asking him. At last he said: "I am not going to give you any." Then the old woman said: "Pretty soon a big cut will be coming your way." . . . That is the way they did if they knew how to smoke, they used to bum tobacco, and matches too. That was the reason why I did not learn to smoke, I might be following somebody, begging tobacco. (Harrington 1932: 269–70)

After contact with white travelers, the use of tobacco among the Karuk began, increasingly, to follow contemporary Western patterns. Smoking was engaged in more frequently and casually, and, most interestingly, a more pronounced dependency became involved with being a tobacco user.

The case of the Karuk, if I have interpreted it accurately, is typical of many Native American peoples. As Wilbert (1987: xvi) proposes, the tobacco plant "had a major impact on tribal value systems until, under the influence of the advancing frontier, the ideological tenets of tobacco beliefs began to shift increasingly from the religious to the profane." After their contact with white travelers, tobacco use among many Native American peoples became more recreational. In relation to this, it became far more common for Amerindian women to smoke (ibid.). Nonetheless, the use of tobacco in shamanistic ritual among some Native American peoples persisted into the twentieth century. The following account of a Cuicuru tobacco shaman in central Brazil serves to demonstrate this point:

> Metsé inhaled deeply, and as he finished one cigarette an attending shaman handed him another lighted one. Metsé inhaled all the smoke, and soon began to evince considerable physical distress. After about ten minutes his right leg began to tremble. Later his left arm began to twitch. He swallowed smoke as well as inhaling it, and soon was groaning in pain. His respiration became labored, and he groaned with every exhalation. By this time the smoke in his stomach was causing him to retch. . . . The more he inhaled the more nervous he became. . . . He took another cigarette and continued to inhale until he was near to collapse. . . . Suddenly he "died," flinging his arms outward and straightening his legs stiffly. . . . He remained in this state of collapse nearly fifteen minutes. . . . When Metsé had revived himself two attendant shamans rubbed his arms. One of the shamans drew

on a cigarette and blew smoke gently on his chest and legs, especially on the places that he indicated by stroking himself. (Dole 1964: 57–58)[12]

Contact with the West, therefore, did not lead to the complete extinction of traditional Native American practices related to tobacco use. In some cases, such practices were adapted and modified, and appear to have existed alongside those adopted from white settlers.

Harrington's conclusion to his account of tobacco use among the Karuk contains some useful observations regarding the transfer of tobacco to Western peoples:

> It is a curious fact that while the whites took over the material tobacco from the Indians, they took with it no fragment of the world that accompanied it; nor were they at first aware that there was such a world, and, again, that after all the generations which have elapsed since its introduction among the whites, it has woven itself scarcely at all into their psychology and mythology. Lady Nicotine is enshrined among the Whites only as a drug, as a taste, as a habit, along with the seeking after mild and tasty forms, while the Karuk make tobacco a heritage from the gods, a strange path which juts out into this world and leads to the very ends of magic. (1932: 12–13)

As Harrington suggests, while material tobacco was transferred to the West, the profound spiritual importance ascribed to it by Native American peoples was not. Most interestingly, it was only the mildest and, to Western tastes, most palatable forms of tobacco that were transferred across the cultural divide. Yet rather than altogether losing all psychological and mythological significance, tobacco use became imbued with a completely *different* set of meanings by its white users: meanings which, contrary to Harrington's comments, were significantly *informed* by Native American beliefs about tobacco. Moreover, the fact that tobacco use was so successfully transferred between such sharply contrasting sociocultural environments is in itself highly significant.

To summarize, *traditional* tobacco use among Amerindians was a highly important, sacred, and 'male' pursuit. Native American peoples cultivated strains of tobacco much stronger than those popularly consumed in the present-day West, requiring an extensive process of habituation. Tobacco was used extensively as a hallucinogen in shamanistic ceremony, and more recreational use was characterized by relatively infrequent intakes of highly potent tobacco at specific times of day. Most important, the traditional use of

12. While the account provided here refers to practices of the twentieth century, Goodman notes that Metsé was performing an ancient tradition that predates European contact with the New World (1993: 19).

tobacco by Native Americans was characterized by a loss of control, by intoxication, in stark contrast with present-day Western patterns of use. It was also a highly ritualized pursuit governed by strict social proscriptions regarding the age and gender of users. However, after the Amerindians' contact with Western peoples, their tobacco use began to change in a number of ways. It became more common for women to smoke, and patterns of tobacco use more closely reflected present-day Western patterns: more frequent intakes of relatively mild "white man's" tobacco. The use of tobacco in shamanism appears to have persisted well into the twentieth century, though practices became adapted and modified.

The question of why people smoke has been reframed in this chapter. On one level, there is indeed evidence to suggest that nicotine self-administration was a central factor in why Native American people used tobacco. But this insight alone tells us relatively little; we are left with only a partial answer to this question. It tells us little about the role of tobacco use for Amerindians—its status, its function, its significance; it provides us with only a partial understanding of the *experience* of tobacco by Native American users; it cannot explain why some users found it easier to abstain from tobacco consumption—to even stop altogether—than their present-day cigarette smoking counterparts; it does very little to explain the difference between patterns of tobacco use among Native Americans and present-day Western users; moreover, a nicotine-self administration model cannot adequately explain changes in *why* Native American people used tobacco, changes in *how* they used it, changes and variations in how they *experienced* it, changes and variations in their experiences of what we might label as *dependency,* and so on.

Of course, a nicotine self-administration model provides us with no insight into the *direction* of changes in Native American tobacco use (and the development of tobacco use more generally) identified in the introduction to this chapter. And yet it is through analyzing this direction of change, as I shall do in the remaining chapters, that we can build an understanding of how the reasons people smoke change, not only over time and between cultures but also within the individual careers of smokers.

In the next chapter, I will consider further the direction of changes in the development of tobacco use by pursuing a number of questions: why were Native American understandings and uses of tobacco prior to Western contact so very different from those prevalent in the present-day West? How was it possible to "transfer" tobacco consumption successfully from Native American to Western societies and cultures? In short, how did the tobacco plant, its use, and its "effects" become adapted to fit into the sociocultural environments of the West? I will examine how tobacco use was originally interpreted and subsumed within Galenic, or humoral, understandings of the body, and explore how the understandings, uses, and experiences of tobacco changed in the West from the sixteenth century onward.

2

Tobacco Use and Humoral Bodies: The Introduction of Tobacco into Britain and Other Parts of Europe

There is some disagreement in the historical literature as to who was the first to bring tobacco and knowledge of its use to Britain,[1] and when tobacco use became widespread there. Sir John Hawkins was one of the first official figures to have brought tobacco seeds (of the species *Nicotiana rustica*) to Britain; he did so in 1565 (Koskowski 1955: 57; Apperson 1914: 14). However, it is quite possible that returning colonists or other travelers may have introduced tobacco some time earlier. Several sources indicate a prevalence of pipe smoking as early as 1573. The social historian, Apperson, draws upon evidence from William Harrison, who wrote in his 1588 *Chronologie:* "[In 1573] . . . the taking in of the smoke of the Indian herbe called Tobacco, by an instrument formed like a little ladell [an early tobacco pipe that had a small, shallow bowl], wherby it passeth from mouth into the head and stomach, is greatlie taken up and used in England" (cited in Apperson 1914: 14).

Tobacco may have also been brought from other parts of Europe that had discovered and adopted its use some years earlier than the date of its reputed

---

1. The bulk of the material I present in this chapter relates to the development of tobacco use in Britain. I intend to use Britain here as a model that typifies the overall *direction* of changes in tobacco use from the sixteenth to the early-twentieth century in Europe as a whole. My choice of Britain is based on practical and substantive considerations. The practical consideration is that since, at the time of writing, I live in Britain, the material most accessible to me relates to this country. The more substantive consideration is that—with the exception of snuff taking— Britain characteristically led the way for many of the changes in tobacco use that later occurred in other parts of Europe and the rest of the world. Significantly, it was one of the earliest countries in Europe to industrialize, and it had major commercial interests in the Americas. Where important differences in patterns of development across European nations are discernible, I have tried to highlight these.

introduction to Britain by Hawkins. For example, tobacco was brought to Portugal as early as 1512 and was already being cultivated there by 1558 (Koskowski 1955: 56). However, it is generally agreed that toward the end of the sixteenth century, smoking tobacco by means of a pipe had become widely known in England.[2] Moreover, the tobacco plant was already being cultivated in Britain by 1573 (Harrison 1986: 554). Cultivation had spread to Gloucestershire, Devonshire, and other western counties by the early seventeenth century (Koskowski 1955: 58). By the mid-seventeenth century, there were said to be over six thousand tobacco plantations in the South of England alone (Harrison 1986: 556).

It is widely accepted that the figurehead of tobacco smoking's popularity in England was Sir Walter Raleigh. It is Raleigh who, in the popular mind, is most commonly associated with the introduction of smoking (Apperson 1914: 14) and bringing the practice into common use. Indeed, there are several folklore stories involving him. One is recounted by Apperson: "The tradition is crystallized in the story of the schoolboy who, being asked 'what do you know about Sir Walter Raleigh?' replied: 'Sir Walter Raleigh introduced tobacco into England, and when smoking it in this country said to his servant, "Master Ridley, we are to-day lighting a candle in England which by God's blessing will never be put out!"'" (15). Another example is provided by Fairholt (1859: 52): "[Raleigh] . . . took a private pipe, and occasioned his servant to cast ale over him as the smoke induced him to fear his master was on fire."

As the above accounts serve to demonstrate, tobacco smoking must have initially looked extremely unnatural, perhaps even disturbing, to Europeans of the sixteenth century. While it is possible that other herbs were smoked before the introduction of tobacco, the practice was likely uncommon. In the above account from Harrison, the author does not seem to have had a word for what we would now recognize as a pipe. Instead, this is referred to as "an instrument formed like a little ladell." Once again, this seems to indicate a relative absence of any previous forms of smoking, particularly by pipe.

It is probable that initially only the more affluent members of society were able to smoke. For the first few decades after its introduction, tobacco was very expensive. As the supply from home and abroad increased, its price fell. Consequently, tobacco smoking rapidly became a popular activity for almost all levels of society (Koskowski 1955: 59; Goodman 1993: 60). For ex-

2. Tobacco was also chewed and snuffed, but by far the most popular mode of consumption in England of the sixteenth and seventeenth centuries was pipe smoking (Koskowski 1955: 59).

Table 1 Tobacco Consumption, England and Wales, 1620–1702

Years	Average Annual Consumption (lb. per capita)
1620–29	0.01
1630–31	0.02
1669	0.93
1672	1.10
1682, 1686–88	1.64
1693–99	2.21
1698–1702	2.30

Source: Shammas 1990: 79.

ample, the following passage was written in 1640: "Tobacco engages, Both sexes, all ages, The poor as well as the wealthy; From the court to the cottage, From childhood to dotage, Both those that are sick and the healthy" (*Wits' Recreations* 1640 in Apperson 1914: 25).

The spread of tobacco use was phenomenal. Per-capita consumption levels are a useful indicator of this success. From the table above, one can observe the dramatic rise in tobacco consumption throughout the seventeenth century.

In order to account for this success, and to build an understanding of tobacco use during and after the early stages of its transfer to the West, I consider five central areas of concern in this chapter. First, I investigate how and why tobacco was successfully transferred from Native American to Western societies and cultures. Second, I consider how tobacco was understood, used, and experienced by early European tobacco users. Third, in relation to these issues, I discuss the increasing regulation of tobacco use by examining the shifting balances of power between its proponents and opponents. Fourth, I examine how tobacco use in Britain and other parts of Europe changed from the sixteenth to the early twentieth century. Fifth, I explore how transformations in tobacco use during this period were linked to broader-scale social processes.

The main purpose of this chapter is to trace further the overall *direction* of changes characterizing the long-term development of tobacco use. Continuing from chapter 1, I explore the move away from the use of tobacco for losing control and escaping normality, and a gradual move toward its increasing use as an instrument of self-control. I consider processes of increasing regulation, both of the tobacco commodity itself and of the practices surrounding its use. I show how rising demands for increased regulation stem in part from the state and the nascent medical profession—both seeking to control the use of tobacco—and in part as a consequence of a *quest for distinction* by tobacco users belonging to higher levels of society. It is in this connection that I present a core part of my argument: that the development of tobacco use has been shaped by processes of *civilization* in the technical, nonnormative[3] sense that Elias (2000) used this term—processes that, to oversimplify greatly, have involved a growing social pressure toward exercising greater self-restraint.[4] I provide an exposition of Elias's work at a point in the discussion where it is easiest to see the links between the development of tobacco use and processes of civilization: in other words, a point at which the ideas will make the most sense to the reader unfamiliar with his work.

In relation to these undertakings, I also explore how, despite being substantially milder than Native American species and varieties, the tobacco widely used in European societies—particularly during the early stages of its introduction—was considerably stronger than the present-day equivalents. In this connection, changing perceptions of the relative status of tobacco and alcohol as intoxicating agents are considered. I show how tobacco itself was initially understood to be an intoxicant, but its status changed as different varieties were cultivated, new methods of curing tobacco were developed, and modes of consumption began to shift. These developments led to the perception that the chief danger of intoxication from tobacco lay not in

---

3. For the reader unfamiliar with Elias's work, it is important to note that his technical use of the term *civilization* is fundamentally different from the more common value-laden everyday use. Elias's use of this term is something akin to the difference between an anthropologist's use of the term *culture* and the everyday usage of the term to denote higher things of the mind—as in the phrase "a cultured upbringing." He is definitely *not* referring to a process involving a form of "social evolution" or "progress."

4. It is, of course, impossible adequately to summarize in one line the ideas of the five-hundred-page, two-volume book *The Civilizing Process,* but the formulation I provide here indicates at least the *direction* of some of the changes that Elias discussed. Elias himself was hesitant to provide overly succinct summaries of his work, partly because he wanted his ideas always to take form gradually, with the uninitiated reader led from one level of understanding to the next; and he always wanted to introduce concepts in relation to historical observations. This was part of a broader attempt to integrate what are currently labeled the empirical and rational components of sociological inquiry: with both equally present in his writing, so as to avoid a separation of theory and research, which itself is problematic. The nearest Elias gets to providing a one-line summary of some of his main ideas is in a postscript (originally a revised introduction) to *The Civilizing Process* written in 1968. In it he describes a core aspect of civilizing processes as "the structural change in people toward an increased consolidation and differentiation of their affect controls, and therefore of both their experience (e.g., in the form of an advance in the threshold of shame and revulsion) and of their behaviour (e.g., in the differentiation of the implements used at table) . . . a change in a specific direction over many generations" (2000: 451).

its consumption but in the fact that it often led to drinking alcohol. Also examined is how, prior to increasing levels of regulation, tobacco was adulterated with a wide range of toxic substances. I consider accounts of people, particularly children, literally dropping dead from smoking several pipes of tobacco in succession.

Another area to be considered in some detail in this chapter is how tobacco was used, understood, and experienced in relation to the prevailing humoral, or Galenic, conceptions of the body; and, indeed, how it was subsumed into those understandings. I explore how prevailing understandings of tobacco began to change, from its initial status as a panacea from the New World, from its role as a prophylactic against the plague, from the identification (and widespread medical acceptance) of tobacco as a remedy to treat the humoral body—to rising medical treatises against the abuse (or immoderate use) of tobacco, to increasingly recreational use, to the growing understanding, use, and experience of tobacco as an agent on the mind to treat the ills of civilization.

Also explored in this chapter are changes in the practices associated with tobacco use: from an initial "smoking *Gemeinschaft*" in which almost all levels of society smoked pipes, toward increasingly individualized and differentiated modes and practices of consumption. In relation to this, I examine the rise of "smoking schools"; "professors in the art of smoking"; the elaborate and ornate equipment that came to be associated with tobacco use; and the intricate, differentiated, and highly individualized set of practices involved in, for example, exhaling smoke or taking a pinch of snuff. I show how the *form* of tobacco itself became individualized through, among others, the mixing of snuff concoctions; and, ultimately, how the *function* of tobacco followed suit. I explain the rise of these practices, as suggested above, in terms of a *quest for distinction* from perceived social inferiors among higher social echelons, in turn related to processes of civilization.

Finally, I explore in some detail the rise of the cigarette as a dominant mode of tobacco consumption. I suggest that, somewhat paradoxically, the cigarette became popular relative to other modes of consumption precisely because its pharmacological effects were comparatively minimal. Its mildness and convenience made it particularly well suited to being consumed as a supplement to other activities. That is to say, in contrast with earlier modes of consumption, the cigarette required relatively little "time out"; and it generally did not intoxicate the user, and so could be smoked in conjunction with a range of activities including, crucially, work. This supplementary role of the cigarette, I argue, was most important because it allowed understandings to break from the idea that tobacco use was almost exclusively tied to leisure activities. In relation to these changes, experiences of tobacco use shifted once again; I discuss how.

Furthermore, I show how the move toward milder forms and modes of consuming tobacco arises not out of concerns for health but partly from fear of embarrassment and pressures to use tobacco in more "distinguished" and "refined" ways. Indeed, I argue that the cigarette itself became popular *in spite of* health concerns. I propose that it can be seen, in many ways, as a quite "civilized" mode of consuming tobacco: in comparison with the media of tobacco use that preceded it, smoking a cigarette involved relatively little physical reaction. The delicate movements involved with taking snuff, by comparison, stood in contrast with the sneezing that accompanied it; or, for example, the expectoration and spitting that accompanied early pipe smoking, and, in the United States, chewing tobacco, was considered vulgar or distasteful by those with more-developed sensitivities. Again, I argue that an examination of these processes can greatly inform our understanding not just of the changing reasons why people smoked but of why they used tobacco as they did, of how they experienced this, of how the utility, purpose, role, and function of tobacco use have changed over time.

The Transfer of Tobacco from Native American Societies

In many ways, it is remarkable that a practice so completely alien to Europeans of the sixteenth century became widespread so rapidly. As I have shown in chapter 1, tobacco had immense spiritual and material significance for Native American peoples. Their practice of tobacco use was embedded within a complex system of customs and beliefs associated with healing, sociability, heritage, masculinity, and other values. A question central to my discussion here is, *How* did tobacco use become transferred from Native American cultures to Western ones?

One of the most important factors promoting this transfer was the predominance of the Galenic, or 'humoral,' system of medicine in late-Renaissance Europe (Goodman 1993: 41). Galenic medical philosophy was central to the cultural framework through which European physicians and herbalists made sense of New World medicines, including tobacco (ibid.). This, in turn, affected how tobacco was transferred from Europe to other parts of the world. Within the Galenic system, based on a conceptualization developed by the second-century Greek physician after whom it is named, human bodies were seen to have four humors: blood, phlegm, black bile, and yellow bile. These humors, like all other matter, had an "essence" formed from the combination of four opposing states: hot and cold, moist and dry. Accordingly, blood was hot and moist, while phlegm was cold and moist (39). Health was defined as a state of humoral equilibrium. A state of humoral disequilibrium, where one humor or state was dominant over another, could affect not only the physical workings of the body but also an individual's temperament or personality. For example, too much dry would lead to a choleric disposition; too much moisture would lead to a melancholic temperament (Hale 1993: 542).

Galenic medicinal therapy aimed to restore humoral balance by drawing out excess humors through bloodletting, purging, vomiting, and sweating. For example, hot remedies were prescribed to cure cold ailments, and wet remedies for dry ailments (Goodman 1993: 40). Around the time of the transfer of tobacco use to the West, Galenic physicians believed in the existence of a universal panacea that, in Galenic medicinal theory, was an organic substance most likely to be a plant (43). They were convinced that the panacea existed, and merely awaited discovery. A parallel can be drawn with the popular myth of the Fountain of Youth prevalent in the same period: "a fountain of water much more precious than wine, by drinking from which anyone becomes young and healthy. . . . It was one of the features looked for by the explorers of new lands . . . indeed, its location had been pinned down to somewhere in Florida" (Hale 1993: 546).

In 1571, Nicholas Monardes, a leading Spanish physician, published a detailed study of all the plants encountered in the New World. The text, entitled (in its English translation) *Joyfull Newes Out of the Newe Founde Worlde,* provided all the medical justification needed to hail tobacco as the long-awaited panacea (Goodman 1993: 44). With this highly influential work, Monardes played a crucial role in establishing tobacco formally as a medical remedy. In it, he defined the humoral essence of tobacco as hot and dry in the second degree (ibid.). Thus tobacco was understood to be ideally suited to treat all the cold, moist ailments so common in northern Europe. Monardes detailed more than twenty conditions that tobacco was said to cure, and provided instructions for its application. The conditions he listed covered a vast range: toothache, sores, carbuncles, flesh wounds, chilblains, "evill" breath, headaches, even "cancers" (Monardes 1925).

The importance of the Galenic medical philosophy in making sense of European tobacco use is abundantly evident from early Western accounts of tobacco use among Native Americans. Consider, for example, the following extract from Thomas Hariot's *A Briefe and True Report of the New Found Land of Virginia* (1588):

> There is a herbe which is sowed a part by itselfe and is called by the inhab-
> itants Uppówoc: In the West Indies it hath divers names, according to the

severall places and countries where it groweth and is used: The spaniards generally call it Tobacco. The leaves thereof being dried and brought into powder: they use to take the fume or smoke thereof by sucking it through pipes made of claie into their stomacke and heade: from whence it purgeth superflous fleame and other grosse humours, openeth all the pores and passages of the body: by which meanes the use thereof, not only preserveth the body from obstructions: but if also any be, so that they have not beane of too long continuance, in short time breaketh them: wherby their bodies are notably preserved in health, and know not many greevous diseases wherewithall wee in England are oftentimes afflicted. . . . We ourselves during the time we were there used to suck it after their manner, as also since our returne, and have found manie rare and wonderful experiments of the vertues thereof: of which the relation woulde require a volume by itself: the use of it by so many of late, men and women of great calling as else, and some learned Phisitians also, is sufficient witness. (cited in Apperson 1914: 15–16)

Tobacco was, Hariot wrote, "of so precious estimation amongst the Indians that they think their gods are marvellously delighted therewith" (cited in Lacey 1973: 101). The above extract demonstrates two key themes. First, to reiterate a central point, it was through the Galenic system that many early European travelers interpreted the unfamiliar practices that they were observing. This is particularly apparent in the statement that tobacco "purgeth superflous fleame [phlegm] and other grosse humours." Second, the great spiritual significance of tobacco for Native American peoples, and its central and wide-ranging role in their healing practices, meant that the European explorers' quest for finding a panacea had, in a sense, already been answered by the Amerindians themselves (Goodman 1993: 49).

Early European Understandings of Tobacco

Through examining early European understandings of tobacco, particularly the processes in which tobacco use became subsumed within a humoral conception of the body, it is possible to see a relatively early stage in the increasing *regulation* of tobacco use. It is this process of increased regulation, the associated rise of humoral understandings of tobacco use, and their relation to early European accounts of the practice that I shall explore in this section.

Following the proclamations of Monardes and other leading medical authorities, tobacco was, indeed, widely recognized as a cure-all from the New World by its European users. Thus, at the time of its introduction, tobacco was understood to be a medicinal plant—one that could be grown locally and used as a remedy against various afflictions. The following extract from the 1615 text *An Advice on How to Plant Tobacco in England* typifies understandings of tobacco at this time:

> I know that [tobacco] is an excellent remedy for the head-ake, for the vertigo & dizines of the head, for moist and Watery stomakes, it prevaleth against the rumes & defluctions, & all the Pains of the joynts therby occasioned, and against all affections of the head, watering of the eyes, and toothake, that it keepes off the gout and sciatica, and taketh away the rednesse of the face, that at sea it preserveth those that take it, both from the calenture or burning Fever, and from the scurvie, that it openeth obstructions, and is exceedingly profitable in the falling sicknesse. The syrope is a good Vomite, and so is a draught of white or redish wine, wherein so much of the leafe as weigheth six pence hath beene steeped all night: the oyle that droppeth out of a foule pipe, killeth tetters, and all of that kinde. (C. T. 1615: c3)

Writers such as Monardes were evidently highly influenced by Native American understandings of tobacco in ascribing the plant the status of a panacea. The Amerindians' identification of tobacco as at once a sacred herb and a medicinal remedy appears to have been of crucial importance in this regard. During the sixteenth century, the belief that illness and disease were a sign of evil was widespread (Goudsblom 1986). Thus, a herb that was understood to be truly sacred[5] would be seen to have the power to heal by driving out this evil. Such ideas were evident throughout Monardes's work on tobacco. For example, he prescribes tobacco as a remedy for "the evill breathyng at the mouthe of children" (bad breath);[6] "the evill of the mother" (labor pains); and "In evill of the joyntes" (arthritis) (Monardes 1925: 79–80). This understanding of tobacco—as a *sacred*, curative herb—can also be seen in the following extract:

> A little whiles past, certaine wild people goyng in their boates to Saint Jhon Depuerto Rico, for to shoote at Indians, or Spaniardes, if that they might finde them, they came to a place and killed certaine Indians, and

---

5. As Fairholt (1859: 46–47) observed, at the time of its introduction into Europe, tobacco became known as the "holy herb" in England, France, and Germany. This understanding of tobacco is evident in some of the literature of the time. Consider, for example, the following extract taken from William Lilly's *The Woman in the Moone* (1597): "Gather me balme and cooling violets, And of our holy herb *nicotian,* And bring withall pure honey from the hive, To heale the wound of my unhappy hand" (cited in Fairholt 1859: 47).

6. While it may seem strange to the contemporary reader for Monardes to suggest tobacco as a remedy for bad breath, the smell of tobacco smoke may well have been savory relative to the odors that people were used to during the Middle Ages.

Spaniardes, and they did hurte manye, and as by chaunce there was no Sub-limatum [a dressing for wounds] at that place to heal them, they did re-member to put upon the woundes the Joyce of the Tabaco, and the leaves stamped [crushed]. And God would, that puttyng it upon the hurtes, the griefes, madnes, and accidentes, wherwith they died, was mittigated, and in suche sort they were delivered of that evill, that the strength of the Venom was taken awaie, and the woundes were healed, of the whiche there was great admiration, the which beyng knowen by them of the Ilande, they doe use it in other hurtes and woundes, that they do take when they do fight with the wild people, and now they have no feare of theym, by reason they have founde so great a remedy, in a thing so desperate. (Monardes 1925: 81)

It is difficult to make sense of the above account. As I understand it, certain "wild people" (Monardes does not specify their nationality) attacked a group of Spanish and Native American peoples, leaving many wounded and dead. The survivors applied tobacco juice and crushed tobacco leaves to their wounds which, Monardes proposed, both healed the wounds and cleansed the injuries of their "evil" origins. Indeed, the distinction I have made here is misleading, as, crucially, Monardes appeared to view "healing" and "delivering from evil" as part of the same process.

The conceptualization of tobacco as the sacred panacea is an excellent example of how central ideas from Native American understandings of this plant and its use were selectively adopted and reworked to fit into the dom-inant European cosmology of the Middle Ages and the early modern pe-riod—in which substantial elements of it continued to survive. Indeed, there was a considerable amount of similarity between some aspects of Na-tive American and traditional European cosmology. The European under-standing of illness and disease as related to evil was not all that different from the common Native American view of illness and disease as caused by malevolent spirits. Similarly, as Wilbert (1987: 156) has observed, for Euro-pean observers the custom of the tobacco shaman "dying" and "returning" as a savior to serve his/her people "was disquietingly reminiscent of the cen-tral doctrine of their own religion."

However, as influential as leading medical authorities such as Monardes were in establishing the widespread belief that tobacco was a panacea, and in locating tobacco use within a humoral medical framework, it would be misleading simply to attribute early European understandings of tobacco to the efforts of these individuals alone. A number of other processes should also be considered. An important one that appears to have been somewhat overlooked in the historical literature is the role of tobacco as a natural model, to use Wilbert's (1987: 181) term. Wilbert proposes that a major factor in the widespread use of tobacco among Native American peoples related to the physical and pharmacological properties of the tobacco plant. For example, a common Native American practice:

> [Extracting] disease agents through the application of tobacco has a natural model in the . . . use of the plant as an insecticide on seed stock and the human body. From there it is only a small step to presume it to be useful also against pathogens of various natural and supernatural causes of illness. This becomes especially apparent in the tobacco shaman's practice of applying tobacco preparations to the skin and the outward mucosa of the patient. . . . Percutaneous absorption of nicotine by passive diffusion is readily accomplished and leads to local and systemic effects. This is true for the passage through the intact skin, the broken skin, and the external mucous membranes. Making use of this route of administration, South American Indians apply tobacco smoke, juice, powder, and leaves not only as an insecticide and vermifuge and for purposes of fertility and fecundity, but also for pain relief and healing. The understanding of nicotine action through topical administration is apt to increase the appreciation of the practice as something more than naïve doctoring. (185–86)

Similarly, physical and pharmacological characteristics of the tobacco plant may have provided a degree of empirical confirmation for its status as a panacea within European society. For example, Monardes's definition of the humoral essence of tobacco—as hot and dry in the second degree—would have been partially confirmed by the warmth and dryness of inhaled tobacco smoke. Furthermore, the expectoration that normally accompanied tobacco smoking would have lent support to the idea that tobacco drove out unwanted cold and moist humors while the analgesic and insecticidal properties of the tobacco plant would have helped to establish it as an important pharmacological substance.

The interplay between these and other more psychological effects of tobacco use may indeed have had significant therapeutic value. The contemporary scientific tendency to reduce the effects and action of tobacco use to generic biological processes very largely overlooks the possibility of considerable variations in how tobacco was experienced in different sociocultural environments, thereby denying the plant a real therapeutic role in the late Middle Ages. Since the tobacco used by European peoples of the sixteenth and seventeenth centuries was substantially different, both in terms of strength and composition, from that of modern day commercial species and varieties, it would be unwise to dismiss all the reputed benefits of tobacco use, promulgated by Monardes and similar others, as mere superstition or quackery.[7] However, it is likely that the physical and pharmacological properties of the tobacco smoked by Europeans of the late Middle Ages and early modern period would have done more to *guide* and *confirm* humoral understandings of tobacco use than to serve as a model for their genesis within an already well-established medical paradigm.

A further set of factors related to the development of humoral understandings of tobacco use is identified by Harrison (1986). Harrison argues that it was very much in the interests of physicians of the late Middle Ages and the early modern period to view tobacco as a powerful therapeutic substance located squarely within the prevailing medical philosophy of the time, as this "provided a rationale for restricting its consumption" (Harrison 1986: 557). Physicians of the time were keen to control the use of tobacco, and warned against the abuse or *unregulated* self-administration of such a powerful plant. Consider the following extract from Burton's *Anatomy of Melancholy:*

> TOBACCO! Divine, rare, super-excellent tobacco, which goes farre beyond all their panaceas, potable gold, and philosopher's stones, a sovereign remedy to all diseases! A good vomit, I confese; a vertuous herbe, if it be well qualified, opportunely taken, and medicinally used; but, as it is commonly used by most men which take it as Tinkars doe ale, 'tis a plague, a mischefe, a violent purger of goods, lands, health; hellish, devilish and damned tobacco, the ruine and overthrow of body and soule. (Cited in Alexander 1930: 89)

These warnings against the abuse of tobacco, in turn, provided the basis for state restrictions on its use, which reflected an altogether different set of interests:

> Behind this idea that men abused tobacco, "as Tinkars doe ale," lay the fear that tobacco smoking, like alehouse drinking, would destroy the productive capacity of labour. There was considerable anxiety, during the early years of James I's reign, about the effect that drinking was having on the discipline and productivity of the labouring classes. In an Act of 1606 which made drunkenness a criminal offence for the first time, excessive drinking was blamed for the "Overthrow of many good Arts and manual Trades," and the "Disabling of divers Workmen." Virtually the same language had

7. In other words, the pharmacological properties of modern-day commercial varieties of tobacco may well be fewer and less powerful than those of the varieties in use in the sixteenth and seventeenth centuries.

been used in 1604, when it had been proposed to reduce tobacco imports through the mechanism of a "good Imposition," or tax, in order to prevent the health of a great number of people becoming "impayred, and theire Bodies weakened and made unfit for Labour." (Harrison 1986: 555)

The comparisons made between drinking and smoking at the time of the introduction of tobacco can also be seen in the language that was used to describe the practice. For example, the smoker was generally said to "drink" tobacco (Apperson 1914: 16; Fairholt 1859: 56). Or, as Lacey (1973: 102) recounts, "at the trial of the [second] Earl of Essex [1600–1601] the French ambassador observed how [a jury of] peers made themselves 'silly' with smoking." There is also a great deal of pictorial evidence available. As Wyckoff (1997) writes, "A first-time tobacco 'drinker' [of this period] had to grow accustomed to the taste, as with alcohol, and the practice tended to be zealously abused like, and often in conjunction with, its liquid counterpart. Image after image of drunken stumbling, vomiting, undisciplined behavior, and dazed reverie as a result of drinking and smoking attest to this connection." Indeed, historical data suggest that the tobacco consumed in the late sixteenth and early seventeenth centuries was considerably more potent than the species and varieties commonly used in the contemporary West (Schivelbusch 1992). Among a wide range of other names, tobacco became known as *Herba Inebrians* (Dickson 1954: 17).

Clearly, the processes involved in the development of humoral-medical understandings of tobacco use were multiple and complex. However, the initiatives aimed at controlling tobacco abuse are of crucial importance to my arguments here: they mark a relatively early stage of an ongoing process in which the use of tobacco to lose control, to become intoxicated, has gradually eroded, and has increasingly been replaced by a move toward tobacco use as a means of self-control. I would now like to begin examining this and other related processes in more detail.

Early European Tobacco Use

As I have shown, tobacco use in Europe during the late sixteenth and, more particularly, the early seventeenth century was, to a degree, actually encouraged by key medical figures, and rapidly became widespread among all social groups; indeed, it had become "common." In this section I shall explore two interrelated processes. The first to be addressed is changes in the practices surrounding tobacco use—toward more differentiated, elaborate, and individualized methods as higher levels of British society sought to *distinguish* their use of tobacco from that of their perceived social inferiors. The second process is a move away from the status of tobacco as an intoxicant in and of itself, and toward forms of tobacco and modes of its consumption that would ultimately allow tobacco to become an instrument of self-control.

As I have argued in chapter 1, Europeans sought the mildest and most palatable forms of Native American tobacco. A short time after the discovery of the Americas, colonists such as Sir John Rolfe in the colony of Virginia began to cultivate milder species and varieties of tobacco, as Native American forms proved to be too strong for European tastes[8] (Koskowski 1955: 58). Yet even these varieties were extremely strong compared with those of today: accounts of smokers literally dropping dead from smoking were not unheard of in the early 1600s. For example, an entry into the *Calendar of State Papers (Domestic)*, 29 December 1601, reads as follows: "One Jackson, who frequented Little Britain Street, has died suddenly, and being opened, it was judged by the surgeons that it was from the smoke of tobacco which he took insatiably" (cited in Harrison 1986: 554). Koskowski (1955: 90) goes so far as to suggest that sudden deaths from smoking were relatively common: "Deaths were fairly often caused by tobacco as a result of bets made on the number of pipes that could be smoked. In those times it was not unusual to see children sitting at the dinner table with pipes in their mouths, and deaths of child smokers occurred quite often." Although it is not clear from these sources exactly how the smokers died, these accounts may indicate the incidence of acute poisoning from the high levels of nicotine that were present in early European tobacco. It is also possible that other toxic substances present in the tobacco may have been responsible. From the early seventeenth century, tobacco was adulterated or "sophisticated" with a number of other substances, to give it extra potency; to flavor or perfume it; or to make a given quantity (of what was a relatively expensive commodity) go further. As Brooks stated:

> The "sophisticating" of [tobacco] practised in England from the later years of Elizabeth's reign, grew to such proportions within a half century that in 1644 the mayor of London was several times petitioned by numerous vendors to represent to parliament their grievances against the "counterfeiters" in the tobacco trade. "Starch, dyer's liquor, oil and spike"[9] were mixed with tobacco stalks and offered as the pure product. The leaf itself was compounded with small coal, dust, etc., etc., and sold as unadulterated tobacco,

8. It is my aim to demonstrate that the European preference for much milder forms of tobacco was not simply a question of "taste."

9. The "spike" mentioned here may have referred to ground maize, wheat, or barley ears. It is possible that this was where the expression "to spike a drink" came from.

at about a quarter to half the prices required by honest dealers. (Brooks 1937–52: 124)

That the practice of adulteration was already quite common by 1612 can be seen in the following extract from Ben Jonson's 1612 play *The Alchemist*, in which he introduces the "Abel Drugger":

> He lets me have good tobacco, and he does not
> Sophisticate it with sack-lees or oil,
> Nor washes it in muscatel and grains,
> Nor buries it in gravel, under ground,
> Wrapped up in greasy leather, or piss'd clouts;
> But keeps it in fine lilly-pots, that, open'd
> Smell like a conserve of roses, or French beans.
> He has his maple blocks, his silver tongs,
> Winchester pipes, and fire of juniper.
> A neat, spruce, honest felloe, and no (userer). (Cited in Mack 1965: 48)

Other sources point toward the adulteration of early European tobacco, particularly snuff (which was more commonly used in Britain toward the end of the seventeenth and eighteenth centuries), with an even wider range of substances. Many of these additives were highly toxic, and included lead, arsenic, hydrogen cyanide, bromides, iodine, mercury, barbitone, antipyrine, chloral hydrate, potassium hydrate, potassium chlorate, benzoic acid, caffeine, strychnine, atropine, stramonium, cocaine, hashish, and opium (Koskowski 1955: 99–100). It is possible that these adulterants—particularly when mixed with high levels of nicotine—may themselves have been responsible for the poisonings referred to above.

The tobacco smoked by Europeans of the sixteenth to eighteenth centuries was thus far more capable of producing intoxication than the commercial species and varieties of today. From the historical data, one gets a picture of tobacco and its use within this period as relatively *unregulated*. Furthermore, these data suggest that this relative lack of regulation and near ubiquity of tobacco smoking was more the case for Britain than for any other European country in the seventeenth century. For example, toward the end of the seventeenth century almost all sections of German society began to pipe smoke *after* adopting the practice from the British (Koskowski 1955: 62). The following account of tobacco use in Britain, cited by the social historian Penn, is provided by a French visitor to the country in 1671:

> The supper being finished, they set on the table half a dozen pipes and a
> pacquet of tobacco for smoking, which is a general custom as well among

women as men, who think that without tobacco one cannot live in England because, they say, it dissipates the evil humours of the brain. . . . I have known several who, not content with smoking in the day, went to bed with pipes in their mouths, and others who have risen in the night to light their pipes, to take tobacco with as much pleasure as they would have received in drinking either Greek or Alicant wine. . . . While we were walking about the town (Worcester) he asked me if it was the custom in France as in England that when the children went to school they carried a satchel with their books and a pipe of tobacco which their mother took care to fill early in the morning, it serving them instead of breakfast, and that, at the accustomed hour everyone laid aside his book to light his pipe, the master smoking with them, showing them how to hold their pipes and draw in the tobacco, thus accustoming them to it from their youths, believing it absolutely necessary for a man's health. (Penn 1901: 78–80)

Penn continued:

That M. Jorevin de Rochefort's [the French visitor] story is not a traveller's lie nor the imposition of perfidious Albion on a too credulous Frenchman is abundantly proved by contemporary records. Hearne, in his diary, after speaking of the use of tobacco during the great plague says "Even children were obliged to smoak. And I remember that I heard formerly Tom Rogers, who was yeoman beadle, say that when he was a schoolboy at Eton that year when the plague raged [1665] all the boys of that school were obliged to smoak in school every morning, and that he was never whipped so much in his life as he was one morning for not smoking." (80)

As Penn proposed, the plague played an important role in increasing the popularity of smoking in the seventeenth century, since tobacco was considered a prophylactic against the disease (1901: 78). Indeed, pipes of the time came later to be known as "plague pipes" (Apperson 1914: 78). The role of tobacco as a prophylactic against the plague can be seen from an entry into one of Samuel Pepys's diaries. After seeing some houses bearing the plague cross, he wrote, "[I was put] unto an ill conception of myself and my smell, so that I was forced to buy some roll tobacco to smell and chaw, which took away the apprehension" (cited in Hirst 1953: 44). During the seventeenth century it was believed that one could catch the plague simply by looking at an infected person (45). Similarly, one could become infected by "evil" smells. According to Hirst, "During the Middle Ages it was supposed that if the humours of the patient became sufficiently replete with corruption they could concentrate their miasmatic poison in the air around them, exhale it from their breath or omit it from their bodies, so that not only actual contact but near approach was risky" (46).[10] Tobacco was believed to counter or "correct" contagious agents via "fumigation" of the evil smells in the air, and by forcing out "corrupt humours" from the smoker's body. The substance was seen to be "Sovereign against Infectious Airs & Distempers, Fogs, Ill-smells, & the PLAGUE by sea or land . . ."; indeed, it was proposed that "no ONE thing is so generally approved of and Recommended by Physicians to Prevent and keep off the PLAGUE or any other Infectuous Distemper, as is the SMOAKING of TOBACCO" (Parker 1722: 13). Such an understanding of tobacco can also be observed in the following account, *A Brief Treatise of the Nature, Causes, Signes, Preservation from and Cure of the Pestillence,* written by W. Kemp in 1665:

> [Tobacco] hath singular and contrary effects, it is good to warm one being cold, and will cool one being hot. All ages, all sexes, all constitutions, young and old, men and women, the Sanguine, the Cholerick, the Melancholy, the Phlegmatick, take it without any manifest inconvenience, it quencheth thirst, and yet will make one more able, and fit to drink, it abates hunger, and yet will get one a good stomach; it is agreeable with mirth or sadness, with feasting and with fasting; it will make one rest that wants sleep, and will keep one waking that is drowsie, it hath an offensive smell to some, and

10. It is important to note that this understanding of contagion was very different from modern germ theory. As Hirst proposed,

> Before Fracastor [one of the first writers to develop a complete theory of infection] no one, and certainly not Galen, seems to have given serious thought to the implications of the idea of contagion, which was inseparably linked in men's minds with both magic and miasma [the idea of disease as located in the "atmosphere"]. Contagious persons were the foci of miasmatic influences, whereas the modern germ theory of disease is radically different. Each infected individual becomes a new and often mobile factory of a self-generating living organism, so that each is capable of initiating a new epidemic, whenever the conditions are favourable for the transmission of the germ . . . according to modern epidemiological science, much does depend on the state of the atmosphere; but in a very different sense to that formerly imagined. (Hirst 1953: 47)

Goudsblom has observed that it is common for historians writing on the subject of the Middle Ages to assume a level of understanding of contagion that was simply not available at the time: "We may all too easily attribute reasons based on modern scientific insight into the mechanisms of contagion and infection, to people who could not possibly have this knowledge. Even such a notable historian of medicine as George Rosen (1958: 63–66) tends to write about the medieval treatment of lepers—isolation—as if it were guided by a well-informed attempt to reduce the risk of infection" (Goudsblom 1986: 165). This, proposes Goudsblom, was simply not the case. People of the Middle Ages would oscillate between the extremes of totally ostracizing lepers, and of "spontaneous acts of love and care." Indeed, on certain holy days, the ban on lepers would be lifted, and they would be allowed to mix freely with everyone else in the community (167). Clearly, such practices were not guided by a modern scientific understanding of germs.

is more desirable than any perfume to others; that it is a most excellent preservative, both experience and reason do teach; it corrects the air by fumigation, and avoids corrupt humours by salivation; for when one takes it either by chewing it in the leaf, or smoking it in the pipe, the humors are drawn and brought from all parts of the body, to the stomach and from thence rising up to the mouth of the Tobacconist [the smoker], as to the helme of a sublimatory, are voided and spitten out. (Cited in Apperson 1914: 76–77)

What is also interesting about this account is that it demonstrates how, in the second half of the seventeenth century in particular, some writers attributed tobacco with a wider range of properties than those initially identified by Monardes and similar others. Tobacco was no longer simply "hot and dry in the second degree"; it was believed to cool as well as to warm, and to quench one's thirst as well as to "make one more fit to drink." Furthermore, the account would appear to attest, once again, to a relative lack of social restrictions on age or gender concerning tobacco use. However, the evidence here is not conclusive. Goodman (1993: 62) proposes that the question of whether there were any gender or age proscriptions on tobacco use before the nineteenth century is still open to some debate. Some medical authorities of the seventeenth century, such as James Hart, following Monardes's definition of the humoral essence of tobacco, advised that children and pregnant women avoid tobacco because they were "hot-brained." Hart maintained that since tobacco had warming and drying effects, its use by children and pregnant women could be dangerous. Instead, tobacco use was most beneficial to older men, "where the brain is cold and moist," and in particular to those residing in "moist, fenny, waterish . . . places; as in Holland or Lincolnshire" (cited in Goodman 1993: 61). As we have seen, a large amount of somewhat anecdotal historical data indicate that such advice, if indeed it was prevalent at the time, might not have been followed. One of the more extreme accounts that can be used to illustrate this point is provided by Apperson, who cites the story of the Leeds antiquary, Ralph Thoresby. In 1702 Thoresby declared that, during one evening spent with his brother at a coffeehouse, he saw his brother's "sickly child of three years old fill its pipe of tobacco and smoke it as audfarandly [old-fashionedly] as a man of three score; after that a second and a third pipe without the least concern, as it is said to have done above a year ago" (Apperson 1914: 92). Even if this account were a vast exaggeration—Apperson casts doubt over whether a child of three years could smoke three pipes in succession—it would seem to indicate than any extant proscriptions were not uniformly observed, and that it may have been the case that even very young children smoked.

Goodman concludes that it is likely that any social proscriptions regarding the use of tobacco, if any existed at all, were largely unimportant. Factors such as price and availability were more influential in constraining the speed and the extent of the diffusion of tobacco use (Goodman 1993: 63). Yet even these factors became less significant with the increasing supply of tobacco from home and abroad. As Goodman argues, "there is sufficient literary and pictorial evidence that attests to the widespread use of tobacco by all social classes from early in the seventeenth century" (60).

As will be apparent, the use of tobacco by Europeans was very different from that of Native Americans in that it was not purely an adult male pursuit: women and children smoked, though the prevalence of this activity is unclear. In addition, the tobacco smoked was mild and weak relative to that used by Native American peoples, and it was smoked in relatively small doses quite frequently rather than in larger doses, generally less frequently, and at specific times. Nonetheless, some aspects of Native American understandings and use of tobacco were selectively adopted by Europeans. In particular, the notion that tobacco was a gift that symbolized a communal bond of friendship became widely popular. Indeed, when the Society of Tobacco-Pipe-Makers was formed in 1620, the motto they chose was "Let brotherly love continue" (Apperson 1914: 44). Even James I, in his famous 1604 anti-tobacco treatise, *A Counterblaste to Tobacco*, bears witness to the prevalence of offering tobacco as a gesture of goodwill; tobacco had become "a point of good fellowship, and he that will refuse to take a pipe of *Tobacco* among his fellowes (though by his own election he would rather feele the savour of a Sinke) is accounted peevish and no good company, even as they doe with tippeling in the Easterne Countries. Yea the Mistresse cannot in a more manerly kinde, entertaine her servant, then by giving him out of her faire hand a pipe of *Tobacco*" (James I 1954: 34).

One could describe early European tobacco use as a kind of smoking *Gemeinschaft* (to use one of Ferdinand Tönnies' salient terms): communities of smokers who gathered, shared pipes together, and exchanged experiences and knowledge of tobacco use. Indeed, smokers would meet in the shops of tobacco sellers, in apothecaries, in taverns or "alehouses," and toward the end of the seventeenth century, in coffeehouses (Apperson 1914: 81; Hackwood 1909: 361). Yet Goodman (1993: 67) suggests that historical data present a mixed picture of pipe smoking. On the one hand, pipe smoking was undertaken in "public" on social occasions, and there were

smoking clubs and even smoking schools in the late sixteenth and early seventeenth century; but on the other, he indicates plenty of pictorial evidence
to suggest that smoking was also undertaken in a more private manner, in
the "confines of home." Goodman speculates that private consumption may
have been more for medical purposes, while public use may have been more
recreational. However, this image is only mixed if one projects—as Goodman appears to—the contemporary understanding of a clear split between
private and public spaces onto the historical evidence from the seventeenth
century. The dividing line between private and public life was not nearly as
highly developed in the seventeenth century as it is in the present-day West.
In many parts of Europe, tobacco use had become a highly sociable practice,
as it was among Native American peoples.

As part of a process that is still evident today, Europeans of the sixteenth
and seventeenth centuries held somewhat ambivalent attitudes toward the
beliefs and practices of Native American peoples: on the one hand, perhaps
more so in the past, many Europeans felt as though they were more "civilized," less "primitive" than Native American "tribes"; on the other, it was,
and still is, often expressed that these peoples had wisdoms that we have lost
or not yet discovered. In the literature on tobacco use of the seventeenth
century in particular, the conflict between these ideas manifested itself in a
number of ways. Opponents of tobacco seized upon this ambivalence in attempts to counter the claims that the plant was sacred. Once again, James I
is a good example in this respect:

> And now good Countrey men let us (I pray you) consider, what honour or
> policie can moove us to imitate the barbarous and beastly manners of the
> wilde, godlesse, and slavish *Indians,* especially in so vile and stinking a cus-
> tom? . . . Shall wee, I say, that have bene so long civill and wealthy in Peace,
> famous and invincible in Warre, fortunate in both, we that have bene ever
> able to aide any of our neighbours (but never deafed any of their eares with
> any of our supplications for assistance) shall we, I say, without blushing,
> abase our selves so farre, as to imitate these beastly *Indians,* slaves to the
> *Spaniards,* refuse to the world, and as yet aliens to the holy Covenant of
> God? Why doe we not as well imitate them in walking naked as they doe?
> Preferring glasses, feathers, and such toyes, to golde and precious stones,
> as they do? Yea why do we not denie God and adore the Devill, as they doe?
> (James I 1954: 12–13)

Dickson (1954: 30) proposed that attacks on tobacco as "an invention
of the devil" may be partially rooted in the use of tobacco in shamanistic ritual observed by Europeans in the Americas. His arguments would appear to

be supported by historical data. Consider, for example, the following account of tobacco in the Island of Hispaniola written by Giralamo Benzoni of Milan in his *History of the New World* (1573):

> When these [tobacco] leaves are in season, they pick them, tie them up in bundles, and suspend them near their fireplace till they are very dry; and when they wish to use them, they take a leaf of their grain (maize), and putting one of the others into it, they roll them round tight together; then they set fire to one end, and putting the other end into the mouth, they draw their breath up through it, wherefore the smoke goes into the mouth, the throat, the head, and they retain it as long as they can, for they find a pleasure in it; and so much do they fill themselves with this cruel smoke, that they lose their reason. And there are some who take so much of it, that they fall down as if they were dead, and remain the greater part of the day or night stupefied. Some men are found who are content with imbibing only enough of this smoke to make them giddy, and no more. See what a wicked and pestiferous poison from the devil this must be. (Cited in Fairholt 1859: 19)

Even Monardes, a key proponent of tobacco, seems to contradict (earlier quoted) statements in which he viewed tobacco as a sacred curative herb. In the following extract, he described the use of tobacco by a Native American shaman:

> [He] toke certain leaves of the Tabaco, and caste them into the fire, and did receive the smoke of them at his mouthe, and at his nose with a Cane, and in takyng of it, he fell doune uppon the grounde, as a dedde manne, and remainyng so, accordyng to the quantitie of the smoke that he had taken, and when the hearbe had doen his woorke, he did revive and awake, and gave theim their aunsweres, according to the visions, and illusions whiche he sawe, whiles he was rapte of the same maner, and he did interprete to them, as to hym semed beste, or as the Devill had consailed hym, givyng theim continually doubtful aunsweres, in suche sorte, that how soever it fell out, their might saie that it was the same, whiche was declared, and the aunswere that thei made.
>
> In like sorte the reste of the Indians for their pastyme, doe take the smoke of the Tabaco, for to make theim selves drunke withall, and to see the visions, and thinges that doe represent to them, wherein thei dooe delight: and other tymes thei tooke it to knowe their businesse, and successe, because conformable to that, whiche thei had seen beeyng drunke therewith, even so thei might judge of their business. And as the Devill is a deceiver, and hath the knowledge of the vertue of Hearbes, he did shewe them the vertue of this Hearbe, that the meanes thereof thei might see

their imaginations, and visions, that he hath represented to theim, and by that meanes doeth deceive them. (Monardes 1925: 85–86)

It may be that in the above account Monardes was describing what he saw as the devil's attempt to appropriate the sacred herb to suit his own ends. That is to say, perhaps Monardes was attempting to convey the impression that the Native Americans he encountered had been led astray by the devil; but, through Monardes's skilful interpretation, this link between tobacco and the forces of evil was only present in Native American shamanic practice. The inherent tension in Monardes's text outlined here arises from his attempt to distance the "disquietingly reminiscent" Native American practice of dying and being born again as a savior from central doctrines of the Christian religion while at the same time appropriating tobacco as a sacred herb.

What is clear from the above discussion is that, in selectively adopting Native American practices, there emerged a need for Europeans to *distinguish* themselves from what they understood to be "rude," "godless," and "animalic" peoples (Brooks 1937–52: 53). Furthermore, as tobacco smoking became increasingly "common" in Britain in the seventeenth century, so the quest for *distinction* among tobacco users of the higher levels of society from their perceived social inferiors became even more pronounced. It is within this context that an increasingly elaborate set of practices relating to tobacco use began to develop.

As Apperson wrote:

Perhaps the most noteworthy thing about smoking in this period [the early seventeenth century] was its fashionableness. One of the marked characteristics of the gallant—the beau or dandy or "swell" of the time—was his devotion to tobacco. Earle says that a gallant was one that was born and shaped for his clothes—but clothes were only a part of his equipment. Bishop Hall, satirizing the young man of fashion in 1597, describes the delicacies with which he was accustomed to indulge his appetite, and adds that, he "Quaffs a whole tunnel of tobacco smoke"; and old Robert Burton, in satirically enumerating the accomplishments of "a complete, a well-qualified gentleman," names to "take tobacco with grace," with hawking, riding, hunting, card playing, dicing and the like. The qualifications of the gallant were described by another writer of 1603 as "to make good faces, to take Tobacco well, to spit well, to laugh like a waiting gentlewoman, to lie well, to blush for nothing, to looke big upon little fellowes, to scoffe with a grace . . . and, for a neede, to ride pretty and well." (Apperson 1914: 25–26)

Tobacco use by the gallant of the seventeenth century involved a highly ornate set of apparatuses, including special boxes for storing the tobacco, sometimes made of gold, silver, or ivory; a case for pipes, sometimes covered with a mirror on one side; a pick for cleaning the pipe bowl; a knife or maple block for shredding cane tobacco; tobacco tongs, for lifting hot coals into the end of the pipe to light it;[11] a ladle, for administering snuff into the nostrils; a priming iron, for preparing the pipe for use; and, of course, the pipes themselves, which were normally made of clay (Apperson 1914: 26–27; Brooks 1937–52: 52–53). In addition, smokers of the early seventeenth century commonly shared pipes with one another (Apperson 1914: 26). Again, this related to the use of tobacco as an expression of sociability; it also appears, much like the drinking of fine wines among connoisseurs today, to have involved a degree of friendly competition over the extent of the gallants' knowledge of the available forms and varieties of tobacco. Fairholt (drawing on Dekker's [1614] comedy *Greene's Tu Quoque*) provides a useful example of pipe sharing:

> The scene is a fashionable London ordinary,[12] where some "fast men" of the day meet, and one asks of another, who is smoking—"Please you to impart your smoke?" To which he replies, "very willingly, Sir." The other, after a whiff [puff] or two, exclaims, "In good faith, a pipe of excellent vapour!" which the donor confirms by declaring it "the best the house yields." To which the other rejoins in some surprise, "Had you it in the house? I thought it had been your own:, 'tis not so good now as I took it for!"[13] (Fairholt 1859: 60–61)

Apperson proposed that

> [t]he properly accomplished gallant not only professed to be curiously learned in pipes and tobacco, but his knowledge of prices and their fluctuations, of the apothecaries[14] and other shops where the herb was sold, and of the latest and most fashionable ways of inhaling and exhaling the smoke,

11. In the absence of matches, this was one of the most common ways to light a pipe. Apperson notes that the practice of lighting a pipe using a live coal held by fire tongs was still in use by "country-folk" at the time he wrote (1914: 42).

12. The "tobacco ordinary" referred to here may have meant either a smoking club, or an after-dinner gathering of smokers "at one of the many ordinaries in the neighborhood of St. Paul's Cathedral" (Apperson 1914: 27).

13. It can be observed here that the practice of sharing the pipe and engaging in friendly competition is very similar to that of the Karuk Native Americans sharing one another's pipes when they met "on the trail" (cited in chapter 1). This is another illustration of how Native American practices in which tobacco was used to express friendship were adopted by Europeans.

14. At the time it was normal for apothecaries to sell tobacco (Apperson 1914: 27).

was . . . "extensive and peculiar." It was knowledge of this kind that gained for a gallant reputation and respect by no means to be acquired by mere scholarship and learning. (Apperson 1914: 28)

Despite Apperson's claims that these refined and particular ways of smoking could not be learned formally, there emerged a number of professors in the art of smoking during the seventeenth century who, for a price, would teach novices everything that they needed to know to become well-established gallant smokers. Brooks has provided the example of a "tobacco tutor's" advertisement from 1600, taken from a play by Ben Johnson, *Every Man out of his Humour,* in which a Signor Whiff made the following claims:

[He] would prepare any newcomer to "be as exactly qualified as the best of our ordinary gallants are . . ." by instructing him in the "Most Gentlemanlike use of Tobacco: at first, to give it the most exquisite perfume; then, to know all the dilicate sweet forms of the [taking] of it: as also the rare corollary and practise of the Cuban Ebolition, Euripus, and Whiffe; Which he shall receive or take in here at London, and evaporate at Uxbridge or farther, if it please him." (Brooks 1937–52: 54)

Apperson, referring to the same example, explained: "Taking the whiff, it has been suggested, may have been either a swallowing of the smoke, or a retaining it in the throat for a given space of time; but what may be meant by the 'Cuban ebolition' or the 'euripus' is perhaps best left to the imaginations. 'Ebolition' is simply a variant of 'ebullition,' and 'ebullition,' as applied with burlesque intent to rapid smoking—the vapour bubbling, but why Cuban?" (1914: 49) "Euripus," Apperson continued, was sometimes used by "our older writers" to refer to a treacherous stretch of water, renowned for its strong and unpredictable currents. Thus, he proposed, "The use of the word in connexion with tobacco may, like that of 'ebolition,' have some reference to furious smoking, but the meaning is not clear" (ibid.). Perhaps *Euripus* referred to "treacherous currents" in the head: a "head rush" in relation to rapid, deep inhalation of tobacco smoke. It is interesting that the term *Euripus* is used—it would appear to imply a degree of bravado, risk-taking, and excitement associated with tobacco use among the gallants. That is to say, *Euripus* may have involved the analogy of brave navigation across dangerous seas as a parallel to a smoker withstanding raging torrents in the head.

Another example was provided by Samuel Rowlands in his *Paire of Spy-Knaves* (circa 1610), in which is recounted the story of how a countryman visiting London was cheated by a knave who pretended to teach him how to smoke: "I'll teach thee (do observe mee heere), To take tobacco like a cavalier;[15] Thus draw the vapour through your nose, and say, *Puffe, it is gone,* fuming the smoke away" (cited in Fairholt 1859: 55).

In a similar manner, a number of apothecaries took on pupils and taught them the "slights," or tricks of the pipe, of smoking, which "included exhaling the smoke in little globes, rings and so forth" (Apperson 1914: 48). Apperson went on to state that "[i]f one contemporary writer may be believed, some of these early smokers acquired the art of emitting the smoke through their ears, but a healthy skepticism is permissible here" (49). Thus, from the historical data one gets the strong impression that smoking by the gallants of the seventeenth century involved a highly elaborate set of practices. Many of the main characteristics of gallants' smoking discussed so far can be clearly observed from the following account, taken from Dekker's *The Gull's Horn-book* (1602):

> Before the meat come smoking to the board, our gallant must draw out his tobacco-box, the ladle for the cold snuff into the nostril, the tongs, and priming-iron; all which artillery may be of gold or silver, if he can reach the price of it; it will be a reasonable useful pawn at all times, when the amount of his money falls out to run low. And here you must observe to know in what tobacco is in town, better than the merchants, and to discourse of the apothecaries where it is to be sold; then let him show his several tricks of taking it, as the whiff, the ring, &c., for these are compliments that gain gentlemen no mean respect. (Cited in Fairholt 1859: 55–56)

I have aimed to show that, to a large extent, the experience and practice of smoking during the seventeenth century were bound up with humoral understandings of the body. That said, there are few direct accounts available of the actual *experience* of smoking tobacco from this period. However, one can begin to assimilate a general impression from the vast amount of popular literature, poetry, and songs that were written on the subject. For example, the following extract is from a song that appeared in John Weelkes's (1608) text, *Ayeres or Phantasticke Spirites:* "Fill the pipe once more, My braines daunce trenchmore,[16] It is headdy, I am geedy, My head and braines, Back and raines, Jointes and vaines, From all paines, It dothe well purge and make cleane" (cited in Fairholt 1859: 74–75). The reference to "purging" and "cleaning" here is indicative of the humoral understanding of tobacco

15. It is interesting that the term *cavalier* is used in this connection. Its use here would appear to indicate a relationship between refined smoking and high status. It may also have anti-Puritan connotations.

16. A popular dance tune of the time (Fairholt 1859: 74).

use as driving out unwanted humoral excess. For a similar reason, it was common for tobacco users during this period to spit quite frequently when smoking; this practice corresponded to the understanding of the purgative character of tobacco. It was also common, and indeed fashionable, for smokers of this time to exhale the smoke through their nostrils (Apperson 1914: 48). Once again, this may have been related to the understanding of tobacco as "dissipating the evil humours of the brain." Both these practices—spitting and nasal exhalation—are documented widely. For example, the following account is from a German traveler to London in 1598: "everywhere . . . the English are constantly smoking tobacco. . . . They have pipes on purpose made of clay, into the further end of which they put the herb, so dry that it may be rubbed into powder; and putting fire to it, they draw the smoak into their mouths, which they puff out again through their nostrils, like funnels, along with plenty of phlegm and defluxions from the head" (Apperson 1914: 32–33). However, it became clear that, particularly toward the end of the seventeenth century, tobacco was being used more "recreationally" and less as a pharmaceutical remedy (Goodman 1993: 59).

Physicians of the time continued to attack the abuse of tobacco, but, as can be seen in the following extract from Simon Paulli's *Treatise on Tobacco, Tea, Coffee, and Chocolate,* they began to realize that their efforts were largely in vain:

> Most people, when only seized with a gentle cough, are so cautious, as not to venture upon a small Dose of the Syrup of Violets, or Liquorice, without consulting their Physicians, Friends, and Nurses; but vast numbers of Europeans, without any Advice, greatly incommode and disturb the Brain, the seat of their Reason, by using the highly penetrating Smoak of Tobacco, in the Morning and the Evening, in the Night as well as the Day, and in all States and Constitutions of the weather, Calm and Serene, as well as cloudy and over-cast. Let us therefore lay aside this barbarous custom, so fatal and prejudicial to Health. (Paulli 1746: 25–26 [1655 original])

Paulli goes on to suggest that many other substances, less dangerous and powerful than tobacco, could be used to drive out unwanted humors equally effectively:

> [A] pipe filled with the burned wicks of candles, gathered out of Snuffers, or with a Piece of a match used in discharging Cannons, or with a Piece of bitumous, fossile Earth, especially that of Holland, will procure as copious a Spitting, as a pipe of the best *Virginia Tobacco.* Soldiers also, and sailours, produce the same Pleasures and Effects in themselves by smoking kindled paper, as are produced by smoking *Tobacco* . . . *Tobacco* stupefies those

who use it, and corrupts the temperature of the Brain, and destroys its tone. . . . Marjoram, Betony, Rosemary, Amber,[17] and other Substances of a like Nature, would eliminate the Phlegm more Safely, and without producing any of these ill consequences. (34–35)

The British government of the seventeenth century continued to introduce measures aimed at reducing the abuse of tobacco. High taxes were levied on tobacco imports, which, as Harrison (1986: 555) argues, were "designed to price tobacco out of the reach of the lower classes, while leaving sufficient supplies for those of the 'better sort' who would smoke in moderation." In a similar manner, legislation was passed by a number of town councils to forbid members of the poorer classes from entry to alehouses or taverns (556)—the places where smokers typically met to drink and share pipes (Hackwood 1909: 377); Harrison argues that such legislation was directed equally at smoking and drinking. The availability of tobacco was also restricted through the licensing of tobacco retail outlets (Harrison 1986: 556).

Restrictions on tobacco use in other countries during this period took a number of different forms, some quite severe. For example, in 1617 Jahangir, the Mogul emperor, ordered that anyone caught smoking should have their lips slit; Murad IV of Turkey threatened smokers with decapitation (Brooks 1937–52: 71–72). In the state of Connecticut, under the Puritanical Blue Laws of 1650, it was ordered that no one under the age of twenty-one would be permitted to smoke and, among people of age, a physician's certificate stating that tobacco would be beneficial to the holder, along with a court license, were required for anyone who wanted to smoke. Even with such documentation, no one was allowed to smoke in public (Apperson 1914: 64–65).[18]

In addition, treatises against tobacco continued to be written, many following lines of thought presented in James I's essay: associating tobacco with evil, and demonstrating the inherent contradictions in Galenic understandings of tobacco use. A particularly eloquent example is provided by Joshua Sylvestro, a court poet, in his 1620 treatise, *Tobacco Battered and The Pipes Shattered*. Consider the following extract:

17. It appears that Paulli was suggesting that these substances should be smoked as a substitute for tobacco. The "amber" mentioned here may have referred to an oil-like substance: perhaps Paulli was suggesting that this oil should be added to a mixture of the herbs he also mentioned.

18. It is interesting to note that a similar set of processes are developing in present-day North America. Smoking has become prohibited in an increasing number of public places.

[Tobacco is] vented most in Taverns, Tippling-cots,
To Ruffians, Roarers, Tipsie-Tostie-Pots;
Whose Custom is, between the *Pipe* and *Pot,*
(Th' one Cold and Moist, the other dry and Hot)
To skirmish so (like Sword and Dagger-fight)
That 'tis not easie to determine right,
Which of their Weapons hath the Conquest got
Over their Wits; the *Pipe,* or else the *Pot.*
Yet 'tis apparent, and by proof express,
Both stab and Wound the Brain with *Drunkenness* . . .
And for conclusion of this Point, observe
The places which to these abuses serve,
How-ever, of them-selves, noysom enough,
Are much more loathsom with the stench and Stuff
Extracted from their *limbeckt* Lips and Nose.
So that, the Houses, common Haunts of Those,
Are liker Hell than Heav'n: for, Hell hath *Smoak,*
Impenitent TOBACCONISTS to choak,
Though never dead: There shall they have their fill:
In Heav'n is none, but Light and Glory still. (Sylvestro 1620: 575)

The above account returns my discussion to a number of central themes. Once again, it can be seen that, during the seventeenth century, tobacco use was strongly associated with drinking, and that the forms smoked were strong relative to those in popular use in the present-day West: tobacco was said to establish "conquest over the wits," and to "stab and wound the brain with drunkenness." Furthermore, Sylvestro was aiming to promote the view that drinking and smoking together caused an "internal battle" between the humoral properties of ale and tobacco. Perhaps he intended to discourage the abuse of tobacco in conjunction with drinking, and to reclaim it as a powerful medicinal agent? Sylvestro appears to have been using humoral theory to highlight what he saw to be an inherent cause of conflict between the two. Perhaps most interestingly, he was trying to undermine the fashionableness of smoking by proposing that those who smoked were "undesirables": "Ruffians, Roarers, Tipsie-Tostie-Pots." [19] He continues this line of attack in a later part of his treatise:

If then *Tobacconing* [smoking] be good: How is't,
That lewdest, loosest, basest, foolishest,

19. I am unsure of the precise meaning of this expression, but it would appear to be equivalent to the more recent "toss pot," i.e., drunkard.

The most unthrifty, most intemperate,
Most vitious, most debauscht, most desperate,
Pursue it most: The Wisest and the Best
Abhor it, shun it, flee it, as the Pest,
Or pearcing Poyson of a Dragon's Whisk,
Or deadly Ey-shot of a Basilisk? (Sylvestro 1620: 575)

The seemingly excessively elaborate and ritualized practices of the gallant smokers become easier to understand within this context; there was clearly a need for the gallants to distinguish and distance themselves from the undesirables among whom smoking was said to be popular. It was this line of argument—that smoking was associated with immorality and vice—that, as I shall show, became the most influential over smokers during the eighteenth century in particular. As the seventeenth century progressed, so tobacco use increasingly became associated with a vulgar and dissolute way of life (Harrison 1986: 554). For example, the tobacco pipe became adopted by brothel keepers as a sign to advertise their houses (ibid.). Nonetheless, tobacco use remained widespread right to the end of the seventeenth century (see table 1.0).

High taxation and numerous moral and medical objections had little effect over the popularity of tobacco consumption. Harrison (1986) has examined why the early campaign against tobacco use was so unsuccessful. He proposes that high taxation was largely ineffective for three main reasons. First, customs duties did not apply to all imports; many of those from newly established colonies were exempt for substantial periods of time—reflecting the Crown's intent to protect its economic interests in the New World. This can be seen, for example, in a 1652 act of Parliament that aimed to prohibit the growth of tobacco in England. It began: "Whereas divers great quantities of tobacco have been of late years and now are planted in various parts of this nation, tending to the decay of husbandry and tillage, the prejudice and hindrance of the English plantations abroad . . ." (cited in Mack 1965: 4).

Second, as can be seen in the above quotation, the availability of cheaper homegrown tobacco seriously undermined price controls over that which was imported (Harrison 1986: 556). Moreover, tobacco planters successfully resisted many of the restrictions that were imposed upon them. In the case of the prohibition act cited above, tobacco planters were eventually successful in lobbying Parliament into accepting a three-pence-per-pound tax on tobacco produced at home (Mack 1965: 5). The prohibition of tobacco growing proved to be extremely difficult to enforce. As Harrison writes:

"the crop was so important to the economy of the West Counties that local magistrates refused to take action; attempts to use the army to destroy illegal plantations led to armed insurrections in the mid 17th century" (Harrison 1986: 446). Tobacco had already become crucial to the livelihood of a wide range of people. This can be seen most clearly in the following extract taken from a translation of Everard's *Panacea, or the Universal Medicine; being a Discovery of the Wonderfull Virtues of Tobacco taken in a Pipe; with its Use and Operation both in Physick and Chyrurgery* (1659):

> If we reflect upon our forefathers, and that within the time of less than one hundred years, before the use of tobacco came to be known amongst us, we cannot but wonder how they did to subsist without it; for were the planting or traffick of tobacco now hindered, millions of this nation in all probability must perish for the want of food, their whole livelihood almost depending on it. So many druggists, grocers, tobacco-shops, taverns, inns, alehouses, victuallers, carriers, cutters and dryers of tobaco, pipe-makers and the like, that deal in it, will prove no less. (Cited in Fairholt 1859: 114–15)

Third, Harrison argues, the manner in which tobacco taxes were collected—by subcontraction to business syndicates—meant that the government had limited control over how the taxation policy was implemented.

Ultimately, the main reason for the failure of the seventeenth-century campaign against tobacco smoking was plain: "The adoption of a strategy which depended upon the co-operation of powerful commercial interests meant that gradually the regulatory policy was subverted, and harnessed to the pursuit of monetary gain" (Harrison 1986: 557). Not only was tobacco a crucial source of income for newly established colonies in the New World, and for those who were variously involved in the production and retailing of tobacco and tobacco-related products in England, but taxation of the plant had become a major source of government revenue by the end of the seventeenth century (556). The government, exporters, growers, retailers, physicians, proponents, opponents, consumers, and others variously involved with tobacco consumption had become bound up in a set of processes involving shifting balances of power, which are still continuing today. Indeed, Harrison suggests, from examining the fate of this early campaign against tobacco, there is "a lesson here for present-day public health campaigners. . . . Many governments still emphasize the need to reach agreement with the tobacco industry over product-modification, and over controls of advertising and sponsorship. Virtually all modern policy options were first tried over 300 years ago." (557).

To summarize this section: I have argued that tobacco use in the sixteenth and seventeenth centuries was substantially different from that of the contemporary West. The tobacco smoked was much stronger than present-day commercial species and varieties, and was more capable of producing intoxication. Tobacco was initially compared to drinking, and much of the language associated with tobacco use at the time reflected this fact. Tobacco became used by all levels of society, with seemingly few social proscriptions regarding the age or gender of smokers. The higher levels of English society sought to distance and distinguish themselves both from Native American tobacco users—who were seen as godless and in contact with evil—and the vulgar, rough, and undesirable characters with whom tobacco use was increasingly becoming associated. Throughout the seventeenth century, there emerged a large amount of literature, much of it written by physicians, aimed at encouraging smokers to use tobacco in a much more regulated, *moderate* fashion. The government introduced a number of policies, including taxation and the licensing of tobacco retail outlets, that were (at least initially) aimed at controlling tobacco use by restricting the supply. These attempts to regulate the practice were largely unsuccessful. One of the main reasons for this relative lack of success was that the governments of the time were both opposed to, and increasingly economically dependent upon, tobacco. Tobacco use remained widespread, and, moreover, had become a highly sociable practice. However, particularly toward the end of the seventeenth century, there emerged distinct signs that the manner in which tobacco was being used was changing. I would now like to examine these changes in more detail.

Changes in European Tobacco Use

Toward the end of the seventeenth century, snuffing began to emerge as a popular means of consuming tobacco, particularly among the higher levels of English society (Brooks 1937–52: 160). The following provides a strong indication of the impetus for this change:

> Nicotia reached its Zenith and began to decline. It had attained a popularity it had never known before, and to which the present age [the early 1900s] is only now approximating. Its very popularity caused its downfall. What the thunders of priests, the logic of philosophers, the warnings of physicians, the satire of wits and the excise duties of kings had not been able to accomplish, fashion performed single-handed. The laws of fashion are aimed at singularity; to be unique, to be different at all costs from the common people, is the aim of fashion's constant inconstancy. Smoking had become common, the pipe was no longer the badge of the beau; the habit

was practised by the very lowest classes of society. And society with a big 'S,' repulsed for its vulgarity the practice it had first embraced for its singularity. The institution of French habits and manners as the standard of social life at the beginning of the eighteenth century—the maxim "They do things better in France" is Sterne's—was a powerful factor in the degradation of smoking. In France snuff had always been preferred to smoking, and Georgian England, repudiating smoking for its popularity began to snuff. . . . The middle classes in time imitated the freak of their social superiors and ceased smoking. But it never lost its popularity among the people, though it was regarded as synonymous with blackguardism and the lowest vices. (Penn 1901: 85)

Penn's argument here is consistent with Norbert Elias's demonstration, both in *The Civilizing Process* and *Court Society,* that the French court had become a model-setting center for the European upper classes in the seventeenth and eighteenth century. Penn's contention that it was "fashion" rather than medical arguments, government interventions, or religious edicts that had the strongest influence over tobacco use is of great importance. The continuing *quest for "distinction"* was instrumental in a decline in smoking, and a rise in the use of snuff. In the early eighteenth century, snuffing became increasingly "fashionable" and, similar to smoking among the gallants of the seventeenth century—but perhaps even more so—came to involve a highly elaborate set of practices and rituals. Indeed, in 1711 a school was opened in London to teach the fashionable the socially 'correct' ways of using snuff (Mack 1965: 8). Fairholt provided the following journalist's account of eighteenth-century snuffing:

A grave gentleman takes a little casket out of his pocket, puts a finger and thumb in, brings away a pinch of a sort of powder, and then with the most serious air possible, as if he were doing one of the most important actions of his life . . . proceeds to the thrust, and keeps thrusting it at his nose, after which he shakes his head, or his waist coat, or his nose itself, or all three, in the style of a man who has done his duty, and satisfied the most serious claim of his well being. It is curious to see the various modes in which people take snuff; some do it by little fits and starts, and get over the thing quickly. These are epigrammatic snuff-takers, who come to the point as fast as possible, and to whom the pungency is everything. They generally use a sharp and severe snuff, a sort of essence of pins' points. Others are all urbanity and polished demeanour; they value the style as much as the sensation, and offer the box around them as much out of dignity as benevolence. Some take snuff irritably, others bashfully, others in a manner as dry as the snuff itself, generally with an economy of the vegetable: others with a luxuriance of gesture, and a lavishness of supply, that announce a moister article, and shed its superfluous honours over neckcloth and coat. (Fairholt 1859: 263–64)

As can be observed from the above account, while snuff use may have been considered refined relative to pipe smoking (which involved a great deal of expectoration, and, perhaps crucially, "invasive" smoke), to modern sensitivities the practice may appear vulgar or distasteful. A great deal of sneezing accompanied the use of snuff, so it was common for a snuff-user's clothes to become discolored both by the substance and by mucus. As Drake states:

> Good fine-powdered snuff when sniffed up into the nostril, instantly produce[d] a strong, almost unbearable irritation of the nasal organ followed by violent sneezing. Snuff-taking surely [wa]s the untidiest form of using tobacco. Historians have always described the clothing of heavy users, such as Frederic the Great as disfigured by being covered with snot and snuff. It took hardy men [and women] with iron constitutions to acquire the habit. Heavy snuffers had permanently inflamed eyes, a sore proboscis, and a weak, damaged sense of smell. Some, who did not want to suffer, but still wanted to be fashionable, only pretended to take snuff. What they really sniffed was a mild concoction of cinnamon and cream. (Drake 1996)

The snuffers' equipment, while still elaborate by modern standards, was considerably more simple than that which was required by the smoking and snuffing gallants of the seventeenth century. Since snuff did not need to be combusted before consumption, no equipment for lighting it was required. In this way, snuffing constituted an altogether more practical, less clumsy means of consuming tobacco (Goodman 1993: 84). In the sense of not involving a risk of fire, it was also less dangerous. However, although the snuffers' equipment was simple relative to that of the gallants of the seventeenth century, its form was often highly elaborate and ornate. Such tools included a "rasp," which was sometimes made of ivory (74), to grate snuff from rolled blocks of tobacco known as carrots (the freshly grated snuff was known as *rappée*) (Fairholt 1859: 257); and highly ornate tobacco boxes, some of which were made of gold or silver and inset with precious stones (260). For those who could not afford these materials, "Agate, pierta dura, rare woods, or mosaics" were used instead (ibid.). During the eighteenth century, particularly in France, snuffboxes were considered items of jewelry. Within aristocratic circles, the practice of giving the boxes as gifts was widespread. Marie Antoinette, for example, was said to have had fifty-two gold snuffboxes in her wedding basket (Goodman 1993: 74).

Snuff was usually consumed as a dry powder that was snorted into the nostrils. However, historical data also indicate the prevalence of other means of consumption. Fairholt (1859: 241–42, 269) provides some interesting examples in this connection, including ocular absorption. He proposed that a number of "Cephalic" ocular snuffs, such as "Grimstone's Eye Snuff," were extensively consumed toward the end of the eighteenth century "from a belief in [their] efficacy in freeing the head of bad humour[s], and imparting clearness in vision, in which [they were] imagined to be 'most sovereign'" (269). Indeed, the use and understanding of tobacco in the form of snuff as a humoral medical remedy persisted throughout the eighteenth century:

> [Snuff] heals colds, inflammation of the eyes, involuntary tears, headaches, migranes, dropsy, paralysis, and generally all those misfortunes caused by the pungency of humours, their too great amount and their dissipation from their normal conduits. Nothing is better to increase the fluidity of blood, to regulate its flow and circulation. It is an unfailing sternutory [sneeze stimulant] to revive those with apoplexy or those in a death trance. It is a powerful relief for women having the pains of childbirth; a certain remedy for hysterical passions, dizziness, restlessness, black melancholy, mental derangement. Those who use it having nothing to fear from bad and corrupted air; the plague, syphilis, purpura, one does not have to guard against approaching those with popular illnesses that are easily communicated. It strengthens memory, it stimulates the imagination. Scholars are never afraid to tackle very abstract and difficult problems with their nose full of tobacco. (Labat 1742: 278–79)
>
> By its gently pricking and stimulating the membranes, it causes Sneezing or Contractions, whereby the glands like so many squeezed Sponges, dismiss their Serosities and Filth. And it serves for a drain to excessive Moisture in the Eyes or Head; so when a sufficient Moisture is wanting, its quick and noble Spirit opens the Vessels that afford Supplies thereto; and pure Snuff put into the Corners of the Eyes is found to alter and destroy the sharp Humours that occasion Bloodshot etc. So beneficial is this Powder for the Preservation of that most dear and valuable of all our senses, the Sight. (Anon. 1712, cited in Goodman 1993: 80)

Most important, as can be observed from the above accounts, in much of the snuff-oriented literature of the period, the substance was seen to have a more specific effect over the "mind," the human brain, and "the head" than the body more generally (as was more the case in the sixteenth and seventeenth centuries).

As mentioned earlier, snuff, more than pipe tobacco, was subject to adulteration. Snuff was not simply mixed with other ingredients to make a given quantity go further; rather, the adulteration process was seen as a way of improving and refining its properties. For example, the following is from a

Table 2 Retail Prices of Wimble's Snuffs

Prices per lb.	s.	d.	Prices per lb.	s.	d.
English Rappee	3	0	Best English Rappee	4	0
Do. do.	3	6	Common do.	2	0
Bolongaro's Hollanda	4	0	Good Plain do.	2	6
English Round Rappee	3	6	Best Scotch	2	6
Strasburgh	3	0	Common do.	2	0
Do. Violet	4	0	Ordinary English Rappee	2	6
Scented Rappee	2	6	High Flavored do.	3	6
English Bran	3	0	Composite do. do.	2	6
Fine English Rappee	3	6	Rappee Bergamot	2	0
High-Flavored Coarse do.	3	0	Low Rappee	1	0
Ordinary English Bran	2	6	Plain Scotch	2	0
Carrot Rappee	4	0	Natural English Rappee	3	0
Romano's Hollande	4	0	High-flavored do.	3	0
Best Dunkerque Rappee	3	6	Cephalic	5	0
Macabao	8	0	St. Domingo	6	0
Scotch	2	0	Brazil Imitated	5	0
Fine do.	3	0	Best Brazil	24	0
Scholten's Best Rappee	6	0	Second do.	20	0
Bolongaro's St. Vincent	4	0	Third do.	16	0
John's Lane	2	0	Best Spanish	10	0
Spanish Bran	6	0	Second do.	8	0
Common Scotch	1	0	Best Havannah	6	0
Fine Irish	2	0	Common do.	4	0

Source: Fairholt 1859: 268–69.

1722 pamphlet: "the Virginia tobacco from which this tobacco is prepared, being here divested of its malignant *ill* qualities, and strengthened in its *good* ones, will, when taken in snuff . . . make an evacuation of offending humours from the head, eyes, &c., without the usual ill consequences of it" (Fairholt 1859: 269–70).

In eighteenth-century England there emerged over two hundred different varieties and mixtures of commercially available snuff (Goodman 1993: 74). The above table of prices from a typical snuff retailer in 1740 provides an excellent illustration of this diversity.

However, snuff was sometimes adulterated with highly toxic substances. As with pipe smoking in the seventeenth century, there is some evidence to suggest that deaths from snuff poisoning occurred during the eighteenth century. For example, in the preface to *Pandora's Box; a Satyr against Snuff* (1719), the author wrote, "I should be glad to be informed how the common salutation, 'God bless you!' when anyone sneezes, became so much in vogue; if it were not from the dreadful convulsions, and sometimes sudden deaths, that have been the fatal consequences of those impetuous shocks" (cited in Fairholt 1859: 267).[20] Another two accounts are provided by Fairholt:

> One instance of the dangers inseparable from scented snuff is given in an anecdote of the Duc de Bourbon, grandson of the great Condé; who took Santeuil the poet to a great entertainment, compelled him to drink a large quantity of champagne, and ultimately poured his snuff-box, filled with Spanish snuff, into his wine. This produced a violent fever, of which Santeuil died, amid excruciating agonies, within fourteen hours after. (256)

> [P]hysicians observe that more people have died of apoplexies in one year since the use of snuff has come up than before in one hundred; and indeed most, if not all, of those who die of apoplexies and other such sudden deaths, upon inquiry will be found to have been great snuff-takers; as it happens usually in Spain and Portugal, where of late years the common disease that carries people off is apoplexy. (*A Treatise on the Use of Tobacco, &c.* (1722) cited in Fairholt 1859: 264)[21]

Historical data point towards the likelihood that it was the adulterants present in many varieties of eighteenth-century snuff, more than the nicotine content of the tobacco consumed, that were responsible for the poi-

---

20. Kanner proposed that the common habit of blessing sternutation by Christian peoples had a number of different explanations. One of the most popular was that sneezing was looked upon by the church as a "momentary palsy" similar to that which occurs in the event of an epileptic seizure, or—more important—a sexual orgasm. All three (sneezing, seizures, and orgasms) were regarded as sacred, and thus were treated accordingly (Kanner 1931: 563–64). Other writers attributed the practice to the outbreak of a plague at the time of Pope Gregory the Great during which prolonged spells of sneezing (as symptomatic of the disease) were often followed by death. As Kanner wrote, "The Pope then, in a special ordinance, is said to have instituted a short benediction to be used every time when a person sneezed, and this habit established itself so thoroughly and permanently that it has persisted to our day [the early 1900s]" (564). However, Kanner proposed that a large amount of evidence pointed toward the prevalence of blessing sternutation sometime before the time of Pope Gregory the Great (the sixth century). Drake expands upon the relationship between sneezing and sexual orgasm. He proposes that sneezing was viewed as a "momentary lapse of consciousness during which demons, or the devil himself, may enter [the body], unless that momentarily disconnected soul is protected by the blessing of someone in the vicinity—even a total stranger" (Drake 1996: 4). It is also interesting to note that in France during the seventeenth century, it was for a time considered improper to bless a person who had sneezed. An entry into *The Rules of Civility* (1685) made this clear: "If his lordship chances to sneeze, you are not to bawl out, 'God bless you sir,' but, pulling off your hat, bow to him handsomely, and make that observation to yourself" (cited in Kanner 1931: 565). Perhaps it was considered rude to draw too much attention to a person's momentary loss of self-control—as sneezing was then seen to constitute.

21. The following footnote is provided to this citation: "The Edinburgh Encyclopaedia ends a short but severe article on snuff with the significant reference, *See Poisons*" (Fairholt 1859: 264–65).

sonings and fatalities referred to in the above accounts. Occasionally the link was made explicitly, as in the following account: "Mr Fosbroke, a surgeon, was very nearly falling a victim to this shameful and poisonous adulteration. Paralysis had commenced, but the lead in the snuff was fortunately detected in time" (Steinmetz 1857: 73). It is extremely difficult to assess the extent to which the snuff popularly consumed during the eighteenth century was, on the whole, 'milder' than the pipe tobacco that was more commonly used during the seventeenth—if indeed it was milder. The relationship between the use of alcohol and the use of tobacco in the eighteenth century may prove useful in this connection. To recapitulate: During the seventeenth century tobacco use was frequently compared to drinking, not simply because no other model for the practice existed at the time, but more because the model of alcohol consumption had a closer "fit" to the use of tobacco than it does in the present-day West. That is to say, the tobacco used in the seventeenth century was far more capable of inducing a state similar to that of drunkenness—of intoxication—than the tobacco popularly consumed in the West today. However, during the eighteenth century there appear to be progressively fewer references to the relationship between tobacco consumption and alcohol in the literature relating to tobacco use at the time. Indeed, when such references do appear, the relationship is considerably more tenuous, and less direct. Consider, for example, the following extract from the 1798 text *A Treatise on the Use and Abuse of Tobacco:*

Axiom I.
Tobacco, whether by the pipe or quid, generally causeth a spitting.

Axiom II.
Spitting, by depriving the mouth of its saliva intended by nature to moisten and lubricate it, will make you thirsty.

Axiom III.
Drought, or thirstiness, calleth for drink to supply the want of ejected spittle.

Axiom IV.
Drinking too frequently (particularly of strong drink) will intoxicate.

Axiom V.
Drunkenness alas! too, too often causes you to fall out with your best friends, and to commit actions, which in your returning sober moments you are sorry for and ashamed of. (Cited in Brooks 1937–52: 180)

It is interesting to note that it is clearly alcohol, not tobacco, that is seen to be the intoxicating agent. This stands in direct contrast to early seventeenth-century accounts, in which both alcohol and tobacco are said to "stab and wound the brain with drunkenness." This is not to say that there are *no* accounts in the eighteenth-century literature in which tobacco is said to be intoxicating, but rather that the above account, written toward the very end of that century, may provide an indication of the overall direction in which understandings and experiences of tobacco were changing.

In much of the historical literature relating to tobacco use, the popularity of snuffing in the eighteenth century is viewed as an aberration, with smoking considered the norm (Goodman 1993: 90). However, the rise of snuffing was much more significant than these texts indicate: in fact, it had become the most popular form of tobacco use throughout Europe in the eighteenth century, and well into the nineteenth (ibid.). Snuffing had become so popular as a medium of consuming tobacco that a number of authors proclaimed that pipe smoking "had gone out" by the 1770s (Penn 1901: 86). However, as Brooks noted, it was probably more accurate to proclaim that smoking had "gone out" among English aristocrats, and the "conventionally proper people"—the fashionable. "The familiar pipe had lost caste" (Brooks 1937–52: 163). Nonetheless, in the eighteenth century, pipe smoking remained widespread among the "common people," within the army and the navy, and at the universities (162).

Indeed, from a very early stage, tobacco smoking became closely associated with military and academic life, in spite of any social proscriptions on the practice. Apperson has provided a number of accounts attesting to the widespread practice of smoking in the universities in the eighteenth century. One example is of a father's letter to his undergraduate son at Cambridge which contains the following sentence: "I would be loath you confirm the scandal charged upon the universities of learning chiefly to smoke and to drink" (Apperson 1914: 102). Another consists of the following extract from Thomas Warton's *Progress of Discontent* (1746), in which Oxford University life of the time is described: "Return, ye days when endless pleasure, I found in reading or in leisure! When calm around the Common Room, I puff'd my daily pipe's perfume! Rode for a stomach, and inspected, At annual bottlings, corks selected: And dined untax'd, untroubled, under, The portrait of our pious Founder!." (cited in Apperson 1914: 103)

Snuffing's displacement of smoking as "the badge of the beau," and smoking's association with the "common people" may also have been related to the decline in the popularity of alehouses in the eighteenth century (Goodman 1993: 72).[22] During this time, alehouses had also become asso-

22. The precise character of this relationship is open to speculation, if indeed any significant relationship existed at all. Goodman proposes that it is possible that since alehouses had been a cheap and available source of tobacco and pipes during the seventeenth century, their demise may have affected the practice of smoking. However, he believes that since the alehouse was

ciated with the lower levels of society. For example, in an extract from an edition of the journal *World* published in 1755, "there is a description of a noisy, hearty, drinking, devil-may-care country gentleman, in which it is said, 'he makes no scruple to take his pipe and pot at an alehouse with the very dregs of the people'" (cited in Apperson 1914: 101).

It is within this context that snuffing increasingly began to be seen as the refined means of consuming tobacco. Unlike pipe smoking, the use of snuff was seen to have its origins in courtly aristocratic circles (Goodman 1993: 81); thus snuff presented a means of escaping the negative Native American associations of tobacco.[23] Goodman's further proposal that practices associated with snuffing were far more *individualized* than those of pipe smoking in the seventeenth century (Goodman 1993: 73, 81–2) is of great importance. Snuffing came to be located within a "complex of soft-drugs" that included tea, coffee, and chocolate and, following the practices associated with these drugs, began to be consumed in a more private manner (82). He writes, "Snuff proclaimed the individual. The range of concoctions was enormous; even those who were forced to purchase from a monopoly or from small retailers could choose specific brands or doctor the standard package to make the product more individual" (ibid.). The individuality of snuffing practices is well documented:

> Each leader of society and the coteries which attached themselves had their favorite snuff, and, in consequence, an extraordinary mingling of scents pervaded each court or ballroom where the well-bred met. In a room where the conversation was punctuated by discreet sneezes, the lady who adored *Jasamena* (made especially precious to her because of the exquisite box from which she took it) would condescend to take a pinch from the proffered box of the dandy who preferred *Orangery*. This she would do in the approved manner, whereby a delicate, bejewelled wrist and a well-turned arm would be displayed to advantage, while her companion, on his part, was in perfect position to indicate the handsome rings he wore, without apparent ostentation. This exquisite technique for the correct means of taking snuff was developed by the French mentors of etiquette, to which native touches were given when the habit invaded London, Rome and elsewhere. (Brooks 1937–53: 159)

---

one of many retail outlets for tobacco and pipes, it is doubtful that their decline as a social institution would have had played a significant role in the corresponding decline in smoking within the same period (Goodman 1993: 72–73).

23. As I have shown in chapter 1, this was clearly a myth about the origins of snuffing. Snuffing had been extensively practiced by a number of Native American peoples at the time of initial contact with the West.

It is significant that the practice of consuming snuff in the form of a dry powder, rather than the other forms that were available—including nasal pellets and "wet" oral snuffs—became widespread in Europe in the eighteenth and, to some extent, nineteenth centuries. Objections to these other forms were not so much based on humoral medical grounds as on the grounds of decency and sensitivity. For example, André Antonil, writing in 1711, discussed the use of nasal snuff pellets; he proposed that if left inside the nostrils, either overnight or throughout the day, the pellets would "draw out moisture from the nasal cavities." However, "one only recommends it to those who, in using it, can avoid the indecency that appears when the pellets, being discharged from the nostrils and the drop of snot that is always suspended, soils the chin and nauseates the person with whom one is speaking" (cited in Goodman 1993: 84). This description highlights the importance of changing sensitivities and delicacies of feeling—in turn related to changing codes of etiquette and manners—in influencing the use of tobacco.

Tobacco Use and Civilization

It is in this connection that the link between changes in tobacco use and much broader-scale social processes can be elucidated. A brief exposition of Elias's (2000) concept of civilization will help to explain some of the processes discussed so far, and introduce a set of ideas that are central to the arguments I present throughout this book.

Elias used the term *civilization* in a *technical* and not a normative manner. Just as anthropologists have sought to distinguish their use of the term *culture* from its evaluative use to express refinement and high mental achievements, so Elias distinguished his use of *civilization* from its normative use to express progress, the triumph of rationality, social evolution, and so on. He used the term to refer to a set of long-term social processes that are visible in changing standards of social behavior in the West. In the broadest sense, and to oversimplify somewhat, the civilizing process refers to processes of state formation, the long-term establishment of monopolies over violence and taxation in the West which, in turn, have involved an increasing social pressure toward exercising greater self-restraint as part of shifting modes of social control. He began his analysis of the civilizing process by examining a highly influential etiquette manual, *De civilitate morum puerilium* (On civility in boys), written by Erasmus in 1530. Erasmus's position in history—between the Middle Ages and the early modern period—meant that he provided data that indicate the *quite specific direction* in which codes of etiquette were changing. From this and other similar sources, Elias traced the gradual changes occurring in *standards of behavioral expectations* among members of the secular upper classes: everything from their manners at the dinner table to how they approached and experienced their emotions and bodily functions.

According to Elias, social life in the Middle Ages was characterized by conduct that, by present-day Western standards, would be considered distasteful. For example, it was common for people to urinate and defecate quite publicly. Indeed, some medieval texts advised that "[b]efore you sit down, make sure your seat has not been fouled" (Elias 2000: 110). Moreover, people normally ate from a common dish, with unwashed hands; broke wind at the table; and spat on the floor (60, 110, 129). In prescribing what one should not do, manners texts also gave an indication of what was commonplace. For example, it was recommended that one should not use the tablecloth to blow one's nose (122). Elias analyzed how the restraints on behavior that present-day Western peoples take for granted actually developed over time. He observes that an increasing range and number of aspects of human behavior gradually came to be regarded as distasteful and were thus pushed *behind the scenes of social life*. Corresponding to this shift, people begin to experience an advancing threshold of shame and repugnance in relation to their bodily functions.

The elaboration of codes of etiquette and manners accompanied a corresponding shift in people's behavior: for example, defecation, urination, and copulation increasingly became conducted in private, closed-off places. Thus a defining characteristic of the civilizing process in the West was that people gradually began to exercise higher degrees of self-restraint. This is not to say that one cannot find any evidence of self-restraint among people of the Middle Ages. Indeed, Elias found extreme forms of asceticism and renunciation in certain sectors of medieval society (such as the self-denial exercised by monks). However, these stood in contrast "to a no less extreme indulgence of pleasure in others, and frequently enough . . . sudden switches from one attitude to the other in the life of an individual person" (Elias 2000: 373). In short, therefore, Western processes of civilization have involved growing pressures for a gradual *stabilization* of human behavior: they have also been characterized by "diminishing contrasts and increasing varieties" (382).

Changes in tobacco use have also been influenced by these processes of civilization. I have shown how the increasing use of snuff in eighteenth-century Europe marks a further stage in the development of tobacco use in the West, a development that follows the *quite specific direction* discussed by Elias. First, tobacco use had moved even further away from early seventeenth-century European, and, more particularly, Native American, practices in which—particularly with the latter—tobacco was used to produce intoxication and a loss of control. Increasingly, the move was toward tobacco consumption in more highly controlled, more formal, increasingly differentiated, private, and *individualized* ways. I have argued that these processes were, in turn, interrelated with an increasing quest for distinction among members of the higher levels of society, and corresponding changes in standards of feeling and delicacy. In other words, many of the changes in tobacco use observed so far have been fundamentally related to *increasing demands for self-restraint*. This is a theme that I would like to develop through a consideration of how tobacco use developed in the nineteenth and twentieth centuries.

Tobacco Use in the Nineteenth and Early Twentieth Centuries

While snuffing remained popular in Britain throughout the first half of the nineteenth century, tobacco-using practices increasingly began to return to smoking during this period. In addition to a dramatic increase in pipe smoking during the 1800s (Goodman 1993: 93), cigar smoking emerged as a popular mode of consumption:

> Until the middle of the last [nineteenth] century there were fewer smokers than snuffers, snuff-taking was as common as smoking was rare when Victoria ascended the throne, though the introduction of the cigar early in the century had rehabilitated smoking with beaux and military men by the substitution of the relaxing cigar for the cumbersome clay pipe which had hitherto enjoyed a monopoly. . . . The reduction of duty on cigars in 1829 from 19s to 9s a pound contributed greatly to the renascence of smoking by placing on the market at a moderate price the elegant cigar. (Penn 1901: 88)

Most interestingly, as the above account serves to demonstrate, clay-pipe smoking increasingly came to be seen as "cumbersome," and outmoded, and the briar pipe emerged as a far more practical alternative. The practice of snuffing declined so rapidly that, at the end of the nineteenth century, snuff constituted only one percent of total tobacco consumption in Britain (Goodman 1993: 93), a pattern that was repeated in many other parts of the West (91). However, there were some quite substantial variations in the timing and character of this process. For example, in Sweden, snuff[24] consumption rose from the late eighteenth century until the 1930s. Moreover, it was only after the Second World War that smoking (cigarettes) began to

---

24. The Swedes generally used wet oral snuff, which was consumed by placing a quantity behind the upper lip (Goodman 1993: 92).

emerge as the most popular mode of consumption there (92). Also, in the United States, chewing tobacco was the most popular mode of consumption from about the third decade of the nineteenth century. It was not until just before the First World War that it was eventually replaced by smoking (Tate 1999: 11). While the cigarette offered few practical advantages over chewing tobacco (which was portable and durable), relief workers promoted it among American troops on the grounds that it did not offend the sensibilities as much as chewing, which, invariably, was accompanied by a great deal of spitting (66).[25]

Historical data point toward a growing number of social proscriptions pertaining to smoking during the early part of the nineteenth century. Penn clearly stated that it was considered objectionable to be seen smoking on the streets during the 1830s (1901: 88). Interestingly, smoking came to be considered a vice that should be practiced in private places (Apperson 1914: 156). Apperson proposed that, during the mid-nineteenth century, it was rare to see people smoking on the streets, and that, after meals, it was common for smokers to "retire" to smoking rooms or the kitchen, where they would wear smoking jackets in place of their normal evening wear and smoking caps to protect themselves from the odor of tobacco – 62).[26] Mack's extract from the early Victorian etiquette manual *Hints on Etiquette and the Usages of Society* (1854) clearly demonstrates how smoking in public was frowned upon at this time:

> The tobacco smoker in *public*, is the most selfish animal imaginable, he preserves in contaminating the pure and fragrant air, careless of whom he annoys, and is but the fitting inmate of a tavern. Smoking in the streets, or in a theatre, is only practised by shopboys, pseudo-fashionable and the

25. It would be interesting to explore in greater depth the rise of tobacco chewing in America. Brooks (1953) goes so far as to suggest that the rise of tobacco chewing marked a general decline of social standards in America, one that possibly arose from the growing social mixing of urban and rural communities: an "era of bad taste when a general sloppiness in American manners was painfully evident. It was a time when a sturdy citizen could (in a phrase quoted by a journalist) stand in his doorway, bite his morning 'chaw' and spit eighteen feet without trespassing on his neighbor. . . . It may be that the intrusion of the frontier upon urban areas and the casual and rough manners of the backwoods had a dynamic effect upon a mixed society whose social habits were diverse and unstandardized" (cited in Walton 2000: 62–63). Dickens in his *American Notes* (1842) was clearly disgusted by the habit of chewing he observed in the United States: "Washington may be called the head-quarters of tobacco-tinctured saliva, . . . I must confess, without any disguise, that the prevalence of those odious practices of chewing and expectorating [have become] most offensive and sickening" (cited in Walton 2000: 63).

26. It is clear that Apperson has a particular smoker in mind in this connection: relatively affluent, and male.

"SWELL MOB". . . . As snuff taking is merely an idle, dirty habit, practised by stupid people in the unavailing endeavour to clear their stolid intellect, and is not a custom particularly offensive to their neighbours, it may be left to each individual taste as to whether it be continued or not. An "elegant" cannot take much snuff without decidedly "losing caste." (Mack 1965: 10)

The above extract underscores several important points. For one, the arguments against smoking in public have a familiar ring to them. In a manner similar to that of the anti-tobacco treatises of the seventeenth century—including the previously cited treatise written by Joshua Sylvestro—the author sought to associate tobacco smoking with the lower levels of society, and with those who were *trying* to be fashionable. Also of interest is the near-endorsement of snuff on the grounds that it was not "particularly offensive" to others—presumably the absence of invasive smoke was implied in this connection. Furthermore, one gets the strong impression that any form of tobacco using, even snuffing, was considered a vice in which one should not overindulge: one "cannot take much snuff without decidedly 'losing caste.'" It is important to observe that this plea for moderation was not based upon health-related concerns. Instead, in conformity with Elias's thesis, it stemmed from concerns relating to codes of etiquette and manners: *the social constraint toward self-constraint*. Finally, the idea that snuff was used to "clear the stolid intellect" is yet another example of the increasing focus on the effects of tobacco on the brain during this period. I shall return to this theme shortly.

There are numerous other examples of quite explicit proscriptions pertaining to smoking in the nineteenth century. Most interestingly, Victorian etiquette dictated that it was extremely bad manners to smoke "in the presence of a lady" (Mack 1965: 9). Many etiquette texts written in the mid-nineteenth century appear simply to have assumed that women did not smoke, and that smoking in the presence of a woman would offend her sensitivities. The following extracts from *The Habits of Good Society* (1868) contain some interesting remarks about cigar smoking:

But what shall I say of the fragrant weed which Raleigh taught our gallants to puff in capacious bowls; which a royal pedant denounced in the famous "Counterblaste"; which his flattering laureate, Ben Jonson, ridiculed to please his master; which, our wives and sisters protest, gives rise to the dirtiest and most unsociable habit a man can indulge in. . . . But I will regard it in a social point of view; and first, as a narcotic, notice its effects on the individual character. I believe, then, that in moderation it diminishes the violence of the passions, and particularly that of the temper. . . . I believe that it induces a habit of calm reflectiveness, which causes us to take less prejudiced, perhaps less zealous views of life, and to be therefore, less irritable in our converse with our fellow-creatures. (1868: 252–53)

But on the other hand, I foresee with dread a too tender allegiance to the pipe, to the destruction of good society, and the abandonment of the ladies. No wonder they hate it, dear creatures; the pipe is the worst rival a woman can have: and it is one whose eyes she cannot scratch out; who improves with age, while she herself declines, who has an art which no woman possesses, that of never wearying her devotee; who is silent, yet a companion; costs little, yet gives much pleasure; who, lastly, never upbraids and always yields the same joy. Ah! this is a powerful rival to wife or maid and no wonder that at last the woman succumbs, consents, and rather than lose her lord and master, even supplies the hated herb with her own fair hand. (254–55)

As it is, there are rules enough to limit this indulgence. One must never smoke, nor even ask to smoke, in the company of the fair. . . . One must never smoke in the streets; that is, in daylight. The deadly crime may be committed, like burglary, after dark, but not before. . . . One must never smoke in a public place, where ladies are or might be, for instance, flower-shows or promenade. One may smoke in a railway-carriage in spite of bye-laws, if one has first obtained the consent of everyone present; but if there be a lady there, though she gives her consent, smoke not. In nine cases out of ten, she will give it from good nature. (255–56)

One must never smoke in a close carriage. . . . One must never smoke in a theatre, on a race course, nor in church. . . . But if you smoke, or if you are in the company of smokers, and are to wear your clothes in the presence of ladies afterwards, you must change them to smoke in. (256)

As can be observed from the above account, it did not need to be mentioned that women should not smoke; it was simply assumed that it was men who would engage in the practice. Furthermore, it was almost as though the rules associated with smoking in the presence of women hardly needed to be made explicit: "As it is, there are rules enough to limit this indulgence." There is an almost tongue-in-cheek tone to the text. The language used is extremely patriarchal: one gets the impression that smoking was considered to be a male preserve, and that while it may have been seen as the "most unsociable habit a man can indulge in," this clearly referred to sociability at a very general level, or perhaps better, a form of sociability involving both sexes mixing. It is clear that postprandial smoking within a specifically allocated area among groups of men was seen as *highly* sociable. What may be a familiar set of processes can be observed in this connection: in general, in the early to mid-nineteenth century it was considered bad manners to smoke in public; smoking within this period became effectively *pushed behind the scenes* of "public" life; the practice, therefore, involved the rejection of a traditional, conventional set of values and norms, which, in turn, strengthened the embrace of an alternative set of values and norms—those belonging to a group that was defined by its *opposition*. This process was neatly summed up by a Dr. Andrew Wilson: "Whenever anybody Counterblasts to-day against tobacco, I feel as did my old friend Wilkie Collins, when someone told him that to smoke was a wrong thing: 'My dear sir,' said the great novelist, 'all your objections to tobacco only increase the relish with which I look forward to the next cigar'" (Apperson 1914: 204). As I intend to show, smokers' identification of themselves as belonging to a community of defiant opposition has reemerged as a dominant theme during recent years. However, crucially, the character and content of the opposition against the practice has been significantly transformed.

Also of interest from the above account is the personification of tobacco as a "mistress": "the pipe is the worst rival a woman can have." As Mitchell proposes, such ideas were characteristic of Western understandings of tobacco at this time:

> [I]n the nineteenth century, it became a cliché for a man to speak of his cigarette or cigar as his lover, a rival of his fiancée or wife. Rudyard Kipling, for example, referred to his favourite Cuban cigars as "a harem of dusky beauties tied fifty in a string." The quotation indicates prevalent associations between the colour of tobacco and that of an "exotic" woman's skin and between ways in which women and cigars were both held in "captivity" to await an owner's need. Thus, the woman on a cigar box label— whose frank sensuality was often surpassed only by pornographic images of the time—became closely identified with a product that was purchased and consumed for pleasure and inserted in the mouth to be "kissed" and sucked. A man might enjoy this pleasure in a solitary situation within his den, office, or smoking room, or he might share the pleasure with other males in a bar or club as part of a bonding ritual. (Mitchell 1992: 329)

During this period, tobacco use was very much viewed as a practice that was *owned* by men. The personification of tobacco as a woman reflected both associations between tobacco use and pleasure, and proscriptions on smoking by women. Mitchell's interpretation of the quotation from Kipling is also interesting. Perhaps, with its reference to the control through captivity of women and female sensuality, it also points toward an understanding of smoking as a means of capturing and controlling *nature*, which has, throughout the history of the modern West, been predominantly depicted as female. That is to say, perhaps the personification of tobacco as a mistress was also a reflection of the idea that, through controlling fire, taming the effect of tobacco, learning to consume tobacco without becoming sick or fainting (i.e., the idea of tobacco use as a male accomplishment), the tobacco user was also seen to be *controlling Mother Nature.*

It is interesting to note that, when cigarettes initially began to emerge in the West as an increasingly popular mode of consumption toward the end of the nineteenth century, advertisers exploited these understandings of tobacco use as the "ownership" of a *representation* of female sexuality:

> The cigarette was used almost exclusively by a masculine clientele[27] in the nineteenth century, and the cards [which were included as free gifts inside the packets of some brands of cigarettes] . . . reflect[ed] the advertisers' keen awareness of the fact. Many sets of cards featured either photographs or lithographs of buxom young ladies in what must have seemed very daring, if not shocking, costumes. Usually these sets were labelled simply "Actresses" or bore descriptive phrases such as "Stars of the Stage," "American Stars," or "Gems of Beauty." Since there was little personal identification by the purchaser with the stars, who were usually unnamed, and since actresses were then accorded with a low place in the social scale of polite America, it seems that such cards were designed for prurient attraction. (Porter 1971: 35)

However, understandings of tobacco—of the cigarette in particular—and its relationship with femininity began to change rapidly, and in a quite significant manner. From the historical data it is apparent that social proscriptions on tobacco use in public, particularly those against women smoking, and men smoking in female company, were gradually beginning to decline toward the end of the nineteenth century. In this connection, Penn, writing at the very beginning of the twentieth century and looking back at the nineteenth, provided some interesting observations:

> It is noteworthy that women have not participated in the renaissance of smoking as they did in the introduction of smoking, on the contrary proving its sternest opponents. [However,] [t]ime may remove [this] objection, and already smoking is becoming common by ladies in the highest society. In a recent number of *The Ladies Field,* Lady Jenne wrote: "The habit of

---

27. As we shall see, it is evident that Porter has overstated the case about the absence of women smoking during this period.

smoking which is so common abroad has now become among many women in England quite as natural a thing, and it is not in the least unusual for cigarettes to be handed round in the drawing room after the women have gone upstairs and left the men to drink their wine and eat their dessert. Hitherto it has been mainly confined to the house, and even the bedroom or the boudoir, but within the last two months two cases of women smoking in public have come under my notice. One day in the Strand a woman, young and pretty, was seen walking and quietly smoking a cigarette, and on another occasion in Richmond Park a woman was enjoying a fairly large cigar with her male companion. These are only isolated cases, but they excited little or no comment, and it seems an indication of a change of sentiment and public opinion on the subject of women smoking." (Penn 1901: 95–96)

Other accounts would seem to indicate that smoking was emerging as a symbol of the "fast" or unrespectable young woman. Porter provided the following account from 1901 in this connection:

The class of girl who likes the irresponsible, dancing, flirting chaperone is not as yet a very numerous one; but yet English Society is well aware of her. She is the "fast girl" who enjoys a cigarette, can toss off a B. and S. [brandy and soda], plays an excellent game of billiards. . . . Men find her an amusing companion. . . . There is a certain degree of laxity in many details of modern society. . . . Men set little store by what is carelessly guarded. They undervalue the fruit that hangs over the garden wall, and long for what is beyond their reach. This is human nature, and the ideal chaperone understands human nature . . . she is careful to suggest to giddy Amy that three times are as often as a girl can dance with the same man in one evening without getting herself unpleasantly talked of. (Porter 1972: 84–85)[28]

Indeed, only a decade or so previous to this description, if a woman were prepared simply to *allow* a man to smoke in her presence, she was considered "fast." A similar account from 1887 is cited by Curtin:

It is true that these young men have in many cases been spoiled by fast girls, who having no respect for themselves, did not exact it from them. If a young woman has "not the slightest objection, and rather like it," men will smoke into their faces, appear before them in none or in scarcely any clothes, call them by their Christian names, say words and refer to things that should be nameless, and in all other ways, illustrate the truth that men respect women as, and only as, women respect themselves. (Curtin 1987: 213)

28. I would like to acknowledge my gratitude to Cas Wouters for providing some of the source material on women smoking in the late nineteenth and early twentieth centuries.

It is interesting to note from the above accounts that a woman's smoking, or even her tolerance of smoking, was perceived to be a sign of her "looseness," or permissiveness and promiscuity. As may also be observed here, the reemergence of women smoking was seen to be intimately related to the rise of the cigarette as a medium of tobacco consumption. Toward the end of the nineteenth century, the cigarette became known as the "female cigar" (Old Smoker 1894: 24). However, as well as being likened to a woman, and, indeed, personified as a mistress, the cigarette increasingly came to be understood as a female *mode* of smoking. The complex and intimate relationship between the cigarette, its perceived "feminine" characteristics and properties, and women smoking is particularly evident in the following:

> The cigarette may indeed belong to the "Weaker Vessels" of Tobacco Smoking, but to the honour of the sex be it said that all are not mere flirts and summer girls, such as she. Sweet, airy, fascinating is this pretty little creature in the fairy garb, delightful to play with now and then, but dangerous as a constant companion. 'Tis whispered by some that she uses drugs for her complexion. Others say that her kisses are perilous from the moisture of her composition, whereby the Nicotine becomes more solvent and absorbable. Like other coquettes, the cigarette is said to afflict her too-devoted admirers with heart trouble. (Old Smoker 1894: 24–25)

This account appears to contain an inherent paradox. While the cigarette is seen to be a relatively weak form of tobacco ("The cigarette may indeed belong to the 'Weaker Vessels' of Tobacco Smoking"), a caution over its constant or excessive use immediately accompanies this statement: "delightful to play with now and then, but dangerous as a constant companion." To the present-day Western reader, this observation may not immediately appear paradoxical; it is, after all, a well-established medical fact that the long-term use of tobacco is hazardous to health. However, it is important for us not to project these recently acquired medical understandings onto the past. At the time when this account was written, significant systematic scientific data on the long-term effects of smoking did not exist. The cautionary proviso in the above account was rooted in an altogether different set of understandings and concerns in relation to the cigarette. I would now like to explore these in more detail.

Interestingly, cigarettes became popular in Britain significantly earlier than in many other parts of Europe and the United States. In 1900, for example, over ten percent of British tobacco sales were from cigarettes, only twenty years after the first machine-produced ones were marketed (Goodman 1993: 93). It is possible that cigarettes may have been introduced into

Britain as early as the 1840s. However, these early cigarettes were very different from those which came to characterize tobacco consumption in the twentieth-century West:

> These early cigarettes were wrapped in tissue paper with a cane mouthpiece attached. But they were very crudely made and it was necessary to pinch together each end to prevent the tobacco from falling out. Accordingly, at that time cigarettes had only novelty appeal. Moreover, dark air-cured and fire-cured tobaccos, most commonly in use, were generally too strong for use in cigarettes. During the 1860s cigarettes made from best quality Turkish tobacco and specially made fine texture paper came on the market, but even these, with their distinctive aromatic flavour, did not commend themselves widely to British tastes. (Alford 1973: 123–24)

Of crucial importance was the later introduction of cigarettes containing "bright" tobacco, a variety that is cured in specially adapted barns containing "flues" or pipes. Hot air is pumped through the flues to dry the tobacco rapidly. Bright flue-cured tobacco produces an acidic smoke that is generally much easier to inhale than the alkaline smoke of the "dark" air-cured and fire-cured tobacco varieties referred to in the above account. Furthermore, the nicotine release of acidic smoke is more gradual than that of alkaline smoke (Goodman 1993: 98–99). These characteristics of bright cigarette smoke, Goodman argues, may have been "critical in influencing new consumers who might have been put off by the adverse initial effects of consuming air- and fire-cured tobacco. . . . This may be one reason why legislation against children purchasing and smoking tobacco was not required before the twentieth century" (99). It was this new type of cigarette that was to become so popular among British, and ultimately most other Western, tobacco users.

Of great importance is Goodman's implicit suggestion that, since the forms and varieties of tobacco available before the twentieth century were generally not as easy to smoke as bright tobacco cigarettes, there was little need in previous centuries for legislation to restrict the use of tobacco by children. This suggestion would appear to be based on the premise that, since the process of habituation involved with pre-twentieth century forms and varieties of tobacco was comparatively extensive and arduous, children would be effectively discouraged from adopting the practice. However, as I have shown, children, even the very young, did indeed smoke tobacco in the sixteenth and seventeenth centuries. While it is difficult to determine the exact proportion of children who smoked, as we have seen, a significant number of accounts written during these centuries attest to the normality of children using tobacco. Yet the issues Goodman raises here are nonetheless important. Historical data would definitely appear to support Goodman's suggestion that there emerged an increasing amount of *concern* in relation to the ease with which cigarettes could be smoked. One of the best examples of such concern is provided by Penn:

> To smoke is one of the delights of the schoolboy, none the less sweet because it is forbidden. By degrees he acquires the habit, until, by the time he is arrived at man's estate, he is proficient in the most "gentlemanlike assumption of tobacco." Of late years the increase in smoking among young boys has been very great. The cheapness of cigarettes, and the prevailing precocity of youth are the factors in this increase. Before cigarettes were to be obtained at five a penny the boy had his first smoke from a pipe or cigar. The resultant lesson was severe enough to postpone for some time a second attempt at nicotian honours. But the cigarette is so mild it can be smoked with impunity. Thus the path to smoking glory is devoid of all difficulties and terrors. (Penn 1901: 291–92)

It is here that the paradox in relation to the emergence of the cigarette becomes clearer. In this account, the author expressed concern, not because the new form of consuming tobacco was *stronger* than those which had preceded it, but precisely because it was *milder*. In part, this may well have originated from a genuine concern for health; the underlying sentiment appears to be that those who learned to smoke via the cigarette would not learn to smoke in moderation, and, if indeed tobacco smoking was dangerous—at the time a large amount of controversy existed over this issue, as it had done during previous centuries—surely it would be better not to smoke in excess? Once again, this account may also embody an expression of the (previously discussed) social restraint toward the exercising of self-restraint in relation to tobacco use. The concern may have been simply that the mildness of the cigarette almost invites excess in relation to its use.

However, another quite distinct sentiment is also evident here. One gets the impression that the author is concerned that smoking is no longer an exclusively adult male preserve; that it is no longer an "accomplishment" to smoke. As Penn appears to have considered it, the cigarette was so mild that anyone could smoke. Viewed in this way, it becomes easier to understand why the more readily learned habit of cigarette smoking was so closely and systematically linked with femininity and youth. There appears to be a quite *conscious* effort in the above account to distance pipe and cigar smoking from cigarette smoking. Such an effort was, indeed, characteristic of many other similar accounts of the time. To the extent that we may attribute it to the influence of "patriarchal smokers," the distinction of pipe and cigar smoking from cigarette smoking had been successfully established. Even today, pipe and cigar smoking are still, in most Western social circles, very much seen as predominantly male activities.

It is important, in this context, not to underestimate the significance of the pipe in the resurgence of smoking in the nineteenth century more generally. In the middle of that century, pipe smoking accounted for approximately sixty percent of British consumption (Goodman 1993: 93). However, even the pipe itself was changing. The long clay pipes, or "churchwardens," and short clays, or "cutties," were rapidly becoming replaced by the briar wood pipe (ibid.). The briar pipe had a number of practical advantages over clays, not least of which was its durability and practicality. When one considers, for example, that it was not possible to walk with a churchwarden in one's mouth, the appeal of the shorter, more durable briar pipe becomes more apparent (Apperson 1914: 162). As Penn stated, the "ease of use" of the briar pipe, the "neatness" of cigars, and the "convenience and elegance" of cigarettes all appear to have facilitated the resurgence of smoking in the nineteenth century (1901: 96). Furthermore, he wrote:

> The invention of lucifer matches led to smoking in the open air. The milder and lighter qualities of tobacco placed on the market created as well as met demand. Manufacturers now [1901] cater for the more refined taste of the upper and middle classes, as well as for artisans and the lower classes, who, until fifty years ago formed the bulk of their customers. Another patent reason is the severity with which society of all classes regards drunkenness, and its consequent decrease. Smoking began to come into favour and practice as it came to be regarded as disgraceful for a gentleman to drink to excess. (96–97)

This extract serves to bring together a number of important points. First, before matches were invented, the only means of lighting a pipe, cigar, or cigarette was by using a candle, hot coal, or one of a range of quite ingenious ignition devices.[29] The development of matches can, in part, be seen to

---

29. In this connection, a particularly interesting account is provided by Meeler:

The advantage of obtaining an instantaneous light, is perhaps seldom more appreciated than by smokers. The articles used until lately for the purpose of lighting cigars, when out, or travelling, were the Amadon, with the flint and steel—the phosphorous box, the pneumatic cylinder:—all of which were, more or less, uncertain or inconvenient, until the invention of Jones's Prometheans. These may very fairly be said to possess a never-failing facility in producing instantaneous light. The Promethean is composed of a small bulb of glass, hermetically sealed, containing a small part of sulphuric acid, and surrounded by a composition of chlorate of potash and aromatics. This is enclosed in paper prepared for the purpose. The light is simply effected by giving the Promethean a

be related to the demands of the increasingly "mobile" smoker, and, in turn, the practical demands of "modern" life. Second, to continue with another central theme of this chapter, the "distance" in the relationship between tobacco and alcohol seems to have increased even further than in previous centuries. The account appears to imply that, since drunkenness had become unacceptable among all levels of society, tobacco smoking was an acceptable alternative to drinking.[30] The author does not appear to feel the need even to mention that, unlike alcohol, tobacco smoking does not cause intoxication. This stands in direct contrast with understandings prevalent in the sixteenth, seventeenth, and, to a lesser extent, eighteenth centuries, when tobacco and alcohol were *both* viewed as powerful intoxicants. Third, a direct relationship is forged between the refinement or class of the smoker, and that of the tobacco he or she consumed. This sentiment reveals a great deal about attitudes toward what were then the new media of consumption, the cigarette in particular. It is significant that the *lighter, milder* forms of tobacco were seen to be more "refined." In contrast with the snuffers of the eighteenth century, the pipe smokers of the seventeenth century, and, indeed, the Karuk Native Americans, the strength or "kick" of the tobacco consumed was now *not* viewed as a measure of its quality or refinement. Instead, it was the relative *lack* of potency that was held in high regard. Correspondingly, "rougher," stronger forms of tobacco were seen to be the taste of male members of the correspondingly "rougher," lower classes, the military, and the like.

The issues discussed here are crucial to understanding the success of the cigarette as a medium of tobacco consumption, and of cigarette smoking as a practice more generally. It is almost as if the refinement of the tobacco medium had begun to catch up with the refinement in the practices associated with its use. That is to say, to take the example of snuffers in the eighteenth

---

smart tap that breaks the bulb, when the acid, coming into contact with the composition, causes ignition. It must be remarked however, the Lucifers or chlorate matches that ignite, by drawing the match through sand paper, introduced by the same inventor, are decidedly bad for the cigar; the fumes arising from the combustion being offensive, are too apt to spoil the flavour of the leaf. (Meeler 1832: 127–28)

It is interesting to note that arguments concerning health or safety are entirely absent from this account. Prometheans are endorsed on the grounds that they do not impair the *flavor* of the cigar.

30. In a similar vein, the YMCA in the United States initially promoted the use of cigarettes in the early part of the twentieth century as a "substitute attraction" to divert young men, particularly soldiers, from drink, drugs, lust, and gambling. According to a YMCA report, troops would "keep sober a long time" given sufficient amounts to smoke (Tate 1999: 72).

century, the highly elaborate and controlled rituals associated with "taking the pinch" stood in contrast to the "animalic" physical effects of the tobacco. As I have shown, there was a considerable amount of conflict between, on the one hand, claiming that snuffing marked the height of refinement, and on the other, transgressing codes of etiquette by placing fingers into orifices, publicly dispelling mucus, dirtying one's clothes, and so on. This inherent conflict was, indeed, seized upon by the anti-tobacco writers of the time. Thus, it may well be the case that, paradoxically, the cigarette was successful precisely because, relative to the forms and media of tobacco use that had preceded it, *it had little immediate effect on the smoker*. The "slightness" of the cigarette; the transience of its effects; the relative ease with which it could be carried around and smoked; its convenience; its "neatness"; its immediacy; were all crucial to its success. The comparative lack of expectoration and other immediately observable forms of physical reaction involved with smoking the cigarette—if, indeed, it is accurate to assume this correlation—would appear more closely to match increasing demands for social "refinement." It is in this way that we can begin to understand cigarette smoking as a particularly "civilized" means of consuming tobacco.

Like the prevailing forms of tobacco consumption that had preceded it, cigarette smoking was initially practiced by the highly fashionable (Brooks 1937–52: 170). However, as Brooks proposed,

> [while] "dandies and snobs" displayed such a preference for this form of smoking, the general public was at first contemptuous of the cigarette and continued to consume tobacco through the "manly" pipe or cigar. This popular prejudice was not of long duration, however, for this nicotian diminutive became fairly common in England by the early [eighteen] 'sixties and prevalent by the middle of the next decade. The pipe began to disappear (its use was even regarded as vulgar a little later!), the cigar began to be popularly associated with the affluent classes (or the office-seeking politicians, etc.) and snuff remained only as small consolation to those who clung to the cherished fashions of the past. (Ibid.)

By 1865, British manufacturers were producing prewrapped cigarettes containing Egyptian and Turkish tobaccos (Brooks 1937–52: 172). However, most interestingly, it was not until the introduction of cigarettes made from bright Virginian tobacco in 1869 that preference for the cigarette as a medium of consumption began to increase significantly (ibid.):

> The consumption of the cigarette increased with a rapidity that astounded casual observers and, demand breeding the invention, there came into existence a machine for the quick production of this article, which demon-

strated its practicability in the early [eighteen] 'seventies. . . . The extraordinary rise in popularity of the cigarette in the later decades of the nineteenth century was more than just a manifestation of a change in taste. The cigarette was something of a symbol of a new age wherein the culminating industrial revolution merged with the advancing mechanical civilization. Smokers responded to the vigorous tempo of the period and called for tobacco in a compact form which would provide immediate effects. The pipe represented a leisurely smoke, and required a certain amount of paraphernalia; snuff (with its essential accoutrements) demanded the deliberations of an aristocratic age, the cigar which had come to be popularly regarded as a luxury, was not to be hastily consumed. Only the cigarette met the need for a transient pleasurable nervine in an age of great activity and among people who had grown impatient with the past. (172–73)

As suggested in the above account, the cigarette began to emerge as *the* symbol of the "modern" age. Most interestingly, the writer makes the link between the pace of modern life and the need for a mild and transient form of tobacco. Other forms of tobacco consumption, including pipe smoking, cigar smoking, and, more particularly, snuffing, are seen to belong to another age. Thus, a second major set of processes are central to the success of the cigarette. Not only was the cigarette more compatible with codes of manners and etiquette of the time, but furthermore, it also met some of the demands of modern social life.

To clarify this point, allow me, once again, to contrast the practice and experience of tobacco use among the Karuk with that of the early twentieth-century cigarette smoker. The Karuk smoker took a great deal of "time out" to smoke, and the effect of smoking tobacco was extremely dramatic and strong. The Karuk smoker may have even fainted after smoking a pipeful of tobacco. In contrast, the early twentieth-century cigarette smoker may have felt only a moderate effect, and would be able to perform any number of tasks while smoking. Indeed, the whole process of smoking a cigarette took less than five to ten minutes. This, crucially, was interrelated with the increasingly dominant understanding of smoking as a *supplementary* activity, and with a move away from the understanding of smoking *as an activity in and of itself.* However, what is still unclear is exactly how these changes in the use of tobacco were related to the demands of modern social life. Brooks's arguments in this connection are based on a series of untested assumptions: it is assumed that the modern smoker has less time available to smoke; it is assumed that the modern smoker requires greater immediacy from the medium of tobacco consumption. Moreover, there is an assumed link between the vigorous tempo of modern life, and the need for a form of tobacco that produced relatively transient effects. The needs and require-ments of the modern smoker are thus seen to stem from the *practical* exi-gencies of modern life. I would like to consider a number of other possibil-ities in relation to the link between the rise of the cigarette and the emergence of modern life.

The key sentence in the above extract appears to be "Smokers responded to the vigorous tempo of the period and called for tobacco in a compact form which would provide immediate effects." However, the phrase "vigor-ous tempo" is somewhat ambiguous. By this, Brooks may have been refer-ring to an increase in the rate of change in peoples' lives, or, perhaps, an in-crease in the number and variety of activities the average person would need to perform in a day. Perhaps it referred to an increase in mobility, both so-cial and geographical. Unfortunately, he has not made this clear. Thus, cor-respondingly, it is difficult to assess exactly what, according to Brooks, smokers of this period were responding to. It is probable that what he meant here is actually an increase in the overall level of what Elias refers to as "stress-tensions" (Elias and Dunning 1986: 41). On one level, all the pro-cesses listed above—an overall acceleration of life changes, increasing rates of mobility, and so on—may be viewed as causes of stress-tensions. However, more important, stress-tensions may also derive from a *sedentary* lifestyle. That is to say, regimented monotony and strict control over, even depriva-tion of, the chance openly and immediately to express emotionality can them-selves be seen to constitute a major source of stress-tensions. If we accept, for the moment at least, that there actually emerged an *increasingly seden-tary* character to modern social life that, paradoxically, grew out of the high rates of change and mobility which accompanied it, then a whole range of further possibilities in relation to understanding the rise of the cigarette be-gin to open up.

Brooks's identification of the cigarette as "a transient pleasurable nervine" embodies an understanding of tobacco use which is characteristically mod-ern. This definition marks a change in how tobacco was becoming under-stood, used, and experienced. Cigarette smokers of the late nineteenth and early twentieth centuries were increasingly beginning to use tobacco not just in more controlled and restrained ways but also *as an instrument of self-control in itself.* The cigarette became seen as a cure for the ills of civilization. There emerged an increasing amount of attention on the effect of the cigarette on the mind, nervous system, and the brain. This attention was not simply the result of shifts in medical understanding but rather reflected a much broader shift in understandings of tobacco use. Tobacco, in the form of the cigarette, was increasingly being used to control feeling states, to combat "stress," to "calm the nerves." However, its understanding and use was not simply limited to that of a "nervine," or nerve-relaxant. In addition, tobacco was increasingly being used as a stimulant to, among other things, *counter the sedentary character of modern life:*

> The action and effect of tobacco depend, of course, upon the individual, the time, and the circumstances. It acts both as a sedative and a stimulant. Some persons it affects in the former, others in the latter way; at different times it acts in both phases on the same person. Its action is quite undoubtedly that of a narcotic or sedative, quieting and soothing the mind and nerves. In other persons it rouses the sluggish mind into activity. Purely as a medicine, smoking is valuable for correcting nervousness and constipation. . . . Its varied and different effects on different individuals render dogma to its use impossible. It disarranges and upsets the nerves of some people by the slightest use; on others excess produces the same effects, while others can smoke to any extent without the slightest ill-effects; hence the use of tobacco is essentially to be governed by that most uncommon of qualities, common sense. (Penn 1901: 301)

Penn's statements here embody a characteristically "modern" understanding of the practice. Furthermore, his comments reveal how the use of tobacco, as with the snuffers of the nineteenth century, was becoming increasingly *individualized.* Crucially, it was the *function* of this use, more than the *form* of the tobacco itself, that Penn saw as varying according to the individual.[31] Thus, we can begin to build a picture of characteristically "modern" smoking as involving—and, indeed, as playing an important role in *maintaining*—relatively *moderate* shifts in feeling states that vary according to the individual, and according to the situation in which she or he finds herself/himself. Tobacco was understood to be predominantly a medicine of the mind that had a direct effect on the central nervous system and the brain. It was sometimes quite consciously (perhaps at other times unconsciously) used by the smoker as either a relaxant or a stimulant, or perhaps for a combination of these effects. It is interesting that Penn also refers to

31. This is not to say that the biphasic (in one instance a sedative, in another a stimulant) properties of tobacco had not been referred to in previous centuries. Indeed, James I wrote in the 1604 *Counterblaste.* "Being taken when they goe to bed, it makes one sleep soundly, and yet being taken when a man is sleepie and drowsie, it will, as they say, awake his braine, and quicken his understanding" (James I 1954: 26). However, one can observe that King James is not so much referring to differences *between* individuals, as to the seemingly contradictory effects upon the *same* individual. The point I make here is not that tobacco was never used as a means of self-control before the twentieth century, but rather that this became an *increasingly* dominant theme from the late nineteenth century onward. Moreover, I am arguing that Penn's observations, while similar to those of James I, are bound up in a fundamentally different set of understandings of tobacco use.

the use of tobacco in relieving constipation. However, the use of tobacco as a medicinal remedy on the "body" more generally was viewed as secondary to its use a pharmacological agent on the "mind."

We are still left with the question of why the cigarette, rather than other forms of tobacco, was particularly suited to being used, understood, and experienced in this way. I have a number of suggestions. First, as has already been mentioned, the increasing understanding of smoking as a supplementary activity—in turn related to the transience and convenience of the cigarette—allowed the smoker to consume tobacco while performing any number of other tasks. This, in turn, was related to the increasing dominance of the view of smoking as an activity that could be undertaken in almost any situation, be it work or leisure time. Smoking became less consistently related just to leisure, and to "taking time out" as it increasingly came to be understood as a practice that could *enhance* the performance of various tasks and activities. Thus tobacco could be used to help one concentrate while working, stimulate the mind during periods of monotonous activity, and relax the mind after stressful events. Put simply, tobacco could be used in a broader range of situations, and came to be associated with a broader range of tasks. In addition, the practice of smoking while working at a desk, for example, involved a whole range of small-scale *movements*. In this sense, cigarette smoking can be seen to be a form of relief from work of a sedentary, immotile character.

Second, the mildness of the cigarette marks a relatively advanced "stage" in the shifting balance between bio-pharmacological and social-psychological processes in the experience of tobacco use. By this I mean to suggest that, for want of a less-crude formulation, since the sixteenth century the increasing move in the West toward the use of milder forms of tobacco has, correspondingly, involved an increase in the social-psychological dimension of the experience of tobacco use, and—in relation to the declining strength or potency of tobacco—a decline in the bio-pharmacological dimension. That is to say, the experience of smoking the milder forms of tobacco—particularly the cigarette—of the late nineteenth and early twentieth centuries was more ambiguous and less "finished" than that associated with the forms that dominated previous centuries. Thus, the modern Western cigarette, more than any of the other popular forms of tobacco before it, was particularly suited to the increasingly *functionally individualized* practices of Western tobacco users of the late nineteenth and early twentieth centuries.

To conclude this chapter, the reemergence of smoking as a popular mode of tobacco consumption and, more particularly, the rise of the cigarette as a medium of tobacco use in the late nineteenth and early twentieth centuries, can be seen to mark a further "stage" in the development of tobacco use in the West; processes already underway during the eighteenth century appear to have continued and accelerated during this period. In particular, the emergence of milder, more "accessible" (in the sense that the habituation process involved with their use was less extensive) forms relates to a further move away from the use of tobacco to lose control, and the increasing move toward its use in highly controlled, differentiated, and functionally individualized ways. Moreover, there also emerged an increasing shift toward the use of tobacco as an instrument of self-control in itself.

The increasing move, up to the early stages of the twentieth century, toward the use of milder forms of tobacco did not arise out of a growing concern about the health risks involved with tobacco use. Indeed, as we have seen, the very mildness of the cigarette initially *increased* concern over possible ill effects. Rather, the shift toward increasingly milder forms of tobacco relates to processes of *civilization.* To reiterate a central point: tobacco was not only becoming used in more highly *controlled* ways, it was increasingly becoming used to maintain self-control. It became understood as a tool to combat the ills of civilized life. The growing individualization of tobacco use which, during the eighteenth century, had been exercised through the mixing of snuff concoctions, became transformed into the *function individualization* of the late nineteenth and early twentieth centuries. Tobacco was being used in one instance as a sedative, in another, as a stimulant. Its function could vary according to the individual, the situation, and, crucially, according to the activity or lack of activity it was being used to *supplement.* Instead of being understood, used, and experienced as a substance that helps one to *escape* normality, tobacco had become recognized as a drug which the individual could use to *return* to normality from a whole range of psychological and emotional states. In relation to these processes, the understanding of tobacco as a medicinal remedy for the body appears to have declined quite sharply during this period. Writings on tobacco use during the late nineteenth and early twentieth centuries, and, indeed, the understandings these embodied, increasingly stressed the role of tobacco as a pharmacological agent on the mind, on the "nerves," and in controlling feelings and moods.

How these understandings changed throughout the twentieth century will be the focus of the next chapter.

3

Tobacco Use and Clinical Bodies: Tobacco Use

in the Twentieth-Century West

A series of reports carried out by the Health Education Authority (HEA) detailed the costs of smoking [for] health authorities and local government districts. These reports estimated [that] hospital admissions due to illness from smoking number 284,000 per year occupying an average of 9,500 hospital beds every day and at an annual cost of over £400 million . . . to the National Health Service. A later estimate by the HEA, including the cost of primary healthcare, put the total cost of smoking related diseases to the NHS at £611 million . . . for England and Wales alone. The Royal College of Physicians estimated, in 1977, that smoking induced illnesses result in the loss of 50 million working days every year. (BASP 1994: 119)

This extract was selected to begin this chapter not because it is exceptional but precisely because it is *characteristic* of late twentieth-century understandings of tobacco use. Tobacco, particularly in the form of cigarettes, has emerged as a major economic and public health concern. Indeed, the distinction between the two concerns has become increasingly blurred. The figures cited above, which detail smoking-related costs to the National Health Service and the cost to industry through the loss of fifty million working days per year, almost beg for a comparison with figures relating to the total revenue the British government receives from, among other sources of tobacco-related income, the taxation of cigarettes (approximately £5,200,000,000 in 1988 [BASP 1992: 9]). Indeed, that statistics have come to dominate current debates surrounding tobacco use is in and of itself significant. It is possible to determine with a high degree of accuracy that, for example, in Britain in 1992, cigarettes accounted for 92 percent of all tobacco consumption (BASP 1994: 117). Or, that while the percentage of adults smoking in Britain has declined quite rapidly in recent years—from 39% in 1980 to 28% in 1992 (113)—Britain still constitutes the second largest domestic market for tobacco in the European Union (123).

These statistics tell us as much about the development of statistical techniques in the twentieth century as they do about the demographic trends they represent. They also point toward important changes in understandings of tobacco use. The very calculation of statistics on the cost of smoking to the National Health Service, or the number of working days lost each year through smoking-related illnesses, indicates fundamental changes in medical understandings, and, moreover, the widespread acceptance of a number of links in what is only recently understood to be a *causal* chain centering on the relationship between cigarette smoking and disease. In a recent paper entitled *Taxes on Tobacco Products,* the question What prevents governments from increasing tobacco taxes? was discussed (BASP 1992: 8). In the several pages that followed, a number of factors were considered: "The impact on inflation," "The impact on the poor," "The impact on jobs," "The impact on government revenue," "The impact on smuggling." The article is indicative of the *lengthening chains of interdependence* involved in the growth, retailing, production, consumption, advertising, marketing, and administration of tobacco. Typically, these chains of interdependence are analyzed by a process of *reducing* each "factor"—the impact on the poor, the impact on smuggling, and so forth—to a statistical trend, which is then compared and contrasted with other trends through correlation, cross-tabulation, and other statistical methods. As we shall see, this *style* of *analysis* has come to dominate current debates surrounding tobacco use.

My central aim in this chapter is to examine how these dominant Western understandings of tobacco use—understandings that center on debates over statistical inference—emerged in relation to a number of processes, including *medicalization, mass-consumerization, individualization,* and *informalization.* In particular, I shall focus on shifts in medical understandings of tobacco since the late nineteenth century, and will explore the interrelationship between these and the development of the debate between proponents and opponents of tobacco use. In relation to this undertaking, I shall explore changes in understandings of tobacco use during the twentieth century and up to the present day: the move away from a focus on the short-term, immediately apparent effects of the practice, toward a preoccupation with the longer term, invisible ones. I examine the implications of this shift not just for how tobacco use became linked to lung cancer and other diseases but to how this shift of focus changed understandings of the practice itself: the rise of clinical understandings of tobacco use as an *addiction,* and as a set of processes that users became "subject to."

Accordingly, I consider the growing prominence of debates concerning "freedom" and "control" that have come to dominate current understandings of tobacco use. I explore the move away from the smoking *Gemeinschaft* of previous centuries and toward, increasingly, a smoking *Gesellschaft,* where smokers smoke alone and where tobacco is used in private, effectively pushed behind the scenes of social life. I also explore the rise of women smoking, and the related use of tobacco as a means of corporeal control— smoking to stay thin. In addition, I continue the analysis of themes from previous chapters: I explore the extension of processes of *individualization* in relation to tobacco use, wherein the practice comes increasingly to be used as a means of *individual self expression,* a means of identity proclamation, a marker of oneself to others. I also continue to trace the increasingly widespread use of progressively milder forms of tobacco and modes of consuming these throughout the twentieth century and up to the present day. Ultimately, my aim is to use these insights, along with the others previously developed in this book, to reflect upon dominant present-day understandings, uses, and experiences of tobacco.

Shifts in Medical Understandings of Tobacco

As far back as 1671, a Florentine scientist and physician, Francesco Redi, had discovered that an extracted "oil of tobacco" would kill an animal if injected into its bloodstream (Goodman 1993: 115). The state of medical knowledge at the time was such that Redi could not identify the active constituents of the oil he had extracted (ibid.). However, over a century later, the practice of isolating the constituent pharmacological agents in plant medicines had become a central preoccupation of the medical profession. Indeed, by 1828 the German physician, Wilhelm Heinrich Posselt, and his partner, the chemist Karl Ludwig Reimann, had successfully isolated nicotine, an active alkaloid in tobacco, and had confirmed its properties as highly toxic (116). The identification of nicotine as a pharmacological agent was to prove central to the development of medical and popular understandings of tobacco. After Posselt and Reimann published their results, a large amount of research was conducted into the chemistry and pharmacology of nicotine. A good deal of this research explored the therapeutic potential of the substance (116–17).

From this large body of research conducted in the nineteenth century, there reemerged a great deal of controversy over whether tobacco was harmful. However, there were a number of important changes to how the anti-tobacco movement began to conduct itself during this period. Rather than the relatively isolated voices of protest and discouragement that character-ized the debates of previous centuries, there emerged a number of anti-tobacco *societies*, particularly in Britain, France, and the United States, which were often headed by well-known, charismatic, and influential figures (Goodman 1993: 117). Some of these societies targeted quite specific groups, in particular women and youths, in what became known as a "pam-phlet war" against smoking (Brooks 1937–52: 173). A salient example in this connection is The Young Britons League Against Smoking who, in a pamphlet entitled *A1 or C3?*, targeted young males in the following manner:

> Do you know that smoking will weaken your sight, your heart, your nerves, your powers of endurance, and your strength of will? If you have any doubt upon these points read what follows from men who know men whom no one would think of calling milksops.
>
> Do you know that the most active ingredient in tobacco smoke is CAR-BON MONOXIDE, a deadly poison. One or two drops in concentrated form can kill a dog.
>
> Mr. A. A. STAGG, of Chicago University, says:—"We have never had a really successful long-distance runner at the University of Chicago who was a smoker."
>
> Rear-Admiral WILLIAM S. SIMS, was the Commander of the Ameri-can Destroyers in European Waters. He has a stalwart figure, surmounted by a massive head, a personality certain to attract attention anywhere. At the age of 57 he was still an athlete, a lover of outdoor games, and neither drinks nor smokes.
>
> HOBBS, the cricketer, says: "Two of the greatest necessities in cricket are nerves and good sight, but there are many thousands of good players who run the risk of shattering both by cultivating the habit of excessive to-bacco smoking" . . .
>
> THE EVILS of SMOKING. Lord Leverhulme has been speaking out on the evils of smoking during business hours, contending that the habit reduces efficiency. The habit, it may be noted, has greatly increased within recent years. In factories, warehouses, shops and offices, smoking is in-dulged in by the workers both by hand and brain. The man who smokes while at work or business, according to Lord Leverhulme, reduces his efficiency; and, if he has a business of his own, will sooner or later go bank-rupt. He remarked further, that smoking was a prevailing habit in the Civil Service—if this could be stopped among the chiefs as well as the rank and file, the work would be accomplished much better and with reduced staffs.

> People could not smoke at work and do the work in the best way. (Young Britons League 1919: 2–3)

A number of central characteristics of anti-tobacco writings of the time can be observed from the above extract. First, it is interesting that carbon monoxide is referred to as the "active ingredient" in tobacco. It is probable that this was indicative of an attempt to avoid altogether the controversy over whether nicotine was a beneficial or a damaging pharmacological agent. Writers of the pamphlet appear to have intentionally omitted any reference to nicotine, and to have instead focused on a compound that was more definitely "bad." Second, one can observe the use of anti-tobacco endorsements by people in positions that (it was assumed) young men would respect and aspire to: a famous cricket player, a rear admiral, a university lecturer. As has already been noted, the use of influential, respectable, and charismatic figures was a distinctive feature of anti-tobacco campaigns of the time. Third, it is possible to discern a direct attempt to counter the emerging understandings of tobacco use first as a supplementary activity and then as an activity that could enhance one's work. It was explicitly stated that tobacco use would, in opposition to these understandings, actually lead to a decline in productivity, perhaps even bankruptcy. It is interesting to note that the argument was not that supplementary tobacco use while working would not enhance the quality of working life more generally, but rather that it would lead to *inefficiency*. Perhaps in this sense the campaign was somewhat misdirected, since as has been argued, tobacco was increasingly being used to counter the monotonous, sedentary character of work in the modern era. Finally, and most interestingly, claims about the health-impairing properties of tobacco were supported only by *anecdotal* evidence. The absence at the time of any widely accepted systematic data linking tobacco use to ill health left few alternatives for the anti-tobacco movement. Indeed, even medical evidence appearing in scientific journals of the late nineteenth to early twentieth century had an equally spurious, anecdotal character. Consider, for example, the following extract from the transactions of the American Laryngological Association:

> At several of our great universities it has been found by exact and scientific investigation that the percentage of winners in intellectual and academic contests is considerably higher in the total abstainers from tobacco. Sammy, the best known newsboy of St. Louis . . . found, other things being equal, that the selling capacity of the boy who used no tobacco was much greater than that of the boy who used tobacco either by chewing or by smoking. (Cited in Mulhall 1943: 716)

As the above account also serves to demonstrate with its reference to intellectual contests, there emerged a growing amount of interest in the effects of tobacco on the brain and the nervous system. While this may, at least in part, have been related to changes in medical understandings of tobacco, it was also fundamentally interrelated with the increasing use of tobacco as a tool to control feeling states (as discussed in chapter 2). A number of articles and texts emerged that considered the question of whether, for example, tobacco could cause mental "disturbances," or conversely, whether tobacco could be used in the treatment of insanity:

> Dr Cortis, who lived in a fishing town and had the opportunity of observing the life and health of local fisherman, stated [in 1856] that they smoked an average of ¼ lb. of tobacco per head per week. These fishermen took very little alcohol, usually one or two glasses of beer every Saturday night. The abuse of tobacco produced in them dyspepsia, nervous troubles, mental depression and paralysis of the tongue, occasionally associated with throat troubles which resulted in difficulty of speech and swallowing as well as of retaining saliva in the mouth. (Koskowski 1955: 950)

> My experience convinces me that the moderate use of tobacco is advantageous in the treatment of insanity; and Dr Conally, the most eminent authority we have on this matter, even recommends tobacco to be given in the middle of the night to patients who are restless. The preponderance of lunatics of the female sex is conclusive evidence against the theory that tobacco either causes or predisposes one to mental disease. (Bucknell 1857: 227)

It is interesting that, in the latter account, the assumption is not only that a low proportion of women smoked, but that women were more susceptible to mental disease than men. It is difficult to determine whether this statement is meant as a flippant remark, or intended to actually constitute a scientific observation. However, it is clear that more generally, a belief in the relationship between women's smoking and insanity appears to have been somewhat influential. Indeed, Carson (1966: 230) describes how a New York magistrate had an actress committed to a psychiatric ward at Bellevue Hospital in 1900 because she smoked cigarettes. The concern about the possibility of mental diseases arising from tobacco use was also particularly focused on younger smokers. An extract from the 9 March 1898 edition of the *Kawakee Gazette* is particularly interesting in this connection:

> A touching incident occurred this afternoon at the central depot when the 3 o'clock train brought in a middle-aged man with a boy in charge. The little fellow cried with genuine feeling as the gentleman inquired the way to the

insane hospital. To an anxious bystander the stranger said that the boy had gone crazy from the effects of cigarette smoking. Though he appeared to be less than 14 years old, the young man who preferred to inhale tobacco smoke instead of pure air, was being taken to the hospital for treatment. It was an object lesson which ought to be impressed on every boy addicted to the habit. (Cited in Bell 1898: 465)

Bell included a number of sensationalist headlines from other newspapers of the same period: "Cigarettes Made Him a Lunatic!", "William Jenkins, Once a Bright Schoolboy, Becomes a Chattering Beggar from their Use," and "Crazed by Cigarettes." As is apparent from the tone of these and the above newspaper account, many of these articles appear to have been written with a quite specific agenda in mind: that of discouraging young people from smoking. Similarly, there also emerged a large number of articles in which were featured numerous examples of youths being *poisoned* by tobacco:

At the age of 22 he was unfit for work, owing to pains in the chest and shortness of breath. From that time he did nothing but eat, sleep, and smoke "fags," he had no liking for beers or spirits; he was content to sit by the fire and smoke, and read the sporting papers.

During the fits he lay quiet until he recovered except for a slight quiver of the mouth. His loss of strength and vigor was gradual.

Present condition (July 14th), eyes are dull and lifeless; the face of a greenish color; cheeks sullen, body emaciated. He has a vacant expression, and appears indifferent to all things. He has now become obstinate, he refuses to put on a clean shirt, and refuses to go to bed; he has not eaten food for several days; he answered my questions in a vacant way; he seemed in a constant dream; he spat up frothy fluid from his stomach; gums soft and swollen, tongue yellow. The following day I was sent for and found him in a fit; he went off quietly while seated in a chair [he died 17 days later]. (Tidwell 1912: 74–75)

[A] youth of 14, having smoked 15 Cents worth of tobacco as a remedy for toothache, fell down senseless and died the same evening . . . a medical student, aged 22, who, after smoking a single pipe, fell into a frightful state—the heart nearly motionless, the chest constricted, his breathing was extremely painful, the limbs contracted, the pupils insensible to light, one dilated, the other contracted. These symptoms gradually lessened, but did not disappear until forty days after. (Trübner 1873: 10)

It may well be the case that these accounts were not complete fabrications. The individuals they refer to may indeed have suffered adverse reactions to tobacco or possibly to adulterants in the tobacco they consumed.

Alternatively, they may have been displaying the symptoms of an altogether different pathology, one which had been mistakenly *attributed* to tobacco use. However, the highly visual, emotive, *involved* language of these accounts, particularly of the former, would appear to suggest that they were written with the intent of discouraging young people from smoking. In this connection, it is important to note that the forms of tobacco in use at this time were, on the whole, considerably stronger than those commonly used at present. Even cigarettes, which at the time were considered an extremely mild form of tobacco, would have yielded higher quantities of nicotine than their present-day equivalents, and may also have contained a number of other toxic substances through adulteration. Writers who were not interested in supporting the anti-tobacco movement and, if anything, *favored* tobacco use also appear to attest to the strength of the tobacco consumed at this time:

> The effects of an overdose of tobacco are well-known—faintness, nausea, giddiness, relaxation of muscles, loss of power in limbs, cold perspiration, and vomiting. Sometimes there is purging, sinking, or depression of the heart. The pupils of the eye are usually dilated, the sight dim, and the pulse weak, with difficulty of breathing. Fresh air and stimulants speedily remove these symptoms. Indeed, the temporary character of all evil effects produced by tobacco is a striking feature. . . . Tobacco never permanently injures the system, whatever effects it may produce, they are temporary, and disappear on smoking being given up. (Penn 1901: 302–3)

Penn's suggestion that these effects were "well-known" is interesting. To the present-day smoker they may not be so familiar, perhaps experienced in a much milder form, and only in the very early stages of tobacco habituation.

The identification of nicotine as the most important constituent pharmacological agent in tobacco, and as a powerful toxic agent, was highly instrumental in an increasing concern about tobacco poisonings. It was, to some extent, appropriated by the anti-tobacco *movement* (as we can begin to refer to it during this period). It is also interesting to note that anti-tobacco writers of this time did not draw a sharp distinction between the moral and medical arguments against tobacco use. A particularly good example in this connection is the following extract from the Supreme Court of Tennessee's anticigarette legislation of 1898:

> Are cigarettes legitimate articles of commerce? We think they are not because they are wholly noxious and deleterious to health. Their use is always harmful; never beneficial. They possess no virtue, but are inherently bad,

and bad only. They find no true commendation for merit or usefulness in any sphere. On the contrary, they are widely condemned as pernicious altogether. Beyond any question, their every tendency is toward the impairment of physical and mental vigor. (Tennant 1950: 134)

While these arguments were not supported by systematic scientific data, they were influential enough to have become embodied in Tennessee state legislation. Similarly, evidence suggests that during this period, the anti-tobacco movement in Britain was also beginning to exert considerable influence over government legislation. For example, Goodman proposes that the Children Bill of 1908, which was passed to ban the sale of tobacco to children under the age of 16 and to empower the police to seize tobacco from children found smoking in public (Welshman 1996: 1379), "had enshrined at least some of the arguments of the anti-tobacco movement" (1993: 118).

As we have seen, during the late nineteenth to early twentieth century, understandings of tobacco use centered very much on the short-term, *immediate* effects of nicotine. This was also related in part to the difficulty of locating tobacco use within the increasingly dominant medical discourses of the period, particularly germ theory (Goodman 1993: 120). During the 1880s the growing dominance and public acceptance of the germ theory of disease associated with eminent scientific figures such as Louis Pasteur and Robert Koch marked a dramatic shift in public perceptions of health, and in the practices related to maintaining health (ibid.). Physicians of the time increasingly advised regimes of cleanliness and hygiene as the key to the prevention of contagious diseases. Within such a medical paradigm, it was extremely difficult to locate tobacco-induced diseases (ibid.).

Most interestingly, physicians of this period advocated the use of cigarettes in favor of chewing tobacco, as the former involved less spitting—which was believed to spread germs (Goodman 1993: 120). It is significant that some of the initial medical resistance against tobacco use centered on the practice of spitting. The medical arguments here were not a great departure from those of previous centuries, in which spitting in relation to tobacco use was discouraged on the grounds of *etiquette, aesthetics,* or *morals.* As I have shown, in previous centuries, spitting was discouraged *despite* the fact that it was considered *beneficial* to health—in the sense that spitting was seen as a means of dispelling superfluous mucus and thus maintaining a humoral balance. Crucially, as we can observe from the above account, in the late nineteenth to early twentieth century, with the growing dominance of clinical, biomedical understandings of the body and the associated acceptance of germ theory, spitting could *also* be objected to on *medical* grounds.

However, since the idea of tobacco use as a disease agent remained somewhat incompatible with the developing medical paradigm, medical researchers initially began to collect *correlative,* relatively crude biostatistical data on the potentially health-threatening effects of tobacco. In particular, there emerged growing interest in the possibility of a link between tobacco use and *cancer.* The following two accounts typify the character of the data which were then being presented in this connection:

> The mucus membrane of the mouth is always more or less inflamed, and when the irritation of the parts is kept up, cancer of the lips and tongue ofttimes results. Dr. J. C. Warren has observed that: "For more than twenty years back, I have been in the habit of inquiring of patients who have come to me with cancers of these parts (the gum, tongue and lips), whether they used tobacco, and, if so, whether by chewing or smoking. If they have answered in the negative to the first question, I can truly say that, to the best of my belief, such cases of exemption are exceptions to a general rule." (Cowan 1870: 30)

> Now there is a well-known form of disease which by common consent has been attributed to the use of tobacco, so much so that *cancer des fumeurs* [smoker's cancer] is the name given to it by M. Bouisson, whose researches on the subject I will now briefly epitomise. Smoker's cancer is a modern malady, and unfortunately, only too commonly met with both in hospitals and private practice. . . . [He concludes that] Tobacco smoke . . . may then be considered, in predisposed subjects, one of the most active provocatives of cancer of the mouth. (English Mechanic 1872: 8)

As with the previously cited articles referring to nicotine poisoning, one can also find nineteenth-century medical articles linking tobacco use to cancer that appear to sensationalize their findings, perhaps with the specific intention of discouraging the practice:

> His tongue, at this time, was enlarged, firm and coated with a white crust, somewhat resembling the confectionery named Kisses . . . the patient put the following question to Sir Astley [the doctor who was treating him]: "Had I come early enough, could I have been cured?" To which Sir Astley replied,—"Sir, there never was a time early enough to have warranted such an operation; every fibre, every papilla of your tongue is diseased; and it would have been merciful to have clapped a pistol to your head the instant the disease began." (Heywood 1871: 10)

It is clear from the above extracts that tobacco was viewed as an "irritant" or "provocative agent." However, the explanations of exactly how tobacco use *caused* cancer were no more precise than this. Interestingly, the focus was on oral cancers rather than cancer of the lungs—presumably because the mouth was seen to have the most direct and immediate contact with the tobacco consumed by smoking or chewing, and also because lung cancer was not given as much attention in the nineteenth century as it would be in the twentieth (this will be discussed shortly). The correlation between tobacco use and cancer was very largely based on rather crude evidence. However, by the 1930s, more systematic and comprehensive biostatistical data began to emerge. The studies of Frederick Hoffman, a medical insurance statistician, in 1931, and Raymond Pearl, a biostatistician, in 1938, in the United States demonstrated a statistical link between smoking and mortality (Hoffman, more precisely, drew the like between smoking and deaths from lung cancer) (Goodman 1993: 124). Once again, a precise explanation of the link was not provided (125). Shortly after the publication of these studies, there were a number of scientific experiments in which researchers attempted to induce cancers in animals by applying nicotine to their skin (ibid.). That nicotine was suspected to be the most likely carcinogenic substance in tobacco is indicative of the central interest then placed in the substance (ibid.). The studies of Hoffman, Pearl, and others also reflect an important shift in understandings of cancer itself. In addition, changes in how cancer was being understood and diagnosed were centrally important. In fact, medicine itself was beginning to change fundamentally: there emerged an increasingly dominant clinical medical paradigm—a *discourse*,[1] which contained a new way of seeing and understanding the human body and disease. The changes in medical consciousness at this time, the rise of clinical medical discourse, are centrally explored by Michel Foucault in his text *The Birth of the Clinic* (1973). Next I will examine Foucault's work in some detail in order to locate changes in understandings of tobacco use within the broader processes of *medicalization*.

Michel Foucault on the Emergence of the "Clinical Gaze"

Foucault examined how the system of classificatory medicine that was particularly dominant before the nineteenth century became rapidly replaced by clinical medicine. The central principle of the former, Foucault suggested, was embodied in J. I. Gilbert's words: "Never treat a disease without first be-

---

1. Shilling (1993: 75) provides the following explication of Foucault's conceptualization of discourse: "Discourse is the most important concept in Foucault's work and it is centrally concerned with, although irreducible to, language. Discourses can be seen as sets of 'deep principles' incorporating specific 'grids of meaning' which underpin, generate and establish relations between all that can be seen, thought and said." The concept will be further explicated in my exposition of Foucault's work which follows.

ing sure of its species" (cited in Foucault 1973: 4). A central concern of classificatory medicine was to organize diseases hierarchically into a profusion of family, genera, and species. Diseases were understood to be semiautonomous from the body, in that their presence in the organ was not what defined them; the body was viewed as a two-dimensional surface upon which the disease could travel from one point to another and still remain the same in nature. What gave a disease its classification was its relation to *other diseases;* the physician's central aim, therefore, was to identify a disease's pure nosological essence. Significantly, death was seen as the ultimate disturbance, at once the limit of the physician's ability to cure and the end of the disease itself (140).

Foucault proposed that modern *clinical* medicine dated (by its own reflection) from the last decades of the eighteenth century. The founding *myth* of modern medicine was that physicians, by removing the blinkers of fantasy, were suddenly able to see what lay before them. A process of *epistemological purification* occurred in which experience began to prevail over theory. The new clinical medicine that emerged was dominated by a quite specific "gaze," or way of seeing, understanding, articulating, and ultimately controlling, the human body. What really made this possible, Foucault proposed, was *not* an act of "epistemological purification" but rather a reorganization of the limits of the *visibility* of disease. Physicians of the late eighteenth and early nineteenth century were gradually able to observe that which had previously lain below the level of vision, not really an "opening of eyes," but a new conceptualization of the body: the emergence of *clinical* discourse:

> Reflecting on its situation [modern medicine] identifies the origin of its positivity with a return—over and above all theory—to the modest but effecting level of the perceived. In fact, this supposed empiricism is not based on a rediscovery of the absolute values of the visible, nor on the predetermined rejection of systems and all their chimeras, but on a reorganisation of that manifest and secret space that opened up when a millennial gaze paused over men's [sic] sufferings. Nonetheless the rejuvenation of medical perception, the way colours and things came to life under the illuminating gaze of the first clinicians is no mere myth. At the beginning of the nineteenth century, doctors described what for centuries had remained below the threshold of the visible and expressible, but this did not mean that, after over-indulging in speculation, they had begun to perceive once again, or that they listened to reason rather than imagination; it meant that the relationship between the visible and invisible—which is necessary to all concrete knowledge—changed its structure, revealing through gaze and

> language what had previously been below and beyond their domain. A new
> alliance was forged between words and things enabling one *to see* and *to say.*
> (Foucault 1973: xii)

The reorganization of the relationship between "the visible" and "the invisible" to which Foucault refers above was, in turn, related to a number of *social* changes. The medical profession was becoming increasingly centrally organized; accordingly, the patient became "enveloped" in homogeneous "spaces": the rise of new forms of medical *institution*—including the new hospitals and the "clinic" itself—and a correspondingly centralized organization of medical consciousness. The locus of medicine was no longer the theory-based lecture hall, but the hospital itself. As experience occurred, it was passed from the doctor to the student. Crucially, Foucault proposes, these changes laid the foundations for a level of access to the body which had previously been unavailable. Physicians were, on an unprecedented scale, able to "open up a few corpses" (Foucault 1973: 124). The black coffer of the body, Foucault proposes, its dark underside, the darkness which had previously hidden and enveloped disease, became dissipated by the brightness of the clinical gaze. That is to say, through the tool of the postmortem, physicians were able physically to "open" the corpse to access its *inside.* Thus death, instead of marking the limits of the physician's ability, became the liberator of the clinical gaze.

Most important, the gaze also consisted of new modes of understanding and expression; it opened up new possibilities for medical knowledge. From these changes a new conception of disease and causality was born. A surface symptom was understood to result from a deep structural lesion. The role of the physician was to locate and understand the disease *mechanism:* its specific *causality.*

Foucault suggests that medicine has become the founding science of all sciences. Accordingly, the biomedical, clinical body, which lay at the center of the emerging medical discourse, took on a role of crucial and central importance and meaning. This shift ultimately corresponds to the processes Foucault outlines in his 1979 work, *Discipline and Punish,* in which he examines changes in how the human body was used as a vehicle for social control. Previously, Foucault proposes, social control was very largely exerted *externally* to the body; however, corresponding to the shift in medical discourse, social control had increasingly become *internalized.* Strict routines from bureaucracy, new "total" institutions, new technologies of power have become "embodied." In Foucault's analysis, the body becomes the locus of a system of *micro politics.* Medicine itself emerges as an institution of social control. It possesses new modes of surveillance, increasingly specialized equipment for penetrating and scanning *below the surface* of the body. Thus, the emergence of strict bodily hygiene regimens—the "healthy lifestyle"—associated with the rise of the germ theory of disease, can be understood from a Foucauldian perspective as a characteristic form of social control exerted through the increasing dominance of specific forms of medical discourse. In the same way, the increasing access to diagnostic tools to probe the inside of the body—X-ray technology, stethoscopes, the increasing use of and access to the postmortem—*all crucial to the development of modern understandings of cancer*—can be located in the shift toward clinical, biomedical discourse that Foucault identifies. Ultimately, he argues, the "clinical gaze" also leads to a proliferation of technologies for the investigation, surveillance, and probing of *society as a whole:* questionnaires, surveys, and, significantly, the biostatistical techniques central to epidemiology.

The clinical gaze, the particular way of "seeing and saying" that it involves, thus has become directed at a growing range of aspects of social life. The expansion of preventative medicine and the emergence of specialized medical institutions directed at specific social groups—for example, child psychiatry, gynecology, geriatric specialists—from a Foucauldian perspective can all be seen to be related to the increasing dominance of clinical discourse. Even within our everyday language, we increasingly use medical analogies: for example the notion of treating society's "ills," or the economist's reference to a "sick economy," or an "unhealthy pound." Later writers have termed this process *medicalization*.

Tobacco Use and Medicalization

As a rapidly growing, highly visible social practice, if we follow Foucault's line of argument, tobacco use was ripe for medicalization. If a link could be established between tobacco use and what was rapidly being recognized as *the* cancer of the twentieth century—lung cancer—perhaps then the practice could be subsumed within clinical medical discourse. The link had to be more systematic than that developed in the circumstantial correlative case studies of the nineteenth century. Indeed, the emerging clinical medical paradigm demanded a precise understanding of the *mechanism* by which smoking *caused* lung cancer. However, as already noted, it was initially extremely difficult to locate the idea of tobacco-induced disease within this paradigm—it did not fit well with the idea of specific causality. As Brandt proposes:

> The municipal laboratory had become [in the twentieth century] the new focus of public health. Even when researchers identified environmental or

behavioral risks, they generally focused on the *mechanism* of the disease. The whole notion of statistical inference was questioned, as research centered on the cellular level. In this respect, exposure to a carcinogen was equated with exposure to an infectious organism. Identifying the health risks of a particular behavior like smoking fitted this model poorly. The length of time before the disease developed was protracted (and equated with an "incubation period"); in addition, the large number of intervening variables confounded notions of specific causality. Everyone *"exposed"* did not get the disease; indeed, most did not; and some who were not exposed did. Also, there was broad cultural discomfort with notions of comparative risk assessment. How dangerous was the cigarette? How did this danger rate vis-à-vis other risks? Finally, medical theory offered few persuasive models for understanding systemic and chronic diseases; the anomalies of cigarette smoking did not fit the biomedical model's idea of specific causality. (Brandt 1990: 160; emphasis added)

However, in the face of changing patterns of disease, medical researchers were forced to implement a further shift in the dominant medical paradigm. Physicians and statisticians viewed the rising incidence of lung cancer as a significant exception to disease patterns as a whole (Brandt 1990: 160). The increase in the United States, like many other parts of the West, was rapid indeed: only 400 cases were recorded in 1900, but 4,000 in 1935 and 11,000 in 1945, with annual rates rising to 36,000 by 1960; by the mid-1980s lung cancer had become the most prevalent form of cancer, accounting for 140,000 deaths per year (ibid.). Observers put forward a range of theories to explain the dramatic increase: improvements in the diagnosis and identification of the disease; better reporting; greater life expectancy—the disease now had enough time to develop, whereas individuals might previously have died earlier on in life of other causes; the growing use of X-rays, and so on (161). But, as Brandt suggests, "some physicians and public health officers pointed to one of the most dramatic behavioral changes in the history of [Western] culture, the rise of cigarette smoking. . . . [This] led to a series of epidemiological studies of the risk of smoking. These studies, in turn, would lead to a redefinition of risk, epidemiology, and public health" (ibid.).

Thus, the articulation of a link between lung cancer and tobacco use required the reconsideration of three questions central to the clinical medical paradigm: the *nature of causality;* the particular *mechanism of the disease;* and the *production of evidence.* The clinical gaze had to be recast within a relatively new framework—that of epidemiology. Accordingly, the idea of specific causality was replaced with a far more complex view of cause, one utilizing criteria based on consistency, temporality, strength, specificity, and the reliability of statistical associations between tobacco use and mortality rates (Gusfield 1993: 58). The mechanism of the disease also had to be reconsidered, from that of a *trigger*, as in the case of a poisonous or infectious agent. Researchers instead adopted the notion of *incubation*. And evidence would have to be collected, not through the process of *going into the body*, but through *going into the body of society*.

It is these three shifts that emerged as central to understandings of tobacco use in the twentieth century. The increasing *medicalization* of tobacco use thus involved a shift away from a focus on the short-term effects of tobacco. I refer again to the previously quoted statement from Penn (1901: 303): "Tobacco never permanently injures the system, whatever effects it may produce, they are temporary, and disappear on smoking being given up." This statement contrasts starkly with the notion of an "incubation period" for disease. The move away from a primary focus on the short-term, immediate, toxic, and psychoactive properties of nicotine toward examining the long-term effects of tobacco as a disease agent, is central to the development of present-day understandings of not just tobacco-induced disease but the development of the smoking practice more generally. As we shall see, this process has, paradoxically, been instrumental in the recent increase in the proportion of young tobacco users. Furthermore, tobacco, like any other potential disease agent, came to be perceived as something that one was *subjected to*. In relation to this, the idea that the effects were not immediately *visible*, were long-term and thus an *invisible*, to be uncovered by the clinical gaze (which had been very largely extended through the techniques of epidemiology), marks another crucial shift in understandings of tobacco use.

Indeed, such ideas were later extended further: the clinical gaze, initially concerned with identifying the role of tobacco as a disease agent, was increasingly applied to the question of why people smoked at all. Just as understandings of cancer became dramatically transformed with the growth of clinical medical discourse, so did understandings of drug use more generally. A term that had been used for centuries, sometimes in relation to tobacco use—*addiction*—rapidly began to take on a new, *clinically medicalized* set of meanings: generic, hidden biological processes from which the individual needed to be abstracted before an understanding could be developed. Ultimately, such a shift in understanding underpins the nicotine self-administration model of the practice that is dominant today. Most interestingly, the idea of tobacco as a disease agent, and that of tobacco use as an addiction, became combined: tobacco use became increasingly identified as *an addictive disease*.[2]

As the extract from Brandt highlights, the entire notion of statistical inference was called into question during the early stages of the rise of clinical medicine. These doubts over the validity of any form of statistical inference, and the inherently conflicting reliance on epidemiological studies in the case against tobacco, were seized upon by pro-tobacco groups of the time, particularly tobacco corporations. Indeed, such doubts continue to feature prominently in current debates about smoking and accountability. As Brandt states, "[T]he debate revealed a deeper discomfort with statistical logic and quantitative methods in biomedicine, a trend which persists today" (1990: 163). But, as the opening quotation to this chapter demonstrates, epidemiological data—in fact, statistics more generally—have come to dominate our understandings of tobacco use. It is ultimately through the growth of epidemiological research linking lung cancer and a range of other diseases to what are understood to be "lifestyle choices," such as our decisions regarding smoking, diet, alcohol, reactions to stress, exercise, and sexual activity, that tobacco use has increasingly become a *moral* as well as a *medical* concern (Gusfield 1993).

Among the first to contribute to the new wave of epidemiological studies relating to tobacco use were Drs. Ernest Wynder and Evarts Graham. They studied the tobacco-using practices of 605 men who were diagnosed as having lung cancer, and found that 96.5 percent had smoked at least ten cigarettes per day for twenty years (Diehl 1969: 22). This research was shortly followed by a British Medical Research Council study conducted by Richard Doll and Bradford Hill (1951). Doll and Hill located 709 hospitalized lung cancer patients, and surveyed their tobacco-using habits. They

---

2. For example, the following extract is taken from a 1957 text entitled *The Disease of Tobacco Smoking and Its Cure:*

Smoking is spread by smokers. Each time a smoker lights up, he proclaims anew his support for the smoking of tobacco and his opposition to non-smoking and little weight attaches to any mere words he may utter in contradiction to the teaching of his actions. Each word of appreciation of smoking also tends to spread the disease. Every smoker is, in fact, actively infectious and makes himself into a gratuitous advertisement for tobacco. Smoking, like pulmonary tuberculosis, is usually a family disease and its development and age of onset largely depend on whether or not a child is exposed to massive infection at an early age, i.e. is brought up in a smoking home. . . . Psychological infection of the non-smoker is completed as a rule by the intimate persuasion of a smoker. "Have a cigarette, old man"; "it'll do you good (or steady your nerves)"; "don't be so miserable (or a cissy)"; "one has to have a *little* bit of pleasure (or comfort) these days"; or "one has to have *one* little vice, it doesn't do to be *too* good.'" (Johnston 1957: 10–11) Interestingly enough, in this quotation the attempt is to portray tobacco use itself as an *infectious* agent, one where contagion is spread through social interaction.

then located 709 patients of the same age and sex, but without lung cancer, and recorded their smoking habits. Their study demonstrated that not only was there a strong association between smoking and cancer of the lung, but, crucially, that a high proportion of lung cancer patients were heavy smokers (Diehl 1969: 22). Another major study was conducted by E. C. Hammond and D. Horn (1954). They found that total death rates were considerably higher among smokers than nonsmokers (Brandt 1990: 162). They also found that the incidence of deaths from lung cancer was 3–9 times higher among smokers than among non-smokers, and 5–16 times higher among heavy smokers (ibid.). Conversely, Hammond and Horn found that smoking cessation substantially reduced the risk of contracting lung cancer (ibid.).

However, it was events of the 1960s which were to prove crucial to the widespread acceptance of a link between smoking and disease. After considering the large amount of research that had been conducted during the 1950s and early 1960s, the Royal College of Physicians in 1962, and the U.S. Surgeon General in 1964, both concluded that cigarette smokers in particular faced a high risk of serious disease, a risk which could be substantially reduced by discontinuing their use of tobacco (Goodman 1993: 126). These events mark an important "stage" in the development of tobacco use in the West not merely because they constitute the point at which the link between tobacco and disease had been officially accepted as "true" by the medical profession but also because they are indicative of the increasingly successful *medicalization* of tobacco use.

The official acceptance of the link between smoking and fatal diseases was instrumental in the development of a wide range of processes:

> First, tobacco was put on the political agenda as it became increasingly clear that there were powerful vested interests involved. Almost immediately, an intense war broke out between the pro-tobacco forces, including tobacco companies, some government agencies, tobacco producers and some consumers, and the anti-tobacco forces, including consumer pressure groups and some other government agencies. The lines dividing the forces have never been entirely clear and shifted over time. The role of the government came under close scrutiny especially since, on the one hand, it had a duty to protect consumers from potentially dangerous substances, while, on the other hand, it acted to protect its own interests, financial and electorate. (Goodman 1993: 126)

From the above extract, we can already begin to observe the libertarian dilemma that continues to lie at the heart of the debate surrounding tobacco use. This dilemma can be presented as follows: on the one hand, should the government intervene to protect individuals from becoming *subject* to a potentially fatal set of biological processes (the clinical-medical argument)? Or, on the other, should the government be restricting an individual's *freedom* to smoke (according to the tobacco companies' response); the freedom of the market; and, indeed, its own interests? From these issues, one can observe how moral debates over whether it is "good" or "bad" to smoke become translated into more "political" arguments, which hinge upon the liberal notion of *individual freedom*. With the dilemma also centering on the *role of the state* in the regulation of tobacco use, one can observe how this shift was, in part, related to the increasing *institutionalization* of the debate between opponents and proponents of the practice.[3]

The tobacco corporations' initial response to the growing volume of systematic medical evidence in the 1950s linking smoking to lung cancer was threefold. First, the corporations challenged the validity of the emerging statistical data, in part by utilizing the more general dissatisfaction within the medical profession with the statistical inference model. Second, they promoted the idea that smoking was an act of "personal choice," an individual liberty, definitely not an *addiction*. Glantz et al. argue that this initiative was essential to the tobacco corporations, since, with this idea firmly established, they would not be "held responsible for adverse health effects attributed to smoking" (1996: 59). Third, the tobacco industry increasingly promoted and developed what were referred to as "safer" cigarettes.

The main vehicle for the tobacco corporations' response to their opponents was advertising. Indeed, the first phase of their responses (as outlined above) took the form of the following advertisement, which was published by the newly formed Tobacco Industry Research Committee in January 1954:

A Frank Statement to Cigarette Smokers

RECENT REPORTS on experiments with mice have given wide publicity to a theory that cigarette smoking is in some way linked with lung cancer in human beings.

Although conducted by doctors of professional standing, these experiments are not regarded as conclusive in the field of cancer research. However, we do not believe that any serious medical research, even though its results are inconclusive, should be disregarded or lightly dismissed.

---

3. Up until the mid-1960s the antismoking movement in the United States and other parts of the West had very much been led by voluntary organizations. It is only since then that the state, particularly through public health agencies, has come to play a central role (Gusfield 1993: 54).

At the same time, we feel it is in the public interest to call attention to the fact that eminent doctors and research scientists have publicly questioned the claimed significance of these experiments.

Distinguished authorities point out:

1. That medical research of recent years indicates many possible causes of lung cancer.

2. That there is no agreement among the authorities regarding what the cause is.

3. That there is no proof that cigarette smoking is one of the causes.

4. That statistics purporting to link cigarette smoking with the disease could apply with equal force to any one of many other aspects of modern life. Indeed, the validity of the statistics themselves is questioned by numerous scientists.

We accept an interest in people's health as a basic responsibility, paramount to every other consideration in our business.

We believe the products we make are not injurious to health.

We have and always will cooperate closely with those whose task it is to safeguard the public health. (Cited in Glantz et al. 1996: 34; emphasis in original)

The advertisement continued by outlining three central pledges to the consumer. First, the tobacco industry would assist (financially and otherwise) the research effort into "all phases of tobacco and health." Second, it would establish a joint industry group—The Tobacco Research Committee. Third, it would place in charge a reputable scientist of "unimpeachable integrity and national repute," and institute an independent scientific advisory board to the tobacco industry. One can observe from this advertisement the already central importance to the tobacco industry of being seen to have nothing to hide, to have the public's interests as a priority, and to be an organization willing to cooperate with the medical profession. Throughout their text, Glantz et al. systematically argue that this image amounted to little more than just a public face to the consumer, in stark contrast with the secret, internal agenda of the industry: to keep the controversy alive, and, ultimately, to protect their commercial interests (Glantz et al. 1996: 36).

Advertising, Mass Consumerization, and the Rise of Women Smoking

The response of tobacco companies during the 1950s was by no means their first reaction to growing public concern about tobacco use. Indeed, throughout the first half of the twentieth century, they responded to and even preempted much of the emerging medical research on the link between tobacco and disease (Glantz et al. 1996: 28). Even as far back as the 1920s, tobacco companies were promoting cigarettes with advertising slogans that suggested their brands were "'healthier" or less "irritating" than others' (ibid.). Lucky Strike advertisements from 1929, for example, claimed that "20,679 physicians have confirmed that *Lucky Strike* is less irritating to the throat than other cigarettes" (ibid.). In the same way, advertisements for Kool cigarettes of the 1930s–40s advised, "For your throat's sake Switch from 'Hots' to 'Kools'" (29). During the 1950s, with the increase in public concern discussed above, cigarette advertisements began to promote filter-tipped cigarettes as a "healthy" alternative. Viceroy's slogan, for example, was as follows: "New HEALTH-GUARD Filter Makes VICEROY Better For Your Health Than Any Other Leading Cigarette!" (ibid.). It is interesting that "healthier" rather than "less damaging to health" was used in this connection. This could almost be read to be an advertisement claiming that Viceroy cigarettes were beneficial to one's health. As Glantz et al. conclude from this evidence:

> These examples of the tobacco industry's advertising claims . . . indicate that the industry began promoting filter and reduced-tar cigarettes during the 1950s primarily to calm public fears about the health effects of smoking. Although the advertisements of the era suggested that the new cigarettes were "healthier," there was no real evidence that this was so. When the evidence finally began to come in (beginning only twenty years later, in 1977), the verdict was that lowering tar with filters had only a very modest effect in lowering the enormous risk of lung cancer caused by cigarettes and no effect in protecting the consumer from the more common threat, fatal heart disease. Today the tobacco industry claims that it markets filter and "low-tar" cigarettes because of public demand, and not because it believes that these products are "safer." . . . However, the industry itself, through its advertising campaigns, has helped to create the illusion that these products are safer. (30)

While Glantz et al. may be right in suggesting that continuing consumer demand for filter-tipped cigarettes stemmed from the tobacco industry's promotion of these as a "safer" alternative to their unfiltered counterparts, there may also be another set of processes involved in this demand. In addition to the growing call for a "safer" cigarette, filter tips were initially successful also because they met the demand for a less irritating smoke (Goodman 1993: 110–111)—a smoke that was milder more in terms of its palatability than its nicotine content.[4] Indeed, mildness was a central theme

4. Goodman also notes that another advantage of filter cigarettes, perhaps one which could ultimately be passed on to the consumer, was that they contained less tobacco, and were thus cheaper to produce (1993: 111).

in a large proportion of tobacco advertising during the first half of the twentieth century (108).

Filter-tipped cigarettes were initially popular with women not so much because they were considered healthier but more because they helped them avoid the "unsightly" habit of spitting out soggy cigarette ends (Jacobson 1981). It is interesting that once again, changes in the medium of tobacco use that have involved, to some extent, an increasing mildness or taming of its effect, were at least partly related to demands of *etiquette*. It is highly significant that fear of embarrassment, more than a concern for health, was central to changes in how tobacco was consumed in the twentieth century, particularly when one considers how influential medical discourse was becoming during this period. According to Jacobson, "Until the Second World War, excessive 'indulgence' in cigarettes was considered unladylike and those who did smoke were expected not to inhale too deeply or to leave too short a stub. Indeed keeping to feminine etiquette was probably partly responsible for holding down female lung-cancer rates until recently" (Jacobson 1981: 11). Not only was women's smoking to be conducted in a highly *controlled* manner, but following the arguments presented in chapter 2, women used tobacco as an instrument of *self-control*. However, this was self-control of a quite specific character. In addition to smoking cigarettes to combat stress or to counter monotony, women also used tobacco as a *means of weight control*. In their earliest attempts to urge women to smoke, cigarette advertisers, made much of this. For example, Lucky Strike advertisements of 1928–29 contained the caption "Reach for a Lucky Instead of a Sweet" (Goodman 1993: 107). Such ideas were endorsed by famous personalities, who attested to the beneficial effects of smoking to a woman's figure (ibid.). Lucky Strike advertisements continued to present this theme in later advertisements, with slogans such as "Pretty Curves Win!" and "Be moderate—be moderate in all things, even in smoking. Avoid that future shadow by avoiding over-indulgence, if you would maintain that modern, ever youthful figure 'Reach for a Lucky Instead'" (ibid.).

From the 1920s to the 1960s, both in the United States and the U.K., the proportion of smokers who were women increased substantially (Goodman 1993: 107). For example, in Britain during the period 1930–39, "the proportion of total tobacco consumption accounted for by women doubled from 5 per cent to 10 per cent" (106). Tobacco companies were quick to target—and were instrumental in catalyzing—the expanding market of female smokers. A number of companies even went as far as to introduce brands of specifically "female" cigarettes; one of these, which was later to become extremely successful, was Marlboro (112). Another, much later, brand was

Virginia Slims, launched in 1968 (ibid.). Once again, the perceived relationship between women, smoking, and weight control is evident from the name of this brand.

Another major theme seized upon by tobacco companies of the 1920s and 1930s reflected changes in attitudes that were generally more pervasive in the West. In line with these changes, the idea that a woman's smoking was a sign of her promiscuity began to decline. Once the occupational symbol of prostitutes, the cigarette began to emerge as an emblem of women's emancipation (Greaves 1996: 18). Once again, tobacco corporations were keen to exploit this image transformation process. A researcher hired by the Great American Tobacco Company to advise on advertising and marketing strategy—the psychoanalyst A. A. Brill—drew the following conclusions in relation to women's smoking in the 1920s:

> Some women regard cigarettes as symbols of freedom. . . . Smoking is a sublimation of oral eroticism; holding a cigarette in the mouth excites the oral zone. It is perfectly normal for women to want to smoke cigarettes. Further, the first women who smoked probably had an excess of masculine components and adopted the habit as a masculine act. But today the emancipation of women has suppressed many of the feminine desires. More women now do the same work as men do. . . . Cigarettes, which are equated with men, become **torches of freedom**. (Cited in Greaves 1996: 19; emphasis in the original)

As part of a process that Ewen (1976) has referred to as "commercialized feminism" (cited in Greaves 1996: 19), tobacco corporations began to devise a number of marketing and advertising strategies designed to exploit these associations. For example, as Greaves recounts, "[T]he 1929 Easter parade in New York city included a company-organized and much publicized group of cigarette-smoking women, lighting 'torches of freedom' as a protest against women's inequality. . . . [C]igarette smoking in the 1920s became a symbol of women's freedom in the dominant culture, and a challenge to Victorian mores. Smoking became firmly aligned with dress reform, bobbed hair, nightclubbing and suffrage" (19). Greaves highlights the paradox that this alignment represented, and, she argues, continues to represent. On the one hand, the cigarette is viewed as a symbol of freedom, equality, and, more recently, personal choice; on the other, tobacco use itself, from Greaves's perspective, constitutes a form of addiction that involves a quite profound "loss of freedom" (ibid.).[5]

5. I shall later challenge the usefulness of this model of tobacco use. I do not wish to argue that tobacco use is in any way a simple act of free will or rational choice, nor, conversely, that

Tobacco Use and Informalization

The relaxation of social proscriptions on women smoking during the early 1920s, in turn related to the rise of the cigarette as a mass-branded, mass-produced commodity, marked an important shift in how tobacco was consumed among both men and women:

> The cigarette marks the convergence of corporate capitalism, technology, mass marketing, and, in particular, the impact of advertising. These forces induced new modes of individual and group behavior. With the rise of consumerism, a new behavioral ethic was defined. From a culture that promoted self-denial and self-discipline in the late nineteenth century—one condemning indulgence in all forms—Americans [like their British counterparts] were now encouraged to indulge. (Brandt 1990: 157)

The broader social processes Brandt indicates here have been examined in some detail by Wouters (1976, 1977, 1986, 1987), who proposes that the Roaring Twenties constituted one of the first of a number of "waves" of *informalization* in the twentieth century. Briefly, the term *informalization* refers to a general shift in codes of etiquette and manners, an increasing permissiveness in society. On the surface, these changes may be seen to constitute a decrease in overall levels of social control; a decline in the *social pressure toward self-restraint*. However, such changes actually involve a high degree of *internalization* of social control by members of a society. In other words, processes of informalization involve a decline in *externally* regulated controls, and a corresponding increase in *internally* regulated self-controls. To make this clearer, consider the example of bathing costumes which Elias provided in this connection. During the first half of the twentieth century, bathing costumes, particularly those of women, were becoming increasingly revealing. In the nineteenth century, Elias observed, a woman wearing such a costume in public would have been socially ostracized. He proposed that, rather than representing a decline in the overall levels of social control, these changes were indicative of "[a] society in which a high degree of restraint is taken for granted, and in which women are, like men, absolutely sure that each individual is curbed by self-control" (Elias 1939: 187).[6]

---

tobacco use constitutes a form of one-way dependence. Rather, I wish to locate the recent debate about tobacco use and individual freedom within the long-term development of tobacco use in the West. My aim, ultimately, is to move toward a conception of tobacco use that centers on the concept of *interdependence*.

6. In some senses, informalization ultimately involves an *intensification* of controls. Consider, as both an analogy and as part of the process of informalization itself, the case of "mufti" days, which are becoming increasingly popular, particularly among large business corporations in the West. On these days, usually once a week, employees can dress as they wish: they do not

Within this context, the increasingly "indulgent" smoking of the twentieth century (more among men), and the general increase in women smoking, clearly exemplifies informalization. If we accept that a major use of the cigarette in the modern era is as an instrument of self-control, we can observe how the relaxation of the temperance norm, and an easing of gender proscriptions regarding tobacco use, in turn involved an increase in behavior that could be viewed as characteristically *civilized*. Moreover, we can also observe a further set of processes in this connection. The standards of socially "correct" behavior at this time were being set less via the traditional, formal institutions of manners texts and etiquette manuals, and more via *informal* determination within *consumer culture*. A key theme of consumer culture is that, increasingly, individuals must know almost *intuitively* how to look, what to talk about, how to dress, what music to listen to—indeed, what to *consume*. Individuals learn socially acceptable behavior in a manner fundamentally different from that of previous centuries. Commercial advertisements, radio, the Internet, television, and film become important conveyors of changes in appropriate modes of behavior for specific groups of people. In relation to these processes, standards of socially correct behavior become increasingly multiple, fragmented, complex, and *individualized*. Indeed, the process of selecting the correct, most appropriate standard of behavior and self-presentation is at once seen as a means of *individual* self-expression, and of affiliation to a specific social group.

Thus, rather than amounting to an overall decline in levels of self-control, processes of informalization involve quite specific changes in the

---

need to wear the company uniform or dress in line with formal corporate policy. There are, of course, considerable variations in mufti days. Some organizations may specify, very loosely, that even on these days, employees must be "business casual." Others may have no *explicitly stated* specifications at all. However, rather than constituting a simple relaxation of pressures on how to dress—an absence of controls—we are immediately presented with *another* set of pressures, and these might be even more intensely felt that those arising from company dress code. We must still dress "appropriately." But what is "appropriate"? We are compelled to ask a series of questions of our clothes: Is this fashionable? Is this the *right* label (interestingly, this refers as much to labels on the inside of our clothes as it does to those emblazoned on the outside)? The questions are expressive of more than just commercial concerns: Is this too trampy? Does my butt look big in this? Is this too nerdy? Too formal? Too casual? Too stiff? Too power-dressy? Too loud? Too dull? Is this really *me*? We are compelled to dress "correctly," not so much according to the formally defined external standard of the corporation, but now according to a blend and balance of internalized and external standards and concerns. We must express both our *individuality* and our *sense of belonging* through our particular way of dressing. On the face of it, we are "free" to wear a track suit to work, but what might "they" think of this? And what would we think of those who did? Thus *informalization* involves a change in the character of demands for self-control, and demands for more *individually nuanced* means of self-expression, emotional display, and affect management.

character and achievement of self-control. As Foucault expresses it, these changes involve *the increasing replacement of "control by repression" with "control by stimulation"* in consumer culture (Foucault 1980). The example he provides in this connection is as follows: "Get undressed—but be slim, good looking, tanned" (57). Individuals, particularly women, are under increasing pressure to make their body "a project" to be developed in accordance with social standards (Shilling 1993). In this respect, tobacco use can be seen as a unique instrument of self-control: as involving both control by repression (to calm the nerves, to combat stress) and, increasingly during the twentieth century, control by stimulation (to stimulate the mood, to "shape the body"). Indeed, tobacco use can be seen to constitute both control by repression and control by stimulation *simultaneously:* the *suppressing* of hunger pangs to *stimulate* the development of a thinner body. The paradox is that *externally,* by social standards, the body may be judged to be healthier as a result of smoking—the thinner body, the *controlled* body is, up to a point, also viewed as the healthier body.[7]

Greaves locates this shift in understandings of women's tobacco use—the emergence of the cigarette as a symbol of women's equality and emancipation—within a long-term process of social change:

> Over this century . . . in industrial countries the cultural meaning of women's smoking as it relates to gender relations has moved from a symbol of being *bought* by men (prostitute), to being *like* men (lesbian/mannish/androgynous), to being *able to attract* men (glamorous/heterosexual). Sexual liberals may argue that this reflects historical differences of power

7. The precise manner in which tobacco use affects body weight has recently been the subject of considerable research. As Krogh (1991) proposes, a number of explanations have been put forward. First, people tend to eat more when they stop smoking, in part as a compensatory behavior—thus, when smokers stop the practice they tend to put on more weight, and conversely, when they resume smoking, they begin to lose weight again (1991: 66). Smoking in this sense can be seen as a substitute for food—as was suggested in many cigarette advertising campaigns of the 1920s and 1930s. Second, a number of studies have found that smokers tend to consume less sweet foods as a result of their tobacco use (ibid.). Third, and most important, research conducted in 1989 found that smoking produces a significant increase in the smoker's metabolic rate, particularly smoking while engaged in activity at work (67). Krogh is unequivocal in his belief that smoking does have a direct effect on body weight, and that this is not simply a perceived effect arising from "folk wisdom" (65). It is interesting that he links the use of tobacco as a means of weight control to workplace smoking. Once again we can observe that this connection has emerged as a particularly dominant theme in the twentieth century with the rise of smoking as a supplementary activity—although the role of tobacco as a hunger suppressant has been known for centuries, particularly by Native American users. In other words, this specific understanding and use of tobacco as a means of weight control can be located, once more, within processes of *civilization.*

and control of a woman over her sexual existence. However, some sexual radicals would see this as evidence of further entrenchment of the institution of heterosexuality, an erasure of sexual orientation issues and a manipulation of the concept of women's power. The tobacco companies cover all this ground by simultaneously appealing to both the equality-seeking, freedom-loving, challenging woman ("You've come a long way, baby" of Virginia Slims), as well as to the heterosexually defined, male-identified woman. (Greaves 1996: 21–22)

To explicate the stages Greaves identifies: the stage in which tobacco was predominantly viewed as a symbol of female sexuality to be appropriated by men is perhaps best embodied in the (previously quoted and discussed) statement of Rudyard Kipling, who referred to his favorite cigars as "a harem of dusky beauties tied fifty in a string" (Mitchell 1992: 329). In this connection, women's smoking more generally was a sign of female sexuality for sale: the prostitute. Greaves proposes that this stage continued until approximately the end of the nineteenth century. The second stage she identifies, the understanding of women's smoking as becoming *like* a man, emerged during the late nineteenth to the early twentieth century. During the early twentieth century in particular, lesbian women, for example, were regarded as having an "affinity" with smoking (Greaves 1996: 20). Smoking was seen still very much as a "masculine" behavior, so women's smoking was viewed as a sign that they were becoming more *equal* to men (ibid.). Indeed, in relation to this, changes in women's appearance, including shorter hair and the popularity of a less curvaceous figure, marked a period in which "an increasingly unisex [or androgynous] trend emerged": "The *masculinity* implied by smoking was a key part of the cultural symbolism challenged by women in the 1920s in industrial countries. Smoking tobacco had almost always been a man's domain, particularly due to the preponderance of pipe and cigar smoking prior to the advent of the manufactured cigarette" (ibid.).

However, women in previous centuries *did* smoke cigars and pipes. The more recent social proscriptions on women smoking these media of tobacco consumption can be seen to be intimately related to the collective effort of nineteenth-century middle-class male smokers to distance their forms of tobacco use from that of women and younger males: cigarette smoking. As has been argued in chapter 2, part of this effort involved the emergence of a number of articles and other writings in which cigarette smoking was portrayed as *distinctively female:* as "belonging to the 'weaker vessels' of tobacco smoking" (Old Smoker 1894: 24). The association being drawn here was that between the relative weakness or mildness of the cigarette and the "weaker sex."

The third stage Greaves identifies, the idea that women's smoking was an activity to *attract men,* emerged particularly in the 1940s and 1950s. Characteristic of this stage were ideas that brought into the popular discourse psychoanalytical concepts, which have continued to have considerable currency in the West, particularly since the 1920s. As Greaves defines it, the cigarette had become "a crucial erotic prop and a way of increasing one's attractiveness to men" (Greaves 1996: 21). Furthermore, advertising campaigns of this period also began to build associations between cigarette smoking and "classy sophistication" (ibid.). Greaves, drawing on Garber (1992) in this connection, presents the argument that this move by the tobacco companies was intended to "obfuscate" questions of sexual orientation in relation to women's tobacco use (a legacy from the complex history of women's cigarette smoking) and to divert attention toward questions of class:

> Such marketing strategies clearly reflect the values of patriarchy and capitalism in that they support the institution of heterosexuality and enhance profits. It was strategic and profitable several decades ago for the tobacco companies to override any lingering associations of women's smoking with lesbianism (or even "manishness"), just as it was strategic and profitable in the 1920s to override the association with prostitution. (Ibid.)

Perhaps Greaves's analysis here overplays the role of tobacco companies in the development of understandings of women's smoking in the twentieth-century West. As we have seen, the move toward a decrease in associations between cigarette smoking and masculinity and a corresponding increase in associations with femininity was, in part, instigated collectively by the "patriarchal" male smokers of the nineteenth century, and thus cannot adequately be viewed as the simple result of tobacco corporations' advertising campaigns. Even within Greaves's own analysis, it is evident that tobacco companies have very largely *responded to* changes already occurring within society and merely exploited these for commercial gain. Consider again in this connection the extract she cites from Brill—the researcher observes emerging understandings of women smoking which the tobacco company could then seize upon.

Thus, while these criticisms do not constitute a refutation of Greaves's thesis, tobacco corporations seem to have had more of a primarily *instrumental* role than a *causal* one in some of the social processes concerning smoking. Even so, it is tempting to view the rise of the cigarette as simply the ultimate in "commodity fetishism," as a "false need" generated by large capitalist, patriarchal tobacco corporations in the twentieth century. While such understandings would, to a degree, help to explain the extremely dramatic rise of Western cigarette smoking during the twentieth century, they would not, for example, so adequately explain the widespread use of tobacco among Native American peoples at the time of contact with the West, nor the role of absolutely central importance the practice had played in Native American societies for millennia before European contact. The political and economic processes involved in the development of tobacco use, while crucially important in the twentieth century, must be understood in relation to the number of other processes that I have discussed.

In the context of this book, Greaves's work once again serves to illustrate how the apparent relaxation of social controls over women actually involved *more fundamental changes in the character of social control itself.* In turn, these changes are related to processes of informalization, individualization, and civilization.

Thus, to summarize, I would like to draw the reader's attention to central themes that I have developed in the discussion so far. First, the increase in the range and variety of cigarette brands in the twentieth century, particularly in the post–World War II era, was phenomenal (Goodman 1993: 112). Brands were targeted at specific groups, portrayed a specific image, and varied according to their tar and nicotine content, filter or lack of filter, and so on. Not only has this marketing strategy continued up to the present day, but it has also been extended. For example, Silk Cut cigarettes offer a Low (tar) version along with Super-Low and Ultra-Low alternatives. Many other brands have introduced "light" versions of their cigarette—for example, Marlboro Lights.[8] Moreover, smokers can buy different lengths of cigarettes: Regular, King-Size, Super-King size, 100s (100 millimeters).

The move toward the mass production and mass branding of cigarettes in the twentieth century—the processes of the *mass consumerization* of tobacco use—constitutes a further stage in the *individualization* of tobacco use in the West. Today's smokers not only can individualize the function of tobacco use—as I have labeled it, *function individualization*—but also can use the cigarette as a highly individualized means of *self-expression.* The brand consumed can be expressive of a quite specific social identity. Moreover, in selecting between brands, to the extent that the information on the cigarette pack is accurate, smokers can choose to the milligram the precise amount of tar and nicotine in the cigarettes they purchase. The present-day smoker, therefore, has an unprecedented ability to select the form, strength, mildness (if this is understood as nicotine content), image, and, to a degree,

---

8. Jacobson (1981) observes that the naming of low-tar equivalents of popular brands as "lights" is also intended to reinforce the association between smoking and weight loss.

"risk" (whether factual or simply perceived), of the tobacco he or she consumes. These processes relate to fundamental shifts in how standards of socially correct behavior are determined and conveyed, which, in turn, relate to processes of informalization and individualization. With a decline in the traditional and formally set standards of appropriate behavior, there also emerges a growing dependence on the informal conveyors of socially correct behavior and self-presentation. Indeed, the presentation of the self is conducted more and more through what one *consumes*. In line with these changes, tobacco use has increasingly become a means of individual self-expression and of expressing affiliation to a specific social group. These shifts do not amount so much to a lessening of self-restraint, but more to an increase in the range of ways in which self-restraint is expressed and conducted. In relation to these processes, we shall later see how the understanding of tobacco use as a means of *identity building* has emerged as a dominant theme in recent years.

Second, it is possible to see how the present-day *dual image* of the cigarette as at once symbolizing both *freedom* and *control* stands as a relatively recent stage of a set of long-term processes. Current associations between tobacco use and personal freedom stem from (among other processes) the development of the cigarette as a symbol of women's emancipation; the neo-liberal state's dilemma over allowing or restricting individuals "freedom" to smoke; and the tobacco corporations' strategy of promoting tobacco use as an act of personal choice (in order to avoid liability for any ill-health effects of smoking). Conversely, present-day associations between tobacco use and control arise from increasingly dominant understandings of tobacco use as a means of self-control; increasing control exerted by tobacco corporations over understandings and individual perceptions of tobacco use; and ultimately, processes of medicalization in which—through the identification of tobacco as a disease agent and as a clinical addiction—the individual smoker is seen to have become controlled by a set of biological processes. In addition, understandings of tobacco have become intimately bound up with the debate between proponents and opponents of tobacco use. The conceptualization of tobacco use itself can be employed to reflect quite specific interests. For example, tobacco use portrayed as a powerful addiction in which the individual has little or no role allows for the promotion of the viewpoint that tobacco companies are simply controlling smokers for their own commercial gain. In the same way, tobacco portrayed as merely an act of free will discourages state intervention into the commercial practices of the tobacco industry, and allows one to "blame" the smoker.

Processes of *medicalization* have, therefore, been central to the development of the debates between proponents and opponents of tobacco. I would now like to further explore this theme by examining a comparatively recent set of processes involving the emergence of the concept of passive smoking.

Passive Smoking and Medicalization

As Brandt proposes,

> Despite considerable gains in stigmatizing the cigarette, the anti-smoking forces had, by the late 1970s, foundered on a traditional American libertarian ethic: "It's my body and I'll do with it as I please." In keeping with this powerful cultural ideal, further governmental interference relating to smoking was seen as constituting the unjustifiable intrusion into individual decisions. The Tobacco Institute viewed such intervention as "health and safety fascism." It was one thing for the government to inform the public about the dangers of smoking; quite another to restrict or ban the behavior. For this reason, scientific studies on the impact of "sidestream" smoke took on special significance. With the publication of studies which demonstrated the risks of exposure to other people's cigarette smoke—in particular, a higher risk of lung cancer—the anti-smoking movement was reinvigorated on the basis of a powerful communitarian ethic: "Do with your own body whatever you like, but you may not expose others to risks which they do not agree to take on themselves." (Brandt 1990: 167–68)

One can observe here how the emergence of the concept of the passive smoker dramatically changed the debate between proponents and opponents of tobacco use. The individual freedom argument effectively became inverted: from being an argument of "As a smoker, I want to exercise my freedom to smoke tobacco," the debate shifted in favor of "By virtue of passive smoking, you (the smoker in public) take away my freedom to be a non-smoker." This shift also made the question of restrictions on tobacco use an increasingly *spatial* issue. Jackson (1994: 423) argues that the emergence of the "passive smoker" in medical discourse was more an act of "production" than of "revelation." Drawing on the work of the social constructionist Ludwik Fleck, Jackson traces the emergence of the concept since the mid-1970s (references to the concept prior to this period, he states, were relatively few). Among the first writers to use the term were Colley et al. (1974), who examined the relationship between child exposure to tobacco smoke and the incidence of pneumonia and bronchitis (Jackson 1994: 431). The authors concluded that infant exposure to cigarette smoke doubled the risk of these diseases (Colley et al. 1974:1031). A number of other similar studies emerged that explored the relationship between infant exposure to ciga-rette smoke and the incidence of respiratory diseases among children up to the age of five, with several drawing similar conclusions to Colley et al. (Jackson 1994: 431).

However, throughout the 1970s the evidence in relation to passive smoking remained somewhat heterogeneous and inconclusive. Indeed, a *British Medical Journal* article of 1978 concluded, "For the moment most—but not all—of the pressure (including many smokers) to have the right to breathe smoke-fee air must be based on aesthetic considerations rather than on known serious risks to health" (cited in Jackson 1994: 432).[9] Jackson goes on to state that by 1988 a review of the "health hazards of pas-sive smoking" undertaken by Eriksen et al. (1988) cited more than eighty references in which passive smoking was linked to disease. He then sets out to address the question of what enabled this rapid expansion of the "evi-dence" in relation to passive smoking. His argument is that a necessary pre-condition for this *act of creation* of the passive smoker was a *discursive dis-section* of tobacco smoke into its component chemical constituents. Jackson proposes that this process of *stylistic reduction* is characteristic of medical discourse (Jackson 1994: 432). Furthermore, he continues, it became neces-sary for medical researchers to measure the dose administered through sec-ondary inhalation of each of these chemical constituents. It was this task, he proposes, that researchers initially found extremely difficult to perform, due largely to the "invisibility" of the passive smoker within medical discourse:

> [I]t would seem that problems of measurement were accompanied by a much more pressing sociological problem, that of the visibility, or more ac-curately, invisibility of the passive smoker. The subject of enquiry, neces-sarily one characterised by connections and relationships, appeared difficult to conceptualise in a discourse which reduced and disaggregated the phe-nomena of its investigations. (434)

Thus, Jackson is arguing, the medical practice of stylistic reductionism—which involves a "disaggregation," or discursive separation, of the subject—rendered impossible the articulation of a subject (here the passive smoker) that centrally involved a conceptualization of connected rather than discon-nected bodies. To overcome this problem, Jackson proposes, medical re-searchers first began to distinguish between two different kinds of smoke: mainstream and sidestream, the former referring to smoke inhaled directly

---

9. It is possible, once again, to observe from this statement how arguments initially based on "aesthetics" become transformed into medical arguments.

from a cigarette and the latter, to the undiluted smoke released into the atmosphere when a cigarette is burned. Researchers began to differentiate between these forms of smoke, proposing that sidestream smoke had a different chemical composition, containing, for example, 2.5 times as much carbon monoxide as mainstream smoke (Jackson 1994: 435). This distinction, Jackson continues, allowed sidestream smoke to possess its own "reality" (sic). This reality was explained scientifically by the myth that it resulted from medical researchers' gaining "increasing access to, and knowledge of, the external [sic] world" (436). In fact, he proposes, this distinction was actually a construction of the "thought styles" involved with medical knowledge, and was developed in order to facilitate a distinction between "[s]moke for the smoker and smoke for the non-smoker" (ibid.).

Second, Jackson proposes, the medical researchers' development of "biochemical markers"—for example, the concentration of cotinine (one of the main substances produced in the metabolism of nicotine) in the urine of nonsmokers—is actually an act of creation—a "stylized connection" of medical discourse (1994: 439):

> Interestingly, FOREST, the Freedom Organisation for the Right to Enjoy Smoking Tobacco, confront science on its own terms on this issue. "Cotinine is not only a derivative of nicotine," they tell us, "it may also be found in the blood after eating tomatoes . . . and various other vegetables" (FOREST 1991: 3). But in a way this reinforces the earlier notion of the stylised reading of the body. It subscribes to a constrained view of the social and implicitly accepts this construction as privileged. (Ibid.)

Ultimately, Jackson argues, the processes discussed above constitute a further effort of medicalization, which has involved "[t]he reconceptualisation of health, a construction which encourages all bodies to come into view; bodies not simply in disease but in potential disease" (Jackson 1994: 439). Thus even the nonsmoker can now come under the "clinical gaze." Indeed, through the distinction of sidestream and mainstream smoke, and moreover, through the development and use of biochemical markers,

> Physical bodies, reduced to mechanisms, organs and substances are still the stuff of medicine, but those bodies now "reveal" the imprint of their connections with other bodies. Even "in health" they are maps to be professionally read. And by its privileged reading of those bodies, medical science legitimises its claims made on the basis of those readings, claims, for example, about the social consequences of individual behaviour. (Ibid.)

Jackson's argument is interesting, as it highlights processes of medicalization and demonstrates some of the ways in which medical knowledge may have been manipulated to further specific anti-tobacco ends. However, there are a number of problems with Jackson's analysis.[10] Most centrally, he does not consider the possibility of "people as *not* affected by passive smoking" as itself an act of "stylistic creation." His arguments present a quite specific account of history: one involving a group of researchers who set out to *create* medical fact, not *reveal* it. For example, he implies that the epidemiological researchers Doll and Hill "set off" in search of identifying tobacco as a "causative agent" for cancer (Jackson 1994: 427). He proposes that, while they considered a number of alternative explanations for increases in lung cancer, these became *stylized,* and soon "disappear[ed] under the welter of information about tobacco consumption"—as he puts it, "Tobacco triumphs" (1994: 428).

But Jackson's account here *in itself* constitutes a highly stylized way of "seeing." He has manipulated events somewhat to allow them to fit his version of "scientific 'discovery.'" When one considers, for example, that, as both Doll and Hill were smokers and "had started their investigation thinking that the suspicion linking smoking with lung cancer was unfounded— 'an old wives tale,' as Doll put it" (Johnston 1957: 18), a slightly different picture emerges. With this in mind, Jackson's implicit image of these researchers setting out to "incriminate" tobacco use does not appear to fit so well with the empirical data. Paradoxically, Jackson's understanding itself appears to be as much an act of *creation* as of *revelation.*

A Smoking *Gesellschaft*

The emergence of passive smoking as a theme in recent debates between proponents and opponents of tobacco has had a number of implications. It is now increasingly possible for nonsmokers *legitimately* to ask tobacco users to refrain from smoking in their presence.[11] Furthermore, the public call for governments to ban smoking in public places has intensified. Consequently, in 1993 the U.K. Department of the Environment commissioned *Smoking in Public Places,* a survey of owners and managers of public establishments. The aim of this survey was to ascertain the proportion of establishments that were following government-recommended policies restricting smoking in public areas. Prior to this survey, in December 1991, the British government

10. For a more extensive discussion of these problems, see Hughes (1996). I have omitted a more in-depth analysis of these issues so as not to alienate the nonsociological reader.

11. As we have seen, it was also possible to make such requests during the nineteenth century. However, the arguments for these requests were made then on the grounds of "good manners"; it is likely that people today would not accept arguments made in terms of etiquette.

drew up a Code of Practice, "providing practical guidelines for owners and managers" on smoking-restriction policies (NOP 1993: 1). In a number of White Papers, the government had set the target that 80 percent of public places "should be covered by effective smoking policies by 1994" (ibid.). Most interestingly, the 1993 research found that this target had already been achieved in some categories of establishment (ibid.). Overall, 66 percent of the establishments sampled had a policy on smoking (ibid.). Thus, even without direct intervention, smoking has become increasingly restricted in a number of public areas.

In a similar manner to that of the eighteenth century, tobacco use has once more been increasingly pushed behind the scenes of "public" life. Correspondingly, we can observe a move away from understandings of tobacco use as a public, collective, sociable activity—the smoking *Gemeinschaft* of, particularly, the seventeenth century, and to a degree, the mid-twentieth century—toward (again to use one of Tönnies's expressions) a smoking *Gesellschaft:* the understanding of smoking as a private, individual, solitary activity.

This conceptualization of the development of tobacco use in recent years may help to explain some of the processes that Greaves identifies:

> Between 1950 and 1970, [cigarette] advertisements less frequently showed women as workers, housewives or mothers. Prevailing values instead encouraged middle-class domesticity. Possibly the emerging evidence about the health costs of smoking forced the advertisers to move away from picturing women in active poses. . . . Women's smoking has become increasingly defined by marketers as a leisure activity and a source of relaxation. In the last two decades, as women's labour force participation has increased significantly, women have been viewed by those in advertising as suffering stress and needing relaxation aids. Cigarettes have been promoted as such aids and tobacco trade journals have particularly targeted stressed women in the labour force as an "untapped market" in the West. (Greaves 1996: 24–25)

Greaves may well be right in suggesting that the cigarette advertisers' move away from portraying women in active "working" poses was related to emerging evidence in relation to the health risks involved with smoking. However, it is my contention that these shifts may also be related to the processes identified: the move toward a smoking *Gesellschaft*. Indeed, one of the advertisements that Greaves uses to illustrate her observations regarding changes in cigarette advertising directed at women contains a picture of a bathtub from which a small portion of a woman's elbow is barely visible; the caption "you are here" is written just above the bath. The suggestion is that a woman is reclining in a relaxing bath with one of her hands behind her head; the other, presumably, holds a cigarette. The overall headline to the ad (which, incidentally, is for Eve Lights Slim 100s—a distinctively *female* brand) is, "It's not just a cigarette. It's a few minutes *on your own*" (Greaves 1996: 25; emphasis added).

The associations this advertisement portrays appear to center upon the notion of "taking time out," of "allowing yourself the luxury of relaxation," of "forgetting the rest of the world for a moment." The bathroom symbolizes a highly private place, and even within this area, the smoker is hidden from view. This advertisement, therefore, depicts a highly solitary, individual, and private scene. Interestingly, the smoker's invisibility reflects a dominant trend in more recent cigarette advertisements. In part due to government restrictions on tobacco advertisements, but also, I am suggesting, because of broader shifts in understandings, cigarette advertisements have decreasingly featured images of people smoking. It is as if these *images*, too, have been pushed behind the scenes. In relation to these processes, consider the following extract taken from the 2 February 1996 edition of *The London Telegraph*:

> Smoking is so frowned upon in middle class America that puffing on a cigarette has emerged as the latest erotic fetish, called "smoxploitation." Videos featuring fully dressed young women sensuously inhaling tobacco are selling by the hundreds at £24 each through a network of small ads and newsletters. Titles include *Smoky Kisses, Sorority Girls Smoke* and simply *Paula,* widely regarded as the hottest example so far. . . . Dian Hanson, editor of the fetish magazine *Leg Show* [states] "Smoking is the fetish of the Nineties. Any time something becomes widely condemned and taboo, it will be eroticised." . . . The hit video *Paula* features an attractive young blonde woman in a slinky black gown. She has mastered the full range of inhaling and exhaling techniques and, half-way through the 30-minute video, engenders new heights of excitement by producing a long cigarette holder. (Laurence 1996: 1)

While this extract does have a slightly tongue-in-cheek tone to it, it is interesting that the emergence of the videos was seen to be intimately related to an increasing social repression and public "invisibility" of smoking. More generally, the article attests to a widespread condemnation of smoking, although it is one particularly prevalent in "middle class America."

Returning once more to the work of Greaves, the idea of smoking as a form of independent relaxation appears to have become an increasingly important one. As Greaves observes, a related theme, that of cigarette use as an expression of individual control and power, has become dominant in Hollywood films:

> For example, in the 1991 Hollywood film, *Basic Instinct,* the main female character uses smoking as a key expression of her personal power. . . . In an era in the West of increased smoking regulations and health knowledge regarding smoking, Sharon Stone's performance in *Basic Instinct,* where she defiantly and successfully continues to smoke in the face of police authority and while under suspicion for murder, stands out as a 1990s testimonial for smoking in the face of oppressive regulations. Having a woman present this message adds power and complexity to the role of women smokers in contemporary times. (Greaves 1996: 28–29)

The central themes in this extract appear to be those of *power, control,* and *resistance.* In the face of growing opposition, smoking has increasingly come to be viewed as an act or gesture of *defiance.* Indeed, in relation to these processes some smokers (perhaps women smokers in particular) have come to view themselves as belonging to a community of *defiant opposition.* For these smokers, smoking involves the rejection of one set of values, which stress the health ethic and mainstream conformity, and the embrace of another set, which involve notions of risk, resistance, and individuality. This shift in values can be central to processes of identity building.

Notions of control, particularly stress control, are a dominant theme in present-day understandings of tobacco use. The relationship between cigarette smoking and stress control is consistently reinforced in film and television. Cigarettes are commonly smoked after or during stressful events, characteristically by "stressed" individuals. Indeed, filmmakers, aware of the powerful symbolism of the cigarette, have frequently used acts of smoking to form a subtext to their films (Klein 1993). As Klein states:

> [S]moking cigarettes is not only a physical act but a discursive one—a wordless but eloquent form of expression. It is a fully coded, rhetorically complex, narratively articulated discourse with a vast repertoire of well-understood conventions that are implicated, intertextually, in the whole literary, philosophical, cultural history of smoking. In the present climate, the discursive performance of smoking has become a form of obscenity, just as obscenity has become an issue of public health. (182)

Significantly, while Klein argues that smoking as a "discursive act" is "implicated" throughout the history of tobacco use, it is suggested here that *tobacco use as a means of individual expression* (as I would formulate it) has become an *increasingly dominant theme* in understandings characteristic of the twentieth-century West. In other words, Klein's conceptualization of tobacco use can be located within a relatively recent "stage" of the development of such use.

Associations between tobacco use and stress control (relaxation) in the form of taking time out, giving oneself space, and the associated theme of smoking as an escape from the mundane are eloquently expressed in the following extract, in which the author reflects upon the meaning of advertisements for Marlboro cigarettes:

> The Marlboro image represents escape, not from the responsibilities of civilization, but from its frustrations. Modern man [sic] wallows through encumbrances so tangled and sinuous, so entwined in the machinery of bureaucracies and institutions, that his usual reward is impotent desperation. He is ultimately responsible for nothing, unfulfilled in everything. Meanwhile, he jealously watches the Marlboro Man facing down challenging but intelligible tasks. . . . Innocence and individual efficacy are the touchstones of the metaphor employed on behalf of Marlboro cigarettes. (Lohof 1969: 448)

The Marlboro Man referred to in the above account was portrayed by actor Wayne McLaren. He appeared in a number of Marlboro cigarette advertisements as a cowboy. As Lohof suggests, these images promoted associations between smoking Marlboro cigarettes and individual autonomy, "tangibility," and a "release from frustration." It hardly needs to be noted, at this point in the discussion, how characteristically modern these understandings of smoking are. In a more recent campaign, Marlboro used the slogan "Come to Marlboro Country" as a caption above images of wide expanses of rugged American landscape. Again, the theme appears to reinforce notions of escape to a less complex, more peaceful place. However, the metaphor of *space* itself may be important. Perhaps this is intended to symbolize a "spatialized" expanse of freedom? Or perhaps, intentionally or unintentionally, it counters dominant trends in which the number of public "spaces" where people are permitted to smoke is diminishing? Indeed, the case of Marlboro cigarette advertisements highlights a more general theme characteristic of trends in contemporary tobacco advertising. Not only are smokers "disappearing" from these advertisements, but the images that take their place are increasingly complex and encoded. It is almost as if these images invite a highbrow decoding on the part of the reader. Perhaps, though, the *decoded* message itself is not what is important for the advertiser, for the very notion of the highbrow decoding of a sophisticated message in itself effectively portrays an image of sophistication.

One of the most interesting aspects of the contemporary understandings of tobacco use is the emergence of a theme that I shall label here as nihilist cynicism. By this I am referring to a process in which the rationalizations for smoking, and the arguments against it, are increasingly converging, centering on notions of risk and risk taking. Consider, in this connection, the following extract from the American comedian Dennis Leary:

> There's a guy. . . . He has a senate hearing in this country coming up in a couple of weeks, and this is what he wants to do: he wants to make the warnings on the packs bigger! Yeah! He wants the whole front of the pack to *be* the warning. Like the problem is we just haven't noticed yet. Right? Like he's going to get his way and all of a sudden smokers around the world are going to be going, "Yeah, Bill, I've got some cigarettes. . . . HOLY SHIT! These things are bad for you! Shit, I thought they were good for you! I thought they had Vitamin C in them and stuff!" You fucking dolt! It doesn't matter how big the warnings are. You could have cigarettes that were *called* the warnings. You could have cigarettes that come in a black pack, with a skull and cross bones on the front called "tumors," and smokers would be lined up around the block going, "I can't wait to get my hands on these fucking things! I bet you get a tumor as soon as you light up!" . . . It doesn't matter how big the warnings are or how much they cost. Keep raising the prices, we'll break into your houses to get the fucking cigarettes, OK!? They're a drug, we're addicted, OK!? (Leary 1997)

Leary comically voices a theme that has a great deal of currency with smokers who stand in a defiant community of opposition. Indeed, he speaks as though he were voicing the opinion of a community—"*we'll* break into your houses," "*we're* addicted." As part of a more general backlash against political correctness, against the increasing idea that smokers are "weak, irrational individuals" (Brandt 1990: 169), Leary fully accepts the arguments of the medical campaigners—smoking will kill you, smoking is addictive, smoking is "bad for you"—but *so what?* "I'm looking forward to cancer," he says. For Leary, smoking is almost considered a sign of strength. It is as though he wishes to embrace the risks of smoking. He jokes, "I can remember a time in this country when men were proud to get cancer, God dammit! When it was a sign of manhood! John Wayne had cancer twice. Second time, they took out one of his lungs. He said, 'Take 'em both! Cuz I don't fuckin' need 'em! I'll grow gills and breathe like a fish!'" (Leary 1997). Leary continues his tirade against the antismokers:

> All these little facts that you dig out of a newspaper or pamphlet and you store that little nugget in your little fucking head, and we light up and you

spew 'em out at us, don't ya? I love these little facts: "Well you know, smoking takes ten years off your life." Well it's the ten worst years, isn't it folks? It's the ones at the end! It's the wheelchair kidney dialysis fucking years. You can have those years! We don't want 'em, alright!? Because you're always telling us, "You know, every cigarette takes six minutes off your life. If you quit now you can live an extra ten years. If you quit now, you can live an extra twenty years." Hey, I got two words for you, OK—Jim Fix. Remember Jim Fix? The big famous jogging guy? Jogged fifteen miles a day. Did a jogging book. Did a jogging video. Dropped out of a heart attack. When? When he was fucking jogging, that's when! What do you wanna bet it was two smokers who found the body the next morning and went, "Hey! That's Jim Fix, isn't it?" "Wow, what a fucking tragedy. Come on, let's go buy some buds." (1997)

For our purposes, Leary's statements can be used to highlight a central paradox in contemporary understandings of smoking. The move toward understandings of tobacco-induced disease as long-term, invisible, and internal has also involved the development of an antithesis. Since tobacco-induced disease, particularly cancer, happens in the long-term, and happens to predominantly "old" people, smoking by the young becomes an expression of death defiance. For the young smoker, death is something a great distance away: the long-term, invisible, internal effects of smoking are almost too far away to contemplate, and yet the relatively short-term, visible, external attributes—mood control, weight control, a means of self-expression—are of central importance. Moreover, Leary highlights that even if one follows the regimens of a healthy lifestyle, one may be equally doomed to die before one's time. In the first extract, he suggests that smokers would still buy cigarettes even if they were called tumors and came in a black packet with a skull and crossbones emblem on the front. In fact, it is now possible to buy such cigarettes—"Death" brand cigarettes, which have precisely that combination of a black packet featuring a skull-and-crossbones emblem. This nihilist cynicism is one example of the convergence between rationalizations for, and rationalizations against, tobacco use that center on the theme of risk; another example is the seductive logo on one side of a Marlboro pack, and the government health warning "Smoking Kills" on another. As Krogh (1991: 37) expresses it, "Americans quite frequently have the opportunity to view what might be called the skull beneath the skin: of taking the beautiful, laughing Virginia Slims woman at the top of an ad and following her shapely figure down to the Surgeon General's foretelling of her future. Youth and beauty side by side with death and disease, one living color, the other in black and white."

I am not suggesting here that today's smokers smoke to get cancer. However, I am suggesting that part of the appeal of smoking, for specific groups of smokers, is that it is seen as a risk-taking activity. Crucially, it is a risk for later in life, and not for the here and now. It can be seen as a way of *expressing* that "I am not investing in my future, I'm *living for now*." This in turn relates to a number of processes, perhaps most important, the increasing emphasis placed on the value of young bodies (Shilling 1993). These processes may in fact help to account for the increasing proportion of younger smokers in recent years. In the U.K., for example, 24 percent of fifteen-year-old boys and 25 percent of fifteen-year-old girls were regular smokers in 1982. By 1986, the figures had risen to 28 percent and 33 percent respectively (Mihill 1997). The proportion of adults smoking in Britain, by contrast, has declined quite rapidly.

Krogh's metaphor of the "skull beneath the skin" eloquently expresses the relationship between the inside and outside of the body, which has come to be so important to contemporary understandings of tobacco use. The processes he points toward appear to center on the notion that the young body is actually the "clothing" of potential disease and of the inevitable—death. Perhaps the ultimate paradox is that, if there were no incubation period for what are understood to be tobacco-related diseases; if the same proportion of smokers contracted disease as a result of their tobacco use, but crucially, *could die at any moment from this disease;* in short, *if tobacco was understood to be more immediately and visibly dangerous,* then perhaps the contemporary picture of tobacco use in the West would look very different.

Summary: Tobacco Use As a Pandemic

The following extract is from a chapter entitled "Staying on an Even Keel" in Krogh's 1991 text:

> The nicotine in tobacco has many uses. But when we begin to ask why it qualifies as humanity's all-time addictive drug of choice, one of the first things we might consider is the idea that it can rescue people from several *different* dysphoric states, returning them to normal from several locations on the psychological map. This is exactly what we would expect of a drug that is heavily used in the workplace, where normal is what's called for and where forces pulling people away from that state range from boredom to stress. (40)

It is first worth noting that Krogh arrived at these conclusions after reviewing a considerable number of clinical studies. Thus, his work is being used here as a particularly good example of present-day medical-scientific understandings of tobacco use. However, despite his suggestion that this understanding of the practice may help to explain why tobacco (nicotine) has become "humanity's all-time addictive drug of choice," I hope to have demonstrated that the understandings embodied by his statements are actually quite specific to a relatively recent "stage" in the development of tobacco use in the West as indeed are the processes that his understandings point toward. When viewed *in the longer term,* Krogh's conclusions indicate a number of processes that I would now like to summarize as part of an overall conclusion to the book thus far.

First, as we have seen, the idea of tobacco as a drug that is used to return to a "normal" state—to "stay on an even keel"—presupposes relatively mild forms of tobacco. Among Native American peoples around the time of initial contact with the West, tobacco was very largely *not* used in this way. The tobacco smoked was, on the whole, a great deal stronger than that used in the present-day West. Among some Native American peoples, it was common for even highly accustomed tobacco users to faint after smoking a pipeful of tobacco. Tobacco was commonly used by Native American shamans to enter a hallucinatory trance: its use was understood to mediate the transition from the normal world to the spirit world. Tobacco use in this context was thus very largely *not* used to return the smoker to a normal state. Only the mildest, most palatable forms (to Western tastes) of Native American tobacco were transferred to the West, and yet, I have argued, even these were considerably stronger than those commonly used today. Tobacco was initially compared to alcohol, not simply because alcohol use was the only model available by which to understand the practice, but because this model was a far closer fit to tobacco use at the time of its transfer (the sixteenth and seventeenth centuries); tobacco use at this time involved a considerably greater degree of intoxication. Even at this "stage," tobacco was very largely *not* used to "get normal." The tobacco used at this time in the West may have also contained a number of highly toxic and psychotropic adulterants. Indeed, when snuff emerged as the most popular mode of consumption in the eighteenth century, adding any number of substances to a snuff concoction was seen as a means of *refining* its properties.

Gradually, the forms of tobacco in popular use became milder to suit perceived changes in tastes. Cigars and pipes became increasingly popular as modes of tobacco consumption in the nineteenth century, but even these modes were changing. For example, pipes generally became shorter, made of more practical, durable materials, and an increasing number had "filters" (Welshman 1996: 1380). In addition, the varieties of tobacco most popularly consumed during this period began to change. There was an increasing use of "brighter," milder, flue-cured varieties. This shift was intimately related to the rise of the cigarette, which, when it initially emerged during the mid- to late-nineteenth century, was considered an *extremely* mild form of tobacco. In the twentieth century, the cigarette itself underwent dramatic change. There emerged filter cigarettes, low-tar filter cigarettes, then extra-low-tar, super-low-tar, and ultra-low-tar varieties. The practice of tobacco "adulteration" came under increasingly strict regulation,[12] as did levels of tar and nicotine yielded from cigarettes. Even within the last few decades, these levels have reduced substantially. The following chart shows, for example, the average nicotine content in milligrams per cigarette between 1965 and 1975:

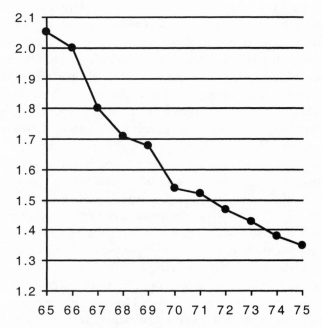

Source: Lee (1976) in Ashton and Stepney (1982: 74).

12. An excellent account of this process is provided by Tanner (1950 [1912 original]): "[A]part from the addition of water to make tobacco smokable, olive oil used in the process of spinning roll [tobacco], acetic acid used as a preservative to pipe tobaccos and certain soluble salts in snuff, all specifically controlled by regulation and permitted to be used only in strictly limited quantities, the article as sold to the public of this country is pure tobacco and nothing but tobacco. Its purity is a trade credential and one of the triumphs of Excise administration. The National Exchequer demands the use of pure tobacco, and no tampering with an article that brings in very many millions of revenue per annum would be tolerated for one moment" (1950: 41–42).

It is important to note that this decline in nicotine content reflects consumer demand in addition to increasing government regulation; ultimately, it is a continuation of a process that began to gather momentum over four centuries ago. Since the time of tobacco's introduction into Britain, as with many other parts of the West, there has been a quite definite move toward increasing *regulations* and *controls* over this "commodity," and a quite definite move toward the consumption of milder strains, varieties, and forms. It was only after the effects of tobacco had been considerably "tamed" in this manner that tobacco would increasingly be actively used in the way described by Krogh—as both a sedative to counter stress and as a stimulant to counter boredom. This move was, in turn, related to another set of processes which, put crudely, have involved a move away from the use of tobacco to lose control, and toward the use of tobacco as an instrument of self–control. In this regard, tobacco has become a tool to control feeling states and, as Krogh points out, to help the smoker "stay on an even keel"—or, as I have argued, maintain the *civilized mean; a stabilization* of the self. For the major duration of these processes, the main driving force behind the changes identified has *not* been health concerns—indeed, quite often changes (including the move toward milder forms of tobacco) occurred in *spite* of these concerns. Rather, the impetus has been the quest for distinction and fear of embarrassment, which are in turn related to processes of *civilization,* while more recently, concerns for "etiquette" have increasingly been *translated* into concerns for health.

Second, the idea of tobacco use being essentially about feeling-state control—as Krogh suggests—also stands at a particular "stage" in the development of understandings of tobacco use in the West. As we have seen, when tobacco was initially introduced into Europe, it was widely understood to be a panacea. Its use was largely understood to be medicinal, as a remedy for ailments ranging from toothache to cancer. However, it was not long after its introduction that tobacco began to be used more recreationally. Indeed, there was a considerable amount of resistance against the abuse of tobacco, as it was understood by physicians of the time. Tobacco use became a mark of sociability, and increasingly became used to mediate social interactions. Although tobacco was still used to maintain health in the form of maintaining a "humoral balance," this practice was understood more as a self-administered folk remedy than a "medicine" as such.

Gradually, understandings of the functions of tobacco began to change. At a relatively recent stage in its development, tobacco use became increasingly understood as a supplementary activity, and became used accordingly—

to *enhance* a range of activities, particularly those involved with work. It came to be seen as an activity that could help the smoker *control* and *counter* both boredom and stress—a cure-all for the ills of modern life. In effect, these understandings became the modern equivalent of the sixteenth-century panacea gospel. The crucial difference, however, is that the understandings had become much more specifically focused on the effect of tobacco use on the mind, the nerves, and the brain. To a large degree, such understandings were accepted by the medical profession in the early twentieth century. Some doctors even recommended the *moderate* use of tobacco as a means of relieving stress—particularly to soldiers during the First World War (Welshman 1996: 1380).[13] This increasing emphasis on the effects of tobacco on the mind has continued to the present day. Thus there remains considerable debate as to whether tobacco smoking is beneficial in the treatment of stress, or, whether it is in itself a stress-generating activity.[14] A number of recent studies have also examined the effectiveness of nicotine in the treatment of neurological disorders. Understandings of tobacco use as a medical remedy for the body more generally have very much declined in the twentieth century—perhaps with the exception of lay conceptions of health in which tobacco use may be seen to prevent the smoker from getting influenza, or to help the smoker expectorate unwanted mucus. However, tobacco is still used as an agent on the body within the practice of smoking as a means of weight control. Crucially, such understandings of tobacco use hinge on notions of self-control and self-presentation, which have become a particularly dominant theme in relatively recent stages of its development in the West.

Third, the understanding of smoking as a means of feeling-state control stands at a particular stage of the *individualization* of tobacco use in the West. As we have observed with the example of the Karuk, the form, function, use, understanding, meaning, and experience of tobacco as assigned to

13. In this connection, Welshman cites a short extract from *The Lancet:* "[T]he significance of the demand from men in the trenches for cigarettes cannot lightly be ignored . . . [as smoking] undoubtedly affords relief and diversion in all nerve-straining tasks" (Welshman 1996: 1380).

14. For example, West proposes, "Many smokers report that they enjoy smoking and also that smoking helps them in various ways—particularly controlling stress and maintaining alertness. There seems to be a tacit acceptance by many researchers that smoking has effects that are psychologically beneficial and that this is due to the fact that it is an effective method of delivering nicotine into the body. Some laboratories have consistently reported positive findings. . . . Yet the evidence by no means unequivocally supports this view. In fact, Spillich et al. (1992) in the September issue of this journal reported that smokers were *worse* at several cognitive tasks than were non-smokers" (West 1993: 589).

it by Native Americans was much more governed by ritual, collectively ascribed beliefs, and Native American cosmology than individual difference: as Harrington described it, "there was little individual variation." During the early stages of the introduction of tobacco into Europe, there emerged great contrasts regarding how tobacco was smoked. The smoking "gallants" of the seventeenth century, for example, developed a set of highly elaborate practices in relation to tobacco using. In a similar manner, snuff takers of the eighteenth century developed a whole range of refined and detailed practices for "taking the pinch." Moreover, snuff takers began increasingly to individualize the form of tobacco by mixing various snuff concoctions. Gradually, approaching the twentieth century, these contrasts in the form and practices surrounding tobacco use began to diminish. The cigarette emerged as a highly standardized form of tobacco. However, crucially, function individualization—individualization of the effect of smoking—came to dominate the character of twentieth-century tobacco use. In other words, the process involved diminishing contrasts in the form of tobacco and practices of its use, and increasing varieties in its function of use. It is here that Krogh's observations must be located and identified as referring to the highly individualized use of tobacco to control feeling states. The process of tobacco use individualization has continued and has become extended. More recently, smokers are able to individualize the image of smoking through brand-specific consumption and, to a degree, the "risk" of smoking through selecting among a range of cigarette brands containing varying proportions of tar and nicotine levels.

Fourth, the increasing variety of the experience of tobacco use relates in turn to a shifting balance between bio-pharmacological and social-psychological dimensions of the practice. Ashton and Stepney (1982: 47) state that "[t]he range of habits which are drug-related forms a continuum of pharmacological involvement from tea and coffee (containing mild central nervous system stimulants), through alcohol (a CNS depressant) and the 'soft' drugs like cannabis, to drugs conventionally thought of as powerfully addictive such as the opiates." I have argued that, since it was introduced into Europe over four hundred years ago, tobacco has moved along this continuum *toward diminishing degrees of pharmacological involvement and towards increasing degrees of social-psychological involvement.* In contrast with the "smack of strength" experienced by the Native American tobacco user (and to a much lesser degree, the early-European smokers), the present-day cigarette smoker receives a relatively mild, ambiguous, unfinished effect from smoking. I have aimed to show that, throughout the history of tobacco, the understandings surrounding its use have profoundly *mediated the experience* of tobacco using—put crudely, these discourses effectively "finish off" the experience. However, such discourses have come to play an increasingly important and dominant role in the experience of tobacco use. This may, in part, account for the increasing varieties of tobacco-using experience, particularly when one considers how function individualization has emerged as an increasingly dominant theme in the last century or so. In this connection, we may begin to understand the move away from the Native American use of tobacco characterized by a large, strong dose (infrequently-consumed ratio) toward the small, mild dose (frequently-consumed ratio) that characterizes present-day tobacco use in the West.

Fifth and finally, Krogh's focus on the action of nicotine rather than tobacco more generally, reflects a process of discursive reductionism that characterizes clinical medical discourse, which has become increasingly dominant in the West since the nineteenth century. This entire approach involves the search for and isolation of generic psycho-pharmacological processes that will account for "why people smoke." However, this tendency to reduce social behavior to static, universal, biological states involves a form of *process reduction*. We have seen that tobacco itself is not and has not been a constant. It has changed significantly since the time of its initial introduction into Britain and other parts of Europe. In other words, it is itself a *process*. In the same way, the manner in which tobacco has been used, understood, and experienced has been substantially transformed. The approach I wish to lay the foundations for here involves examining the *development* and dynamic *interplay* of these processes. Medicalized understandings of tobacco use have been drawn upon throughout this book as both a subject and object of inquiry. It has been argued that such understandings themselves have come to dominate contemporary discourses surrounding tobacco use, and, consequently, have increasingly come to influence the dominant experience of tobacco use and of being a tobacco user. The present-day smoker may very much experience tobacco using as an "addiction," as involving his or her "enslavement" to a set of powerful biological processes. Medical advice on stopping smoking[15] characteristically involves a process of further discursive reductionism. The smoker is, as it is understood, "weaned off" his/her addiction by substituting the cigarette with *nicotine* chewing gum, *nicotine* patches, or, more recently, noncombusting nicotine inhalation de-

---

15. For example, Russell (1983) recommends nicotine chewing gum to facilitate smoking cessation.

vices. These smoking cessation products may, ironically, point toward the future development of tobacco use in the West. In the following extract the unveiling of the first "smokeless" cigarette is described:

> And so, in September 1987 amid much media hype, the company [R. J. Reynolds] staged a New York press conference, complete with information kits, charts, and cutaway diagrams of the new cigarette. The chief claim for it was that it looked, lit, tasted, and smoked like other cigarettes but had no ash, produced virtually no smoke after the first puff or two, and if left alone, would extinguish itself rather than igniting any surface with which it came into contact. It was an ingenious contraption, a cylinder of tobacco wrapped around a carbon rod that was ignited and burned down, warming the air drawn in by the smoker's inhalation and passing over a small aluminum capsule implanted in the center containing beads of tobacco extracts, nicotine in particular, and flavorants. A cellulose acetate filter was attached, but what value it had for an essentially smokeless cigarette was not explained. In lawyer-crafted language, Horrigan [a chief executive in R. J. Reynolds] stated that since the tobacco did not burn, the compounds normally produced by cigarettes "are eliminated or greatly reduced, including most compounds that are often associated with the smoking and health controversy. Simply put, we think that this is the world's cleanest cigarette . . . [and] addresses the desires and perceptions of many of today's smokers." (Kluger 1996: 599–600)

Perhaps to state the obvious, the emergence of the "smokeless" cigarette marks an even further stage in the medicalized "dissection" of tobacco into its constituent parts. It is tobacco "extracts," not even the entire compound, that will be used for the new cigarette. However, most interestingly, the smokeless cigarette is endorsed on the grounds that it is the "world's cleanest cigarette"—an aesthetic argument, and it is "safe" in the sense that it is unlikely to cause fire if left unattended. Kluger continues:

> But when he tried to elaborate on the nature and purpose of the radical device, Horrigan lapsed into language that disclosed the manufacturer's dilemma in presenting it to the public. "We're not saying it's a safe or safer cigarette," he said. "We're saying many allegations about the burning of tobacco and elimination of those compounds should be greatly reduced with this product." Beneath that double-talk was the unmistakable implication that here was a less hazardous cigarette—otherwise, why was Reynolds going to market it? Just to meet "the perceptions of many of today's smokers"? That would make the product a mere piece of trickery? (Kluger 1996: 600)

Despite Kluger's suggestion that the smokeless cigarette represents just another attempt by the tobacco industry to fool consumers into thinking it has invented a safer product, in keeping with the arguments I have presented throughout the first three chapters in this book, I would suggest that R. J. Reynolds's invention did indeed meet a real need of the smoker—not so much the concern for health, but more along the lines of *meeting changing standards of socially acceptable behavior.* Why the filter? Perhaps to help the smoker avoid spitting. The "smolder-out" feature? So that the smoker is less likely to cause fires. The lack of ash? So that the smoker leaves no "mess" behind. But most important, why the absence of smoke? Precisely because this is what makes tobacco use "intrusive"; what makes smoking a "spatial" issue. Viewed in this way, the smokeless cigarette actually does fulfill some of the desires and perceptions of the present-day smoker: to be able to meet the demands of political correctness—to be able to smoke in the presence of others without communicating *disease.* One can only speculate as to whether the smokeless cigarette will ultimately come to be the most popular form and mode of tobacco consumption, despite the ill fate of R. J. Reynolds's invention. However, these processes clearly are a response to the most fundamental paradigmatic shift with which I have been concerned in this book: tobacco use, widely understood to be a panacea at the time of its introduction into Europe, is now widely considered a *pandemic*—an addictive disease that spans the globe.

4

Becoming a Smoker

In this part of the book my focus shifts to consider the development of tobacco use at the level of "individuals." My aim, following the work of Becker (1963) outlined in the introduction to this book, is to develop an understanding of some of the processes involved in becoming a smoker in order to build a general model of the career of the present day Western tobacco user.

In this chapter, I will draw extensively upon a piece of Economic and Social Research Council–funded research that I conducted between February 1995 and March 1996. I will shortly provide a full description of this research, and explain the rationale behind it. However, I would like to note at this point that when I set out to explore the development of tobacco use at the level of individuals, I had very little idea of what my conclusions might be. What I found was absolutely fascinating. I began to realize that the development of tobacco use at the level of individuals (at least those that I researched) typically followed a very similar direction to that of the long-term development of tobacco use in the West as a whole.

Below I explore in depth this direction of change through the exposition of a five-"stage" model of smokers' careers—from Beginning Smoking to Continued Smoking to Regular Smoking to Addicted Smoking and, finally, Stopping Smoking. I argue that (like the long-term development of tobacco use in the West) the "lose-control" effects of tobacco, dizziness, nausea, and vomiting, are more confined to the early stages in the development of individual smokers' careers. I propose that for the more experienced smoker, there is a move away from the use of tobacco as a *marker to* others—that is, for predominantly social reasons—characteristic of the Beginning stages of respondents' tobacco use (and, correspondingly, characteristic of the smoking *Gemeinschaft* of the seventeenth century), accompanied by a move toward the use of tobacco use as a *marker to* oneself. In relation to these shifts, I suggest that there is typically an increasing move toward individuals smoking alone as their tobacco-using careers develop (again, as is characteristic of a smoking *Gesellschaft*). In addition, I explore how, within the span of their individual smoking careers, users exhibit a growing *individualization* of the functions of, and rationalizations for, tobacco use, particularly within the Regular Smoking stages. The use of tobacco in the individual construction of identity—as a marker *of* oneself—emerges, I suggest, as an increasingly important theme toward more advanced stages in the development of individual smokers' careers. Also in relation to individualization, I observe how, in the development of tobacco use among individuals, there is a move toward increasing *individual control* over the effects, indeed, the whole *experience,* of tobacco use. In relation to this I discern, in the development of smokers' careers, a shift towards the use of tobacco *as a means of self-control* (corresponding to the long-term shifts observed at the societal level of tobacco use development). Finally, I explore as a dominant theme among respondents at a relatively advanced stage in their smoking careers the increasing understanding and experience of smoking as an addiction, something one becomes *subject to.*

Research Overview

The research consisted of fifty semistructured "depth" interviews with a mix of smokers, nonsmokers, and ex-smokers. The sample interviewed was not selected randomly, and thus cannot be considered, in the positivist sense of the word, to constitute a group that is statistically representative of a broader population. While this sample may fall foul of specific methodological standards, it is important to note that I have challenged the assumptions and indeed the *rationale* that many of these standards are based upon.[1]

A total of two nonsmokers, nine ex-smokers, and thirty-nine regular smokers were interviewed. The interview length varied considerably: the shortest took approximately ten minutes, while the longest took over an hour. Respondents were given the opportunity to elaborate on themes as much as possible. The central agenda of the interviews with smokers was to elucidate the processes by which the respondent became a smoker. I also

1. My choice of method here reflects a more fundamental rejection of the positivist approach to sociological research, at least in the way in which the term *positivism* came to be understood following the initial formulation by Comte. I have provided a defense of this methodological strategy, and a discussion of the sociological issues informing this elsewhere: see Hughes (1996).

sought to understand how these respondents' understandings, uses, and experiences of tobacco began to change as they continued to smoke. Another part of each interview was devoted to examining experiences of stopping smoking. Interviews with nonsmokers (used in the research presented here to refer to people who had *never* been smokers) were centrally concerned with why each respondent never became a smoker, and with examining what the nonsmoking respondents' attitudes were toward smoking. Interviews with ex-smokers focused on the process by which these respondents stopped smoking, and whether they now felt themselves to be nonsmokers or ex-smokers—and if, indeed, there was any significant difference between these terms as they are commonly understood.

The questions asked in the interviews were based on a set of assumptions, some of which I would like to make explicit here with the benefit of insights developed in the book thus far. Drawing upon these insights, it is possible to observe how the questions I asked in the interviews were specifically oriented toward characteristically "twentieth-century" patterns of tobacco use. For example, a large section of each interview with smokers and nonsmokers was devoted to asking how the effect of smoking a cigarette, roll-up (hand-rolled cigarette), cigar, or pipe *varied* (with the proviso "if at all"). While I state the obvious here, the interview questions were very much based on the understanding that *the experience of smoking does vary, and that it varies significantly enough for the smoker to be able to describe this*. As I have aimed to show, the increasing variety of experiences of tobacco use characterizes a relatively recent stage in its development in the West.

More important, the questions were also based on the assumption that there would be some form of *development* to respondents' smoking—that their smoking would actually involve a set of processes, and that users would be able to distinguish between different "stages" in these processes. In particular, it was assumed that smokers may not have considered themselves to be smokers until they had reached a certain "point" in the development of their smoking. The term *smoker* itself is, after all, not as unproblematic as it may first appear. When does one actually become a smoker? The moment at which the first cigarette (or other medium of consumption) is placed into the mouth? After the first cigarette (or otherwise) has been consumed? The first time one buys tobacco? Is a smoker simply someone who is smoking? Do smokers become nonsmokers or ex-smokers when they extinguish their smoking material? If not, for how long must they abstain before they can be considered ex-smokers or nonsmokers? These are important questions; however, they cannot be adequately answered without recourse to empirical investigation. Simply to apply an external, *logical* criterion—for example, to define a smoker as someone who *regularly* smokes tobacco—would direct the researcher away from a number of important processes. A more adequate way to address some of these issues is to view smoking *processually,* and to attempt to understand smoking *"through the eyes" of smokers themselves.* The questions asked can be adjusted accordingly: at what point does the tobacco user come to see him- or herself as a "smoker"? This formulation is partly based on the assumption that there is a quite specific self-image, identity, and set of experiences associated with being a smoker. Again, the understanding of tobacco use as a means of *identity-building* has emerged as a particularly dominant theme in recent years.

Furthermore, perhaps the word *point* (as in "at what point does the tobacco user come to see him- or herself as a smoker?") is in itself misleading. As we shall see, respondents found it difficult to identify a particular moment or definite point at which they *became* smokers and instead indicated a set of processes, which shall be explored shortly. Correspondingly, some respondents felt they would *always* be smokers whether they had stopped smoking or not. Thus, the application of a-priori conceived external categories would be highly problematic. Moreover, it would mean that issues that have emerged as central to understanding tobacco use would simply be overlooked.

My interviews, while not statistically random, were conducted with people from a broad range of backgrounds: unemployed people, an ex-convict, students, an air traffic controller, lecturers, a management consultant, a secretary, a laborer, and so on. The respondents' ages ranged from fourteen to sixty-five years. Interviews were predominantly conducted in Leicester within the workplaces or residences of the respondents themselves. A number were also conducted in Manchester, London, and in various parts of Kent. I knew some respondents before conducting interviews with them. However, a number were conducted with respondents whom I had not previously met, and was put into contact with on an informal, opportunist basis. A proportion defined themselves as variously belonging to Asian, Afro-Caribbean, or mixed-race ethnic groups. Twenty-eight respondents were female, and twenty-two were male.

The transcript data were analyzed in the following manner: after first reading through every transcript to familiarize myself with the data, I read through them all a second time and began to identify a number of central themes. After reading through approximately twenty interviews, the number of distinct themes had reached "saturation point"—the point at which I could discern no further themes. The themes can be divided and analyzed according to a number of somewhat artificial stages in the development of individuals' tobacco use. Each stage shall be identified by specific labels derived from understandings of present-day tobacco users: Beginning Smoking, Continued Smoking, Regular Smoking, Addicted Smoking, and Stopping Smoking. These labels are as much the subject as they are the object of the stages and themes which they serve to separate. Within each section my intention is to highlight the *range* of responses that I elucidated from the transcript data, and ultimately to relate these to the themes I identified in the discussion presented in the preceding chapters of this book.

Beginning Smoking

As we have seen from examples presented in previous chapters, the first smoke is a well-documented experience. While most respondents remembered feeling nauseated by their first cigarette, one respondent remembered actually enjoying it. Overall, however, respondents suggested that the first smoke involved considerable physical discomfort. In one interview I made a mistake in asking the first question: I asked the respondent when she had first started smoking, although my normal opening question was, At what age did you first experiment with tobacco? Her response is significant:

> *I'd first like to talk about the beginning—when you first started smoking. At what age did you first experiment with tobacco?*[2]
>
> My very first experience, or when did I first start *smoking*?
>
> *Very first experience.*
>
> I think I was about twelve and my granny used to smoke. I had one of my really good friends from school over and we stole one of her cigarettes and went to the bike shed and I hated every minute of it. I hated it. I tried to tell her how you do it, showed her. . . . I hated it, really did not like it.
>
> *Why did you do it, what motivated you to do it?*
>
> I really don't know. I've absolutely no idea, I think it's just being inquisitive, because my brothers are six years and four years older than me and some of their friends smoked—at that time my brothers didn't at all but . . . I don't know, maybe I thought I just wanted to find out what it was like. But, oh God I hated it, it was foul. (Rosie, 23, student)[3]

In the above account, the respondent makes a definite distinction between her first experience of tobacco, and when she "started *smoking*." Her

2. The standard format I have adopted in all the transcripts is to present my speech in italics, and that of respondents in normal type.
3. Each of the "labels" I use to describe respondents—student, secretary, ex-convict, etc.—are drawn from the question, How would you describe yourself?

account also serves to raise an important question: why do smokers (by definition) continue to use tobacco after having such unpleasant first experiences of it? Laying aside for the moment the range of reasons people initially try tobacco, at a very basic level, common understandings hold that one must first become *accustomed* to tobacco before one can enjoy it—*one needs to learn how to smoke.* As has been discussed in the introduction to this book, Becker found in his 1963 study of marijuana users that users needed to learn the *technique* of smoking, and to *perceive* the effects of smoking marijuana in a positive way, for their use to continue successfully to further stages of the marijuana user's "career." A similar process can be observed with the smokers in this study:

> One thing I do remember as being very distinctive was that for the first six months I didn't actually know how to inhale! I tried to swallow the smoke, so it was quite uncomfortable. (Angela, 26, a postgraduate researcher)

Can you describe the first time you tried tobacco?

> Well it wasn't very nice, I used to smoke . . . sort of just put a cigarette in my mouth and not inhale, just blow it out and everyone said to me "that's really unfashionable," and so they taught me how to take it back and I nearly choked to death! That was on my school playing field. (David, 33, salesperson)

So in general what was it like being a smoker when you very first started?

> I don't know, it was quite exciting, I thought I'd grown up! It was just something new. And it is a skill that you have to learn to do it properly so that people don't say "she's not inhaling properly, she's not smoking." You have to learn how to do it. I'd *achieved* something. (Anita, 22, bar worker)

> When I first started I just used to do it . . . it didn't seem to do anything to me. I can remember I was sick a few times from smoking too many. I was about ten. I didn't really know how to do it, and before I knew it I'd already smoked about twenty fags[4] in about two hours, so I came in and I was ill. (Brian, 15, student)

While the technique involved with learning to smoke tobacco may not appear to be as complex as that involved with learning to smoke marijuana, it nonetheless needs to be *learned*—it is not something smokers are simply "born with." As we can see from the above accounts, it is important to learn how to inhale properly; not simply to take the smoke into the mouth, but further down, into the lungs. It is also important to learn how much to

4. For the U.S. reader: the word *fags* is a widely used UK English slang for cigarettes.

smoke, and how frequently one should be smoking. In the case of the second and third accounts, it is explicitly stated that these techniques were learned through reinforcement within peer groups (as was also the case in Becker's study): in other words, learning the "correct" way to smoke. In effect, in these early stages, users were beginning to *accustom* themselves to tobacco smoke, to become increasingly *tolerant* of it—I would like to refer to this process as habituation (and later to explore this in more detail).

Again, following Becker's study, it is important that users learned how to *perceive* the effects from smoking and to distinguish the "desired" effects from the "undesired" ones:

> To start with I didn't know what I was meant to do with it or what I was supposed to be experiencing. I knew people did smoke and it was forbidden and, therefore, a quite daring thing to do, but at the same time I didn't know why one would smoke. I didn't know, had no idea, what it gave to people. (Mike, 30, researcher)

The respondent reports not knowing what he "was *supposed* to be experiencing"—"what it gave to people." The implication is that this emerged over time—it, once again, had to be *learned*. This account also serves to steer the discussion toward another central question: for what reasons do people start smoking? In Mike's account it is evident that there was a certain amount of illicit appeal from smoking—it was seen as a form of rebellion against authority. This is a theme that was often repeated:

> *Why did you start?*
>
> Hmm, probably because again: going out with my friends, everyone was doing it, and I think it was, hmm . . . about the independence thing—as I could see the adverts and think, well, that's what I want to be, I want to, you know, take my own life into my own hands, I want that risk—I mean, I enjoy it. It was more about sort of rebelling . . . my parents were really antismokers. I mean, my dad would do the sort of thing where we'd be in a restaurant, if we were stuck at a table where there was someone smoking he'd get up and walk out and he'd make the biggest fuss ever. So to me it was sort of a taboo and I thought well what's the big deal about this—and again it was just rebelling. I think if they hadn't made such a big deal about it I wouldn't be so interested to try it. And again, when you're going through that sort of teenage phase and you want to do anything to sort of like get away from what your parents believe, smoking was sort of one of those, well, one of the escapes that I used. (Sam, 24, schoolteacher)

In the above account, smoking was seen to be a means of asserting independence from parental controls. Indeed, Sam suggests that the very fact that these controls were so strict made cigarette smoking all the more appealing, and made it appear to be all the more an act of rebellion. At the same time, she viewed it as a means of asserting her maturity, both to herself and to other people. It was also "risky" and "exciting." She continues:

> I think it was because everybody was doing it and it was cool at the time. I had a boyfriend who smoked who was a lot older than me so it was a symbol of being, you know, older and being able to smoke and because you have to buy cigarettes—you have to be sixteen to buy cigarettes and I was just turning sixteen—I thought, well, you know, it's something to do. You know, to look older as well. . . . At that time it meant that you were hard enough to sort of, I dunno, not *hard*, it's hard to describe it actually. It meant that when you went to the pub and you were drinking, you were smoking as well, you were splashing your cigarettes around. I don't think it was a money thing—that you could afford it—though you would, at times, look at people who had a packet of ten and say, well, stingy, like that, sort of thing. But there was something, some status, that was definitely there that you felt more . . . I don't know, more independent. Like I was saying before, definitely more sort of in control because you could choose to smoke and you *were*. I think it was that sort of image. (Sam, 24, schoolteacher)

Thus, for Sam, becoming a smoker was intimately related to becoming more of an adult, and to becoming "independent." It was, in a way, seen to be a kind of freedom, a symbol of her being in control of her life. Put another way, smoking was a *rite de passage*. This idea of a period of *transition* is particularly well illustrated by the following account:

> You tend to be—at that sort of age—in this kind of limbo between thinking, you know, "I'm not a child anymore, but I'm not an adult"—you've got a foot in each camp. And it's also, obviously, illegal and ma and pa say "don't do it." (Sarah, 32, secretary)

It is important to note that such ideas are quite specific to smokers who start during their teenage years (as was the case for the majority of respondents in this study). It is apparent that such ideas of adulthood, and rebellion from parental controls, would not be as dominant a theme among smokers who had started sometime later. However, a common theme that does emerge from the transcript data is that starting smoking is also associated with other periods of transition:

> I remember when I was doing my finals I was going out with a young woman who was a smoker; on her suggestion I (to do with prefinals

nerves) bought a pack of cigarettes one day. But then I decided, after the way I smoked them—I consumed a whole pack in one day, they were "Senior Service"—that this wasn't for me and that I would do better to counsel my nerves in some other way. But when I became a postgraduate student, at the end of my first term my supervisor—Norbert Elias—asked me to produce a summary of what I had achieved in that first term. I remember going into the research students' common room and [finding] the woman I was very friendly with there (she wasn't my girlfriend, by the way) who was a smoker, doing a higher degree in English, and I said I've got to do this for Norbert and I'm, you know, very concerned about it. She advised me to smoke, and I thought yes I would. Part of what made me decide at that point to smoke, even though I was still involved in university football and cricket, part of what made me decide to accept her advice at that point was the fact that I was changing my image of myself, I was changing my image from being a sportsman who also happened to be a good student with some ambitions in that direction (I hope I said a *good* student with some ambitions in an academic sense). I found myself changing my definition of myself towards someone who was *primarily* an academic and had the vision of academics like artists, living in a garret, suffering poverty, suffering for their art, suffering for their subject. Smoking seemed to fit in well with being a postgraduate student. (Derek, 59, university professor)

At a very general level for many smokers in my study, starting smoking was intimately related to changes in their self-image, in their identity—be it from child to adult, or, as in Derek's account, from sportsperson to academic. In direct relation to this, a dominant theme in the Beginning Smoking stage is the use of tobacco for external appearances: processes of identification are directed both to the self and to others. Indeed, for many smokers at this stage, smoking was a central part of social life, and of sociability within specific groups:

It was really, really important to smoke being a—not even a—young woman! A teenager who just started drinking alcohol, who started going out, started wearing a lot more make-up. I also started wearing contact lenses when I was fourteen; that made a lot of difference to my self-image. I was quite sort of punky I suppose (I was the first person to wear a studded belt at the *Fan Club!*) and smoking was all part of that. . . . Yeah, it was part of the social life. It was about being a teenager, it was about going out with boys, snogging in recreation grounds and passing cigarettes out. I remember one incident smoking menthol cigarettes, there's a certain sort of menthol cigarette—I can't remember the name, it begins with "C" [Consulate]—and they're white with white filters, there's no distinction between one end or the other. I remember being with one of my first boyfriends and him lighting it up the wrong way. . . . It might even have been me lighting it up the wrong way! And us all falling about. So the actual going and smoking was all part of that behavior, was all part of rebellious teenage behavior. As far as my self-image was concerned I think that continued, particularly with mixing with older people, going to the pub a lot. It made me feel more grown-up to have B&H [Benson & Hedges cigarettes] with me at the time. (Angela, 26, postgraduate researcher)

It was common for less "established" smokers (those who did not readily identify themselves as "regular" smokers) in my study to define themselves as predominantly "social" smokers—that is, smokers who do not smoke a great deal on their own, and who smoked primarily within a sociable setting. For example:

I do it on a social . . . I've never been addicted, if I want to stop—and I have stopped basically, I had some last night but that was on a social level. It's really silly, that's why I ought to stop because I'm not addicted to it and so there's no point in me doing it at all. In my first year when I was in halls a girl who I was really, really good friends with and her boyfriend both smoked and I didn't smoke for two terms. I do go through spurts like when I started university, I didn't smoke for months and months and months and then I spent so much time with those two and other people that smoked that I gradually started smoking again. But I'm not the sort of person who would sit in my room going, "Oh God I need a cigarette." I'd just go out and I'd have them.

Do you see yourself as a smoker?

I don't like to think that I am but I suppose I am. I don't smoke during the day and stuff really but yeah, I suppose I am a smoker. (Rosie, 23, student)

Here the respondent does not immediately identify herself as a smoker, but when applying an external label, believes that she could be classed as one by other people. It is interesting that she says, "I ought to stop because I'm not addicted to it and so there's no point in me doing it at all"—it is almost as if one should *only* smoke if one *has* to. I would like to explore this theme in more detail shortly. Another example of the relationship between smoking and sociability during the early stages of becoming a smoker is provided in the following account:

It was part of talking, very much part of talking with other people and the intimacies with other people, you know, sitting in a car, waiting for something to happen, share a cigarette, in a group of people talking, articulating. And it was certainly also to do with getting on with members of the opposite sex, that was also something you did by offering cigarettes and you had shared a cigarette, it was part of the process of interaction. I think that was what attracted me about it. I liked it, the taste was okay, I did enjoy the taste, although I always hated smoking out of doors, I always hated the taste of that. But it was the "social process" that always brought it back to me, kept me a smoker during that stage. (Rick, 51, senior lecturer)

Thus, to summarize the themes that have been elucidated from the transcript data as particularly dominant in the Beginning Smoking stages, the focus is characteristically on the social aspects of tobacco use. It has been argued that the technique, perception, and practice of smoking appear, to a large degree, to be *socially* learned. Furthermore, of particular importance during the beginning stages is the use of tobacco as a "marker" to others. Smoking is used to mark transitions in social identity: as a sign of adulthood, or as indicative of a particular social identity. These transitions of identity often involve the rejection of, or even rebellion against, one set of values, rules, and understandings and a corresponding embrace of another set. In relation to this, another dominant theme in the Beginning Smoking stage is the use of smoking to facilitate social relationships; to reinforce social bonds; and to express affiliation to a particular social group.

Continued Smoking

In general, respondents reported that as their smoking continued they began to smoke more frequently (though one respondent proposed that he actually smoked less), and in a more "stable" manner—their tobacco-using practices began to settle into more *consistent* patterns. Interestingly, many respondents reported using the cigarette for different purposes at this stage in the development of their smoking careers:

So how did your smoking behavior change as you continued smoking?

I started to use cigarettes to deal with stress much more, in a sense it was dealing with stress before, but it was dealing with oiling wheels in the social situation. Something to do in the social context. But I started to smoke much more on my own, when I was working, when I was under pressure of some kind or another, if I had something to do, a big deadline, I'd buy some cigarettes and sit and smoke and work on it. So I started to use it much more as a sort of more . . in getting things done, getting through pressures. (Rick, 51, senior lecturer)

Initially it was in the pub, it was a definite social thing with the type of people that I was hanging about with. And then it becomes a stress thing, definitely, sort of stop here or, this person's winding me up, I need to get

out of here, the good sort of physical break from something. Get out of
the house and have a cigarette, and then it kind of carried on from that,
come out of a tutorial that I thought was appalling, I'll have a cigarette,
because it's a sort of clear your mind, do something different. (Chris, 20,
student)

From these accounts it is possible to observe several key changes that
characterize the Continued Smoking of respondents in this study. First,
smoking was increasingly something that was engaged in by respondents *on
their own*. Second, smoking was increasingly being used as a means of self-
control. Its role as a marker to others, while still important, was becoming
less so; and its role as a marker to oneself to "do something different" and
to change one's emotional state had become more significant. One respondent explains this understanding as follows:

> I think it's more . . . it's almost like something you . . . it's not a simple
> thing where you take a tablet or drug which has a specific effect which
> gives you control, it's more like something you . . . a story you tell to your-
> self. It's more like a superstition that you use as a way of telling yourself
> you will deal with a situation. It's like a marker to yourself, it's a way of
> mobilizing resources you have already, it's like the cigarette gives you the
> power to do something you couldn't do before. It's like "You will do
> this!", it's like a flag: the flag in battle does not give the army the power to
> do things, but it's a way of stating "You will do this!"—it's an assertion.
> And it signifies to yourself that you will mix, you will work hard, it's not
> that the cigarette itself has some sort of property which gives you an extra
> power, so you might have the illusion it does because you focus, because
> you concentrate, because you exert yourself in that situation. (Rick, 51,
> senior lecturer)

The question emerges of whether smoking regularly, or smoking alone,
is what defines one as a smoker. The dictionary definition of the term *smoker*
is perhaps interesting in this connection: "**Smoker** *n.* 1. a person who ha-
bitually smokes tobacco" (*Collins English Dictionary* 1991: 1459). By this
definition, a user becomes a smoker when he or she begins to smoke out of
habit. The term *habit* itself would appear to imply some degree of *compulsion* or *regularity*. With these issues in mind, consider the following extracts,
in which "being a smoker" is effectively defined:

At what point did you come to see yourself as a smoker?

I suppose not until I was about seventeen—after another year or so,
properly.

And what was it that changed that made you feel like you were a smoker?

155

Cos I think I was more addicted to it. When I first started smoking I didn't actually need it and it was just something to do. After about a year or so, then I did actually crave more, so I think it was about then. (Rachel, 21, researcher)

Well, I didn't actually smoke properly until I would've been, I would say, sixteen, and at the time I started going out to parties and drinking and would be offered cigarettes and started smoking properly. Other people would have cigarettes and they would offer them in a different way from how they'd been offered previously, not in a sort of "go on, dare you" sort of way but as an actual mature gesture. I occasionally smoked and decided I quite liked it. I didn't actually become a *smoker* until the latter part of my sixth form, so I was a very occasional smoker—I would smoke if I was out, if it was offered to me—cigarettes, or, as I say, cigars, at parties, but as regards to actually buying cigarettes as a habit . . .

Eighteen?

Yeah, towards the end of my sixth form.

So you're making the distinction here between being kind of a casual smoker and being a kind of "real" smoker.

Yeah.

The distinction being?

The distinction being that I bought them, bought the things myself and made a conscious . . . was consciously aware of wanting a cigarette rather than just having one presented to me. (Mike, 30, researcher)

Perhaps the first thing to note is how remarkably consistent the definitions from the above accounts are with the previously cited dictionary definition. Reflecting dominant understandings of tobacco use, it is by definition apparent in the extracts from respondents that one becomes a smoker when one becomes *habituated*. Thus, the whole identity of being a smoker involves the idea of dependence, of habitual compulsion, of addiction. Perhaps to state the obvious, respondents found it difficult to identify a particular moment at which they came to see themselves as smokers. Rather, it was described as a gradual process in which particular kinds of feelings were increasingly experienced. Of interest from Mike's account was the importance placed on buying cigarettes; the actual act of purchasing a packet was, he appears to imply, a sign that he was becoming dependent—that he increasingly *needed* them. Also, Mike describes another central shift with his continued smoking: a move away from childlike cigarette offerings as a dare, to be naughty, and towards more offerings of cigarettes "as an actual mature gesture," as it appears to have been implied, something which one would wish to consume *for its own sake* more than for the defiant or risky act it embodied. It is clear, therefore, that a number of the changes identified above are actually related to more general life changes: to entering adult life.

Thus, the dominant themes that I have elucidated from the Continued Smoking stage of respondents in this study are as follows. First, users increasingly smoked on their own. Second, in relation to this, the importance of smoking as a "marker" to oneself began to increase. Smoking was used more and more as a means of self-control, as a device to control feeling states. It was used as a signal to oneself to mark changes or counterchanges in moods, to "take time out," or "to do something else." Finally, respondents in this study felt that they only became "proper smokers" after they began to experience a longing or need for tobacco. By definition, a central part of smokers' identities was the experience of what was understood to be increasing dependence. Such understandings can be located within the long-term shifts in understandings of tobacco use in the West. The pervasiveness of the idea of smoking as an "addiction" can be seen as manifest in the notion that one cannot even be considered to be a "real" smoker until one has actually experienced feelings of *dependence*. These understandings mark another crucial shift in the careers of tobacco users: away from predominantly experimental and voluntary tobacco use, and toward the more compulsive use of tobacco to *relieve* withdrawal-related feelings.

Regular Smoking

The key theme expressed by respondents who came to see themselves as regular smokers is that this stage involved the *increasing individualization* of their tobacco use: individualization of the function of smoking; individualization of the rationalizations for smoking; individualization of the smoker's self-image and identity; and, indeed, individualization of the effect of smoking. This stage appears to be characterized by *increasing varieties and diminishing contrasts* in experiences of tobacco use.

Just as tobacco use increasingly became a marker *to* oneself for respondents during the Continued Smoking stage, so in the Regular Smoking stage tobacco use increasingly becomes a marker *of* oneself. From the following extract, it is possible to observe how tobacco use can come to form a central part of the user's identity:

> I remember in Austria going for the really strong fags I was . . . I did identify very much with smoking the strongest cigarettes that I could. I think that's got a lot to do with me wanting to be a very strong, hardened person and wanting to be seen as that. I've always felt, you know, it's like be-

ing proud of the capacity of what you can drink. I know that I can put a few drinks away and I also like strong cigarettes, but I think part of that is wrapped up with wanting to be a hard and strong individual woman. These cigarettes in Austria called "Red Hands"; I remember waking up in the morning with this man I was sleeping with and smoking one of those straight away. They've got no filters on and they're virtually black tobacco leaf and they're just rough! That was all part of it, it was all part of being sort of, as hardened as possible. . . . I smoke filter cigarettes now, I smoke them to their end; not right at the end, near the end. I usually stub them out by folding them over. I'm aware of things like . . . the different ways of putting out a cigarette is like part of your personality. Lots of things about it that are very important. Going back to me being "hard," when I go around glass collecting I've got a cigarette drooping out of my mouth, I don't mind that. . . . I'm not worried that it might make me look rough. There's the old Ms. Fag-ash, the sort of cleaner with the cigarette drooping out of her mouth. I don't mind because that's part of my image in the pub as a big, strong woman; who you don't mess with! So if I'm going 'round glass collecting I've got a cigarette sticking out of my mouth with my hands full. I'm not worried about that, I don't think that's going to take away from my image. In some ways I s'pose it might even add to it. (Angela, 26, postgraduate researcher)

For Angela, "being a smoker" is intimately related to her identity as a "strong woman." Indeed, in a manner similar to that of the Karuk Native American tobacco users, the strength of tobacco is viewed as a metaphor for physical and mental "strength"; for "toughness." This is a theme that emerged quite frequently, particularly among young female respondents. For example, another respondent expresses a similar set of understandings:

I like it because I don't feel girlie when I'm smoking it.

Can you explain that?

If you're walking about it just makes you look a bit rough I think, so you're not being a girlie-girlie, all soft and clean and giggly. . . . You're being like Debbie Harry sort of thing. (Anita, 22, bar worker)

The above two respondents have very largely not *internalized* the popular idea that smokers are "weak" and "irrational." Indeed, Angela continues at a later point in her interview:

Generally, I s'pose even I have taken on board this idea that it's more mature not to smoke. Because I suppose it means that you can make key decisions about your body and your health based on fact, and stick to them. So in some ways smoking's a bit of a weakness, but I think I don't . . . I agree with that, but I don't necessarily believe it regarding myself. In some

> ways smoking is a strength for me: people that smoke are stronger. That's
> bound-up with this idea of roughness.

Stronger in what way?

> Harder, I suppose. That must be because of the whole movement of light-
> ing cigarettes, of putting them out: you're dealing with dirt, you're dealing
> with ash. People who smoke are a lot cleaner, they don't smell as much.
> It's almost prissiness. I think that's a view that I have constructed for my-
> self, which justifies it for me just about. It isn't really, if you think about it
> rationally, but I can use that one. (Angela, 26, postgraduate researcher)

In relation to a theme highlighted in my earlier discussion of nihilist cynicism (chapter 3), Angela appears positively to embrace the idea of smoking
as having "rough" effects, and as being a symbol of roughness and toughness. In the above extract she clearly demonstrates that she is aware that her
smoking is a mark to others as well as a mark to herself. While she agrees that
smoking can be seen in a negative way at a very general level, she does not
believe these ideas regarding herself. Thus the role of smoking as a *mark to
herself* and *a mark of herself* appears to be *more important* to Angela than the
role of smoking as a *mark to others* (to the extent that these can be seen as
separate). She is quite aware of the highly individualized way in which she
constructs[5] the rationalizations for her smoking. She explicitly states that "I
think that's a view that I have constructed for myself, which justifies it for
me just about," and places this in contrast with what she might believe if she
were to think about it *rationally*—perhaps, the way others might see her
smoking. In short, Angela is quite aware of the *active role* she plays in the
continuation of her tobacco use. It is also clear that this respondent views
the *brand* of her cigarettes as another integral part of these processes:

> I smoke Embassy Filter, which is a slightly shorter but stronger cigarette.
> I've been smoking them quite a while now, they feel like "my fags." Even
> though a part of that is to do with, I know that they're called "Scally
> fags," they're a big Liverpool thing. They've got a slightly rebellious,
> more working-class element to them as well. They've just come at the
> right time for me. (Angela, 26, postgraduate researcher)

What is particularly interesting is that these associations with Embassy
Filter cigarettes are very different from those related to Embassy Number
One expressed by another respondent:

5. It is also clear that in the process of this "construction," the respondent may be drawing
upon specific images from broader discourses—the previous respondent, for example, makes
an explicit reference to the pop singer Debbie Harry—the idea of a "tougher" kind of woman.

You've got the Southeast of England and Embassy Number Ones, and the "Bennie" smokers will smoke Benson & Hedges because it's a sort of lower-class cigarette.

Really?

Oh yes, without a doubt.

And Number One aren't a lower class . . . ?

No, God no. That's the sort of "achiever" image, I think, Embassy. And the gold box Bennies are kind of a street cigarette. Taxi drivers smoke them, even walking on the street you see lots of them, but in cafés, you get to the Marlboro Lights, and then in pubs, you get the pool-playing, rugger-bugger "Marlboro red" smokers, and then you get the fruitcakes who smoke obscure cigarettes.

What about Silk Cut, who smokes Silk Cut?

Occasional smokers, social smokers.

And what do students smoke?

It depends where they are from and where they go.

Yeah?

Occasional smokers: Silk Cut, without a doubt, and varying colors of Silk Cut. You know, "Oh I'm trying to give up," and they smoke the white ones and . . .

They're the weakest aren't they?

Yeah, yeah, or the yellow ones or whatever, different phases. And people doing sort of "achieving" subjects, that they come from a sort of . . . "I'm going out to rule the world," the economists and so on, largely Embassy smokers, then the "arty" people, archaeologists, lots of archaeologists smoke menthol, and English students and language students and then you get into the trendy thing. Girls in clubs who wear plastic knee-high boots and short skirts smoke Marlboro Lights. Rugger-buggers smoke Marlboro reds. And then people who are into Hip Hop will smoke Bennies. Definitely. (Chris, 21, student)

The above respondent views a different cigarette, "Number One," also made by Embassy, as having a completely different, more affluent image from that which was expressed by Angela about Embassy "Filter" cigarettes. It may well be the case that this contrast in images is consistent with many smokers' understandings. However, it may also be possible that different smokers have quite different understandings of the associations with any particular brand. Indeed, other respondents in my research proposed that archaeology students would never smoke menthol cigarettes, and would only ever smoke roll-ups (hand-rolled cigarettes). Similarly, another respondent proposed that Benson & Hedges cigarettes have a very affluent image and are anything but a "street cigarette." What is important to recognize is that, whether or not it is possible to discern consistently coherent associations with any particular brand, respondents clearly understood that branding itself is seen to be a marker of smokers' socially indexed identities.

It is also apparent from my research that some smokers chose among different brands for a number of quite practical reasons, which included cost and availability. However, some chose a particular brand because of its length, the type of filter it had, and how much tar and nicotine each of its cigarettes was said to yield. Indeed, this may have been part of a strategy to reduce the *risks* associated with smoking. In the following extract, the respondent describes how he and a friend decided upon the brand they were going to smoke:

> I actually got a leaflet which gave you a list of every brand of cigarette you could possibly think of and it told you the amounts of tar, the amounts of nicotine, you know, and we actually went through the process of matching up the "flash"-sounding name with the one that seemed the least harmful . . . it was a real conscious decision to actually work out which good brand name went with the least amount of risk in terms of tar and nicotine. (Simon, 28, lawyer)

Rather than embracing the risks associated with smoking, Simon carefully balanced considerations of the image of a particular brand with considerations of the amount of tar and nicotine contained within its cigarettes to find a compromise between the least "risky" and most "flashy" cigarette. This stands in direct contrast with previously cited accounts, in which the "strongest" and "roughest" cigarettes were actively sought out. A number of other respondents described a similar process. However, quite interestingly, instead of relating to a concern about long-term risks, respondents chose among different brands based on concerns about the immediate effects of smoking: smoking the "wrong" brand could variously cause a sore throat or have an unpleasant taste, or it would not produce the desired effects:

> I started with Silk Cut—very weak—and then I went on to Benson & Hedges, and that was for quite a long time, and now it's menthol cigarettes because since meeting Matt [her partner], again, it's . . . they taste fresher, don't they? And they're a bit weaker than Benson & Hedges as well. But now I don't like smoking normal cigarettes—they taste dirty. They [the menthol cigarettes] taste nice, it's like when you have a menthol cigarette it feels like you're breathing fresh air instead of tobacco. And they

> don't leave a bad taste in your mouth afterwards, not that I can notice,
> Matt probably can. (Becky, 23, dentist's assistant)

It is very interesting to observe, once again, that individual changes in tobacco use—the preference for one brand over another, the preference for
low-tar or filter cigarettes—do not simply relate to a concern about health,
but also to reasons of taste and aesthetic considerations.

Dominant understandings—such as those embodied in the ideas behind
government health warnings on cigarette packets, or behind many of the
health promotion advertising campaigns targeted at discouraging people
from smoking—hold that if smokers only knew the risks involved with smoking, they would be more likely to stop. The idea seems to involve the notion
that if smokers are made to feel frightened—if they are shocked by the "hard
facts"—they will be discouraged from continuing. However, as we have seen,
such ideas are effectively turned on their heads by some smokers, who positively embrace the risks of smoking. Similarly, some respondents suggested
that the very fact that they were told that they should no longer smoke,
seemed to *compound* their desire to do so:

> If I want to smoke I will smoke. Whether I go outside and smoke—which
> I do if I'm in somebody's private house. If I'm in a restaurant, I only pick
> restaurants that I know that I can smoke in. Same as airlines. I only go on
> airlines that I know that I'm allowed to smoke on—be it in the back of the
> plane. I will go on an airline that I know will allow me to smoke. I don't
> use buses, I use my car. If anybody wants to get in my car they have to ac-
> cept that I smoke and people who come to my house—I wouldn't make it
> uncomfortable for them if I know they're absolutely against smoking—
> can't stand smoke—then we (the respondent and her husband) wouldn't
> smoke. But, it is *my* house and I will smoke if *I* want to. The emphasis is
> on *if I want to*. I can stop to be polite—if they're my friends I would stop.
> But if I want a cigarette I will smoke. The more people tell me I shouldn't
> smoke, the more I smoke. Quite literally. I have this thing that "I am me"
> and if I want to smoke, I will smoke. I don't obviously smoke in people's
> houses—friends' houses—if they don't like smoking. You have to respect
> their views, obviously. My doctor says I shouldn't smoke because I have
> had two heart attacks and I have angina. I've had two heart operations but
> I still smoke. I think basically it's if somebody says you're not to do that
> thing, you do it—I do. (Brenda, 53, housewife)

Perhaps these remarks may be related to notions of smoking as an act of
defiance? Or perhaps it is more related to understandings of smoking as a
liberty, an individual freedom? Indeed, this same respondent continues:

"Everybody's an individual. I'm an individual—a forthright individual, which you can probably tell from what I've said. So therefore I will do what I want to do. If I smoke, I smoke." These understandings of smoking can be seen to be related to fairly recent debates over whether one should be "free" to be a smoker or a nonsmoker. As I have argued in chapter 3, such debates have become increasingly dominant in relation to the emergence of the concept of "passive smoking." One respondent actually makes the link explicitly:

> I think you should be allowed to smoke; I appreciate there is a lot of evidence to suggest passive smoking is dangerous, but then again a lot of other things are dangerous. You walk out there, it's a polluted world, I mean you are consuming a damn sight worse than you would from cigarette smoke just by walking along the Welford Road in the rush hour. I just think it is going over the top, and I would just like to see people just ease out and be slightly more rational about it. . . .

So in what ways have your attitudes and other peoples' attitudes affected your smoking behavior?

> Ah, well now, this [she holds her cigarette in the air] is crack, isn't it? Because you are not allowed to smoke, you are determined you are going to buck the system and you smoke. A classic example of it was on an aircraft fairly recently, when I did not get the choice whether I wanted smoking or nonsmoking and I had paid for this airline ticket and they had actually got ashtrays in the seat as well. So I just took out a cigarette and the steward came along and he said, "Excuse me, you cannot smoke in this area," although they had ashtrays in the seats. "Well, this was before we sort of introduced this policy," he said. "If you want to smoke, you can squeeze in at the back there, the last three rows, there might be a spare seat." I took instant umbrage to this as I said, "I have paid the same money for my flight ticket as everybody else, and now I would like to be able to enjoy my flight in comfort." He said he would go down the back to see if there was a seat. And there was one wedged between two people, so I would have had to cross two people—and I would not do it! I was being bloody minded for the sake of it! I did not light another cigarette up for about an hour and a half, I will be honest, but when I did light one up I was actually watching how close this guy was getting, and I was wafting the cigarette smoke so he would not see it. But I was determined that I was going to smoke simply because I was not allowed to, I did not like the way he said that I could not, again with this "you are a leper, for goodness sake you cannot do that here." So I suppose it makes you more determined and more dogmatic. A certain arrogance comes into it then. So yes, I suppose I'm much more determined now. (Pippa, 35, mother)

Not only were the images and associations with, and rationalizations for, smoking highly *individualized* by respondents during the Regular Smoking stage, but they also pointed toward their increasing *individualization* of the actual effect produced by smoking during this stage. The effect produced varied significantly: according to the situation in which the tobacco was smoked; the mood respondents were in before consuming tobacco; what respondents were *expecting* the cigarette to do for them. As one respondent proposes:

> Sometimes it's a calming-down thing, it is getting away and "Just going to have a cigarette now folks," and then it is a sort of "Huhhhh." But if it's towards the end of the evening, and you're in the pub, "can't keep my eyes open," "I'll have another cigarette": it's something to *do*. It's something to do with your hands, it stops me chewing my fingers, so that's different, I suppose that's more of a kind of "This'll pick me up at the end of the night when I'm shattered," rather than a kind of "Go and calm down, have a fag" thing. (Chris, 21, student)

Another respondent explains this process as a kind of mood *stabilization:*

> Yeah. In general I would think it probably had a kind of stabilizing effect. So if I was feeling lethargic it would (i.e., in the morning) it would pick me up and if I was feeling overworked, stressed, it would relax me, so it has a stabilizing effect. And certainly that's true of the example I just gave because, obviously, the reason I was wanting something to do with my hands in a nightclub is because I felt self-conscious, so it would make me feel less self-conscious; and in terms of how it would make me feel, it would have the same sort of effect on me—unless I had too many. (Mike, 30, researcher)

It is interesting that in both of the above accounts (and indeed, a number of others) smoking is seen to be "something to do with your hands." It is a way of being active both to counter boredom in a mundane, sedentary situation, and perhaps also to appear less alone in a social one. That is to say, to appear as though one had a purpose for standing alone, so as to appear to be less isolated, to be *joining in with an activity* which others are pursuing in that context. Once again, both of these examples can be seen to be related to the use of cigarettes as a source of *emotionality,* as discussed in chapters 2 and 3. What is also clear from the above accounts is that the respondents felt that the effect of smoking varied according to different social contexts, and according to *what the tobacco was being used for within each context:*

Well, let's say I've got a mega crisis at home, say one of the kids has just cut themselves and require rushing down to the Royal Infirmary, well then the cigarette there is "oh my God," and you have the cigarette and it's keeping you charged: you've got to do this, you've got to get here, you've got to ring that person, get them down there. A cigarette then is being used in a sense that it's keeping you active, it's keeping you going while this particular crisis is being dealt with. Take the same cigarette two or three hours later when the crisis is over, and you sit back and you light the fag and you go "phew" and then it has a relaxing effect, but it's exactly the same cigarette, out the same packet as the one that was getting you going at a hundred miles an hour and allowing you to go at hundred miles an hour, is the same as the one that's now calming you down. . . . Very often you'll think to yourself, "I must have a cigarette now, I've got to go and find somewhere to have a cigarette." It's not because you've got the actual craving inside you, it's just like you owe it to yourself—you have a tryst with your cigarettes—you've got to go and have your cigarettes. . . . You use it for the purpose that you want it . . . the purpose of "a" or the purpose of "b." (Pippa, 35, mother)

The above account demonstrates how the respondent *actively experiences* the effects of the cigarette in a variety of different ways. Also of great interest is how some smokers *actively* control the effects of their smoking through *abstaining* from using tobacco:

When I smoke my first cigarette of the day, it's very stimulating. For instance, this morning I smoked the first cigarette, I think it was 12:00—it was very stimulating. The second one, perhaps, is a form of controlling, but I know if I smoke another cigarette I won't smoke a second for ten minutes afterwards—I can't enjoy it. There's no stimulation, so I look for a kind of smoking to have time between smoking the second, the third cigarette, and if I'm going to smoke, for instance, if we have a meeting or I'm going to the pub and so on, and I smoke one cigarette, perhaps after half an hour I stop smoking because there is no stimulation. Stimulation is a very important point. (Sigo, 62, visiting German professor)

Interestingly, Sigo proposes that he could only enjoy smoking if he *abstained* from the practice for sufficient periods. If we once again follow the addiction model, of tobacco use, a central part of Sigo's enjoyment at this stage of his smoking appears to involve the *relief* of withdrawal-related feelings, since he could not enjoy too many cigarettes smoked in succession. The pursuit of specific effects from smoking was a theme that characterized the Regular Smoking stage of respondents in my research. One respondent understood this process very much within the terms of the addiction model itself:

> There are certain trigger moments. When I wake up in the morning, I reach for a cigarette, it's the first thing, it gives me . . . I get a little bit of a buzz out of the first one in the morning, that seems to be the best one of the day. Cos it's out of your system for a while and "wham," it gives you a little peak there, and you can go off and have your shower and get up. It has a stimulant effect. (George, 34, ex-convict)

Other respondents reported that they did not smoke until sometime after waking up. A number of these respondents appear positively to have avoided the feelings that George points toward. One explicitly states, "If I have a cigarette in the morning and I spin out, I don't like it. I don't smoke cigarettes to be spun out." For some of the smokers in my research, getting the desired effect involved striking a *balance* between extremes:

> [I]f you've not had one for a while, a short while, it's very enjoyable to have a cigarette. If you've gone an extremely long time without a cigarette, then you're going to feel giddy for a couple of minutes and that's when it highlights to me just how much of drug it is, cos you, sort of "whoooo," and I won't say that's particularly nice either, it's a very off-putting experience when you're feeling wobbly. There's all different times. . . . If you smoke too much that's equally unpleasant and that as I say is the stupidity of it, because you will actually find yourself taking cigarettes when you don't really need the cigarette, you've only just had a cigarette, so why are you taking another one? It's just the fact that somebody may come along and offer you a cigarette and because you are a smoker you take the cigarette, you don't necessarily need it. It's something . . . I've always felt, "Why are you doing this? You've just put one out, for God's sake!" and you can get what I define as "smoke-die," which is not nice at all actually. It can make you feel a bit "ugh" and feel a bit sick actually, and "better go and eat something." (Pippa, 35, mother)

The above accounts point toward the highly individualized control of the effects of tobacco. Also, it would seem that once again the techniques involved in these processes of control need to be *learned* by smokers. The notion of tobacco use as essentially involving individuals passively receiving unambiguous pharmacological effects is far too simplistic. Not only do users have a significant degree of control over what may be seen to be the pharmacological effects—through protracting periods of abstinence and, as other respondents suggested, by taking deeper and more frequent puffs, or vice versa—but also, in relation to these processes, their understandings and expectations profoundly *shape the very experience* of tobacco use. To quote one of the respondents in this connection, "I think I'm not sure at all that the physiological reaction, the physiological 'kick' from smoking was a clear, unproblematic, unambiguous thing, I don't think it was at all. It could be seen in various different ways, different moods and feelings influence the experience" (Rick, 51, senior lecturer).

To highlight what is by now a familiar theme, the Regular Smoking stage for respondents in my research involved not only a move toward *increasing control* over the effects of tobacco, but also *the increasing use of tobacco as a means of self-control*. As can be observed from the above accounts, the understanding of smoking as a stress-reliever is a dominant one among participants in my research. What is interesting, however, is that for some respondents, while the role of tobacco use as a stress-reliever was increasingly dominant in their Regular Smoking stage, the associations between smoking and stress relief seem to have been made *before* any first-hand experiences with tobacco. Consider, for example, the following two extracts:

> I was inside, in a place called Grendon. Which is a psychotherapeutic community prison—not a "nuthouse" or anything like that. Just about everyone there smoked roll-ups. I was into fitness training, did a lot of weight lifting, stuff like that, so I always saw smoking as being something, not just that I disliked the smell of, but something that was bad for you. . . . In one situation I was under a lot of pressure, under group therapy, you know, where I'd been given a bit of a battering by the other group members. I forget what the actual point was, but it was something where I'd really stormed off from the group and this guy had come running up after me to try and calm me down and given me a cigarette. . . . There was actually a motion put forward to stop people smoking in the groups because they were seeing it as an "out," you know, if someone's able to smoke, they're able to take the stress off themselves and therefore the therapy isn't working. That never succeeded because people insisted on smoking. (George, 34, ex-convict)

When did you first try tobacco?

> It was when—the Israeli customs are a bit dodgy anyway—and because we were on a chartered flight they started bringing the Israelis through to do their own security checks and they were all really objectionable anyway. They didn't understand that two girls were traveling together who weren't related. . . . Why was my father there and my mother in Britain? And all this, and they were just really nasty to both of us, and we came out of there really stressed, got to the departure lounge, and went "cigarette!", for no apparent reason, cos neither of us actually smoked at the time. That's when it started. (Alex, 25, personal assistant)

I use these examples to illustrate how dominant understandings of to-bacco use can strongly reinforce the association between it and stress relief and, moreover, ultimately shape the effects that are actively sought out by users when smoking, particularly in their Regular Smoking stage. Indeed, one respondent explains how he began to question the *direction* of the re-lationship between smoking and stress, believing that tobacco use may have been more of a sign to himself that he was "stressed" or "pressured" than an effective method of dealing with that stress or pressure.

> I think I began to feel, maybe because I was using cigarettes to deal with stress as I went on in my twenties and thirties, the pressure; I began to as-sociate cigarettes with stress and pressure, so I began to wonder if it really did any good, because if I'm sitting there smoking, I'm feeling "Christ, I must be pressurized, I'm smoking my head off!" (Rick, 51, senior lecturer)

While smokers have a degree of control over their tobacco use, particu-larly in determining the effects produced by smoking, this is not to suggest a *voluntaristic*, free-choice model of smoking. In other words, this is not to deny that many smokers feel *compelled* to smoke. Rather, such ideas are based upon the understanding of tobacco use as involving *cycles of interde-pendence which give rise to an order that becomes more compelling than the in-dividual will of the user*. To make clearer exactly why I have used this partic-ular formulation in place of concepts such as nicotine dependence or tobacco addiction, I shall now discuss exactly what respondents understand by the term *addiction*. Then I will examine respondents' experiences of to-bacco withdrawal and stopping smoking.

Addicted Smoking

In order to examine what respondents understood by "addicted smoking," it may again be useful first to consider the dictionary definition of the term. "**Addiction** *n.* the condition of being abnormally dependent on some habit, esp. compulsive dependency on narcotic drugs" (*Collins English Dictionary* 1991: 17). As was the case with the definition of *smoker*, respondents' un-derstandings of the term *addiction* appear to be quite consistent with the dictionary definition of the term. Consider the following extracts:

> *Did you become addicted, or, at what point did you become addicted—if at all?*
> Well, yeah, I'm certainly addicted now. I don't know, probably I would say the time that sticks in my mind is by the time I learnt to drive, which is when I was just about seventeen. I would say by that stage I was addicted. I would have found it hard to give up at that stage . . . there's been a long

period of time now where I've been addicted to cigarettes, as I see it anyway, where the addiction has been the same but it certainly grew initially, in
my view anyway. There were times when I lit cigarettes when I was probably in what you might call the initial curve towards becoming fully addicted,
where I was perhaps smoking when I didn't really feel I needed to, and if I
hadn't had one it wouldn't have made any difference to me. But certainly
for a number of years now, it's been steady. (Simon, 28, lawyer)

And when do you think you became addicted—if at all?

Oh, I don't know. I only noticed it the first time I tried to give up and I
couldn't—I failed. When I was at home in the winter and I had to wait till
2 o'clock in the morning to have my first fag of the day. It was a fucking
freezing-cold night, the wind blowing a gale and I had to hang out my
window, and I thought, "Yeah, I must be addicted, then, if I'm going to
those lengths." (Anita, 22, bar worker)

In these accounts, which are characteristic of many respondents in my
study, a fundamental part of becoming an addicted smoker involves smoking against one's own will. Put very simplistically, these understandings of
addiction appear to involve the idea that a set of powerful processes has
taken control over the tobacco user, and he or she no longer smokes so
much out of *wanting* to, but rather because she or he *has* to. A mark of addiction is seen to be that one can no longer "give up"—this will be examined shortly. Another mark, as is evident with the second extract, is that the
addicted smoker is prepared to go to great lengths to smoke. Also, of great
interest is the first respondent's statement that "I was perhaps smoking
when I didn't really feel I needed to, and if I hadn't had one, it wouldn't
have made any difference to me." This appears to involve the idea that addicted smoking becomes partially automated. It is as though the practice becomes blindly functioning.

A central part of the agenda of the interviews I conducted was to elucidate how the compulsion to smoke was *experienced*. I asked respondents
to describe what this "felt like" to them. I received some very interesting
responses:

Yes, and again I mean I do not know whether it is physiological or psychological, you will obviously get a huge desire to smoke and if you know you
cannot smoke, then that does compound the fact that you want to smoke.
I have always sort of said personally that the only thing worse than having
a lighter and no cigarettes, is to have a cigarette and no lighter! If you can
be that close to it but not actually be able to light up a cigarette, then it
compounds the desire for one. I would say, I probably could do without it,

I am not going to drop dead if I do not have a cigarette or anything or go crazy. But certainly in your head you start thinking . . . you know you can't have one, the desire to want one just gets bigger.

Could you describe to a nonsmoker what that "desire" is actually like—to want a cigarette, to be craving for a cigarette, to need a cigarette. What levels does it work on?

Well, obviously there is a physiological aspect in the sense that you do actually get a "craving." This will probably show itself, you might feel angry, tense, annoyed, have a very low tolerance threshold. Whether that is more psychological I do not know. I mean, I personally, I do not get shaky, but I know people that do. I suppose then you become in a sense *obsessed* with this single act of having to have a cigarette, you feel that you cannot do anything else well unless you have a cigarette. It is an absolute *must* to have a cigarette before the activity in order to do the activity as well as you might do it. From the psychological point of view it is mind over matter, your head is completely dominating you now, that you must have a cigarette. That this is a good thing to do and it is going to be wholly fulfilling for you, is probably not the case, you probably could manage very well without it. But I am certain that the mind plays larger tricks upon you. I know people who attempted to give up smoking and after two or three weeks they were worse than when they first started, although there was now no physical cravings left within them, it is their mind now that is really giving them the cause for concern because they see other people smoking and think, "Gosh, I would love one, I have got to have one." It's a great *relief* to be able to light up a cigarette.

So for somebody who has never smoked, it's an obsession: you just get obsessed, I suppose about the fact that you can't do anything as well as you would if you had the cigarette. . . . It's your friend, it's your mate, you can't . . . you need to see the friend, it's as simple as that, it's become so much a part of your life that the absence of it is very badly missed. (Pippa, 35, mother)

So, for the above respondent, the "need" for a cigarette was experienced as a kind of *preoccupation*—an *obsession*—and the experience when a cigarette was finally smoked after a period of *abstinence* was one of *relief*. However, of great importance is her suggestion that the *conscious* understanding that she was *unable* to smoke—perhaps because she had a lighter without cigarettes, or vice versa—seemed greatly to *compound* her obsession. Thus, it is the *conscious* feeling of *deprivation* that has emerged from the above account, and, indeed, much of the interview data, as a central part of the *compulsion* to smoke. What is even more interesting from Pippa's remarks is the statement that tobacco is "your friend, it's your mate . . . you need to see that friend." It is as if notions of dependence have a *dual* meaning to her. On one level, she admits that she is addicted. On this level, notions of dependence can variously mean "enslavement" or "powerlessness." However, on another level, the meaning of *dependence* for Pippa seems to involve the idea that tobacco is something that one can *depend upon*. Put in another way, *"It is something that will always be there for me"* (more than "me" for "it"); it is a stability, a source of security—perhaps better, an *emotional resource*.

When one considers how Pippa started: in her teens, rebelling against parental controls, aiming to break with the emotional dependence on her parents, and replacing it with a form of emotional dependence on tobacco—to control feelings, to promote identification with a different group, as a *rite de passage* to adulthood, as a resource to be accepted and to be able to cope within the adult world as she perceived it—to gain *independence,* it becomes easier to understand why she *relates* to tobacco in this manner. Pippa drew upon her tobacco use as a *resource* to facilitate the transition between crucial junctures in her life, cope with stressful events, reward herself for work well done, and comfort herself during periods of anxiety. It is not surprising, therefore, that she considers it "so much a part of [her] life." In other words, in her use of tobacco, in her understandings of tobacco (which, as we have seen, are intimately related to broader sets of understandings of tobacco use), and in her *experience* of tobacco there has been a systematic reinforcement of the role of tobacco use as an *emotional resource*. Thus, for Pippa, to be "denied" the use of tobacco is almost to deny a central part of herself.

It is the *associations* between tobacco use and a range of different processes that seem to play a central role in the compulsion to smoke:

> It's a very substantial part of my identity still, I'm aware of that and I'm aware that that's going to cause me a lot of difficulty when I "give up." I think of myself as a smoker, and I have done for a number of years. And I'm actually scared of actually not thinking of myself as a smoker. In some ways I don't want to be a nonsmoker. It doesn't feel like me. (Angela, 26, postgraduate researcher)

Again, for Angela, tobacco use was considered very much a central part of "me." Part of the compulsion to smoke may also be related to the ritualized associations with tobacco use:

> Well, obviously there is an addiction, after all the smoking time I've done I'm obviously addicted to smoking. I'm not going to say to nicotine be-

cause those peculiar chewing gums and patches that are supposed to help you with your nicotine cravings, personally speaking, they're crap.

Why are they crap?

> Because they don't . . . whoever's saying to themselves let's get smokers off cigarettes, has never smoked. I'm quite convinced of that because it isn't so much the nicotine it's the actual act of drawing on the cigarette. . . . You draw in on it and it's a relaxation exercise. So if you've got a patch or chewing gum (the chewing gum tastes revolting, anyway), while it might be fulfilling a physiological need, you don't actually feel that it is, it still hasn't taken away the *desire* to put this thing in your mouth and pull on it. And I think for a lot of smokers they actually like that, it's that act—perhaps the smoke might be less than the actual cigarette. You like to see the smoke being. . . . The smoking act—it's probably more important that the cigarette is in the mouth and being drawn upon than anything else. Although having said that, if it's a low-tar cigarette it is like pulling on fresh air. But then again, you can still be satisfied with that. . . . It's the actual *act* of smoking. (Pippa, 35, mother)

Thus the respondent would appear to suggest that the *desire* to smoke does not simply occur on a physiological level; there is much more to the process than this. Ritualized associations seemed to be particularly important to noncigarette smokers in my study. Some roll-up smokers, for example, described how they enjoyed the whole process of rolling the cigarette, of actively creating something that they could consume.[6]

Thus, while the term *addiction* may be useful as a label to apply to a specific set of experiences, it is somewhat inadequate as a model with which to understand these experiences. It is argued here that the process which we currently label as addiction involves much more than a simple one-way dependence. The process of addiction is at least partly dependent on the continued reinforcement of understandings of tobacco use as an emotional resource, a psychological tool, or whatever. To make this point clearer, I shall now examine respondents' experiences during the Stopping Smoking stage.

Stopping Smoking

Consider the following extract:

> *Was it initially difficult to stop?*
> Oh yeah.

6. Nonetheless, I do not wish to deny the physiological level to the practice. To understand the appeal of smoking *purely* in terms of the activities and rituals associated with it would be highly problematic. Such a limited insight would not explain why tobacco, and not other leaves, was being consumed in this process.

What was difficult about it?

> It was absolutely horrendous, I mean . . . one of the things that did strike me at the time was, you imagine . . . say tomorrow was the first day you stopped. You don't have one at breakfast, which is hell, you don't have one with coffee, and then you don't have one at lunchtime. And I always thought, before I did stop, that the effect would be cumulative, so it was like an increasing scale. By the end of like two weeks, you'd just be insane. Of course, it isn't like that. You know, you get over a cigarette period where you want one. So instead of having one with breakfast you just walk out of the house. And the craving's gone until the next time. That was quite surprising, but it drove me to distraction—those times in the day. I think it was the consideration that I was never ever going to have that comfort again that I was craving, and that was the difficult thing to get over. It's really true that you've got to take it day by day because if you think "I'm never ever going to experience that comfort or relaxed feeling again," you'd just start smoking again. That's the way it happened to me anyway.

So the hardest thing to get over was to get your head round this whole idea of being without cigarettes—for the rest of your life you're never going to be able to have that?

> Yeah, that's it, definitely.

What kind of situations were likely to trigger those kind of "I would like to have had a cigarette now"—what situations, what times. . . . How did that work?

> As I said, every meal, breakfast certainly. After every meal, they are key times when I crave a cigarette. For the first six weeks, obviously I didn't go out, so I was never in the situation, and there was no real stress cos I was at home doing absolutely nothing apart from sport, but after that, when I started going out again, it was definitely the social scene—particularly if I was with somebody else who smoked. If I sat down for a drink in a pub with a friend who smoked, it drove me insane. It was the most difficult thing to control. It was strange because if I was thinking to myself, "I'll pass this one, or I won't have the next one," I'd got to go through the whole of the night and feel like it all night. And then you think to yourself, "I've got to go out all these times in the future, and it's going to be like this." It's that which makes you cave in. (Simon, 28, lawyer)

Once again, for the above respondent, it was the *conscious associations* with tobacco use that seemed to generate the greatest *compulsion* to smoke. Simon clearly associated tobacco use with particular times of the day, and with particular activities. He proposes that in the context of those situations, or at those particular times, his cravings for tobacco would get much worse. Furthermore, he proposes that what made him eventually return to regular smoking was the *fear* that he would never be *able* to smoke again. It was a fear that he would always have longings for tobacco—that he would never *lose* the associations with tobacco use and particular times and situations as a particular kind of resource. This may help to explain why some respondents suggested that they would always be smokers, even if they had stopped. They felt that although they may stop the act of smoking, this would not stop them from *being* smokers:

> I think that I will always be a smoker whether I smoke cigarettes or not, I think I will always, would always, like to have one.
>
> *Why?*
>
> Because I'll always, whether I will or not, will always *want* to have a cigarette. Whether I "crave it" or whether I've got over that stage . . . I've got over the craving and the stage, I think I would always still think of having one. (Rachel, 21, researcher)
>
> The thing that puts me off trying to give up is the fact that it's like being an alcoholic: once you've become addicted, you will always end up smoking. That's quite a negative attitude, but I will always want a cigarette, so there's no point. (Adrian, 22, unemployed)

From these accounts one gets the distinct impression that these respondents thought that there was very little point to stopping smoking because they felt that they would always be "addicted." It is as if these respondents were now smoking *because* they were addicted—an almost tautological understanding of the practice (if we accept user's definitions of these terms). It is argued here that what this apparent tautology actually points toward is a degree of "self-fulfilling prophecy" involved in the *cycles of interdependence* that are recognized as addiction. These respondents, particularly Adrian, appear to have attached the label of "addict" to themselves; it is as if they are no longer responsible for their tobacco use. They see themselves as simply powerlessly dependent—as driven by an *involuntary* need for tobacco. Thus, to put it very simplistically: popular understandings of addiction and one-way dependence become *internalized;* for some smokers, such understandings become reinforced—effectively confirmed—when they attempt to stop but experience a great, almost irresistible, compulsion to smoke. Feeling that they are powerlessly dependent, that they have no role in what has become an almost *automatic* process, these smokers resign themselves to continue smoking. In other words, they are smokers because they are addicted, but they are addicted because they continue being smokers.

However, perhaps paradoxically, these smokers actually play a very *active* role in the construction and maintenance of their addiction. It is significant that stopping smoking is, for smokers, the ultimate *deprivation* of their tobacco use. Therefore, if we follow understandings discussed earlier, this is the stage at which their longings for tobacco are likely to be the most *compounded*. Indeed, one respondent discussed how he had previously gone for several days without smoking a cigarette. Then, when he made a concerted effort to "stop," he was only able to last for several hours. A related paradox is that some respondents viewed their smoking as an individual freedom, yet at the same time no longer felt that they were free to become nonsmokers. Indeed, it is apparent that respondents felt that becoming a nonsmoker involved something different from becoming an ex-smoker:

> *Do you see yourself as a nonsmoker now?*

> No, I see myself as an ex-smoker. Smoking is always your failure clause, isn't it? Smoking is always the bit about you that says to people, "You know, I'm only human," you know what I mean? It's the little bit of you that however professional you are as a nurse, or fantastic you are as a student, however brilliantly you cope with doing all this kind of stuff that people are always telling you, smoking is always this sort of failure clause. . . . If I was to say, "No, I'm a non-smoker," then you set yourself up to failure, don't you? I'm an ex-smoker, and hopefully a reformed smoker. (Michelle, 38, student)

Again, such ideas seem to involve the understanding that it would be wrong for smokers to tell themselves that they will *never* smoke again, that this will almost encourage failure. I asked another respondent what it would mean to become a nonsmoker:

> The easy answer to that is never wanting a cigarette. But I think that's probably a bit idealized. I can't contemplate never *ever* wanting a cigarette, and even when I've given up for four or five months previously I started smoking again because I went through a personal trauma—seemed to be dying for a packet of cigarettes at that time! But prior to that happening I'd been sort of five months without a cigarette and even then I was occasionally wanting one even though I suppose I could consider myself a nonsmoker at that stage, so I think it's a bit naïve to say never *wanting* a cigarette. But I suppose being a nonsmoker, it would just be a question of not thinking of smoking as an issue in everyday life. You know, from my point of view, broadly speaking, it makes absolutely no difference to me whatsoever whether other people smoke—at the moment it does because it reminds me that I'm not smoking. When I get to the stage when I don't perhaps notice that the bloke sat next to me is smoking . . . at the moment . . . ? (Mike, 30, researcher)

Clearly, becoming a nonsmoker would involve no longer thinking about smoking, no longer drawing associations between stressful events and smoking. Indeed, the above respondent described how he returned to smoking after experiencing "personal trauma."

A number of respondents who had stopped smoking described feeling as though part of "them" was missing when they quit. This may again indicate that smoking had become a central part of respondents' identities, or had consistently been drawn upon as an emotional resource. Several respondents feared that they would replace this "emptiness" by *substituting* food for tobacco; in fact, this concern became a major factor in returning them to smoking. As one respondent put it:

> Actually, I should mention probably that one of the things that's making me not want to give up is because a lot of people tell me you start eating a lot and I don't want to get fat. You know, I don't want to start eating loads of chocolate and stuff, so I'm worried about that as well, that maybe I'll replace it with food. (Steve, 21, clerk)

For other smokers it was more the fear that they would lose an important means of weight *control*. While this reaction emerged from both male and female respondents, it is important to note that, as has been argued in chapter 3, this has been a particularly dominant theme for women smokers throughout the twentieth century.

It is also important to note that I am not proposing that the smoker's progression from the Beginning, to Continued, Regular, "Addicted," and Stopping Smoking stages I've outlined above is a *universal* process—one that *all* smokers go through, and in the *same* way. Rather, I am suggesting that while respondents in my research had a large variety of different understandings and experiences of tobacco use, they nonetheless identified themselves as having passed through at least some of the "career" changes identified. Some identified more closely with relatively early stages of smoking—for example, with remaining as a predominantly social smoker—others, with much later stages. However, my central aim in this chapter (and, indeed, throughout the book as a whole) has been to examine the overall *direction* of the changes identified. As suggested in the introduction to this chapter, to a degree, this direction follows, in microcosm, the quite specific direction of the long-term development of tobacco use in the West. As part of an overall conclusion to the book as a whole, in the next chapter I shall examine whether this observation amounts to more than just coincidence.

Conclusion

In trying to understand why the direction of change in the processes of becoming a smoker as identified by respondents in my research is very similar to the direction of the long-term development of tobacco use in the West, a number of possibilities can be considered. To begin, I would like to explore a range of plausible explanations in turn. I will then go on to consider the policy and practical implications of the arguments presented in this book as a whole.

Civilization

It may well be the case that the development of tobacco use at the level of individuals follows a similar path as the long-term, broad-scale development of tobacco use in the West because both are influenced by processes of *civilization*. Consider, once again, the arguments of Norbert Elias:

> By a kind of basic "sociogenetic ground rule" individuals, in their short history, pass once more through some of the processes that their society has traversed in its long history. . . . This expression should not be understood to mean that all individual phases of a society's history are reproduced in the history of the civilized individual. Nothing would be more absurd than to look for an "agrarian feudal age" or a "Renaissance" or a "courtly-absolutist period" in the life of individuals. All concepts of this kind refer to the structure of whole social groups.
>
> What must be pointed out here is the simple fact that even in civilized society no human being comes into the world civilized, and that the individual civilizing process that they compulsorily undergo is a function of the social civilizing process . . . since in our society each human being is exposed from the first moment of life to the influence and the moulding in-

tervention of civilized grown-ups, they must indeed pass through a civilizing process in order to reach the standard attained by their society in the
course of its history, but not through the individual phases of the social civilizing process. (Elias 2000: xi)

Allow me to elaborate: from the respondents' accounts presented in chapter 4, one can observe how important tobacco use was as a mark of *transition*,
typically from childhood to adulthood.[1] In relation to this transition, how tobacco was used began to change. Particularly during the Beginning Smoking
"stages," tobacco use had a predominantly social purpose—it was used to express affiliation to a particular social group, often as an act of defiance against
parents or society as a whole. This could, in some ways, be seen to be similar
to the smoking *Gemeinschaft* of seventeenth-century tobacco use in the West
in which the practice was understood to be a mark of sociability and also of
defiance against religious edicts, moral treatises, and medical arguments.

However, as respondents began to move into adult life, and into social
circles in which different kinds of demands were placed on their behavior, so
they began increasingly to use tobacco for a number of other purposes in addition to its social "functions." They perhaps began to feel an increasing
amount of pressure or stress as they faced the growing responsibilities associated with life changes and, in relation to prevailing understandings of tobacco use, began to see smoking as a way to deal with this. In short, respondents faced increasing demands for *emotional independence*. Indeed, some
explicitly understood their smoking to mark a break from the *emotional dependence* on their parents. One can also understand this practice to mark a
move toward a growing *emotional dependence* on tobacco.

Another crucial stage appears to have involved respondents' use of tobacco in connection with their work, salaried or otherwise.[2] In relation to
these changes in use, respondents began increasingly to use tobacco as a relaxant to counter stress and pressure; as a comforter to counter anguish; as
a stimulant to counter boredom (perhaps in undertaking repetitive work);
and as an energizer to help spur them into action. As I have shown, such uses
of tobacco may correspond to a stage in its broad-scale development when
understandings of the practice as a supplementary activity, as a psychological tool, were becoming increasingly dominant toward the end of the nineteenth and the beginning of the twentieth century, particularly with the
emergence of the cigarette as a popular mode of consumption.

1. But also, as we have seen, to other transitions in identity.
2. I have housework and child rearing in mind in this connection.

From this stage in the development of their tobacco use, respondents characteristically reported an increasing move toward smoking alone. For many, the more social functions of tobacco had declined in importance, while the more psychological functions became more significant. In relation to this change, respondents increasingly began to *individualize* the effects of tobacco by adopting any one or a combination of a number of different strategies. This appears to correspond to fairly recent stages of the long-term development of tobacco use in which *individualization* has come to be an increasingly dominant theme.

Finally, in relatively advanced stages of their tobacco use, many respondents began to adopt quite negative understandings of the practice—as an addiction, as a biological dependency: one involving the regular, consistent, compulsive consumption of tobacco. This stage can be seen to roughly correspond to the smoking *Gesellschaft* identified as marking a relatively recent "stage" of the development of tobacco use in the West. Most interestingly, some respondents proposed that their use of tobacco at this stage was no longer even conscious; it became almost automatic, blindly functioning, internalized.

Thus, from this generalized model of tobacco use at the level of individuals, one can observe an increasing move toward the use of tobacco in a more regulated manner, and also the use of tobacco as a *means of self control*: to maintain stability and self-regulation, and further, toward a growing internalization of tobacco use as a means of self-control.

As we have seen, these processes roughly follow the long-term development of tobacco use in the West, and, in turn, processes of *civilization*. Indeed, the increasing *internalization* of controls was seen by Elias to mark a relatively advanced stage in processes of civilization. However, to say that tobacco use was being used in an increasingly *controlled* manner does not mean that tobacco users were more in *control* of their "addiction," any more than increasing degrees of self-control by members of civilized societies necessarily allow individuals to be more in *control* of their societies. Indeed, the reverse is often more the case.

Increasing Opposition

Perhaps another reason for the correspondence between the direction of change at the "macro" and "micro" levels of tobacco use development is that for many respondents, their smoking histories have taken place within a broader social context of *increasing opposition* to tobacco use. Consider the following extract:

I mean I think you feel a pariah as a smoker. Nowadays a whole variety of people (strangers!) feel empowered to come up to people who are smokers and . . . even in public contexts where smoking is still allowed. I mean I've had it twice while I've been watching football matches: I've had people complain about me smoking my pipe; I've had people come up to me in an airport lounge . . . well not actually come up to me, but to say loudly in my presence in an airport lounge—where I was smoking in a *permitted* area—"Oh that's disgusting!". Or in restaurants, people would come up— that would not have happened in the fifties and sixties when I started to smoke because, as I said, smoking was permitted, and was in fact a dominant pattern of behavior in that period. (Derek, 59, university professor)

One can observe from this account how some respondents have felt under an increasing amount of pressure to *regulate* their smoking behavior. Such changes can also be seen to be related to increasingly dominant understandings of the effects of *passive smoking* (and the general acceptance of this concept), and also (over a much longer period) the growing dominance of understandings of smoking as an addiction. Consider, for example, the following response:

And what type of smoker do you see yourself as?

Somebody who's addicted. I don't really do . . . it's not to do with anybody else, it's purely to do with me. I'm a reluctant smoker now, certainly, somebody who wants to give up, somebody who's *embarrassed* about it really. I don't really think it fits into—you know, I like sport, I try and take care of myself, try to think of myself as healthy and yet I do something which is as ridiculously destructive as smoking. It just doesn't fit with my own image of myself anymore, how I see myself. (Simon, 28, lawyer; emphasis added)

This respondent is almost *ashamed* of his smoking. He understands his tobacco use to be "ridiculously destructive." As he sees it, it is somehow an *irrational* thing which he does, when he knows he should not. It is this shame or embarrassment that has perhaps driven him increasingly to smoke *alone,* in private.[3] This would appear to correspond to part of a more general shift

3. For some respondents, an increase in smoking alone was intrinsically related to the fact that they had left home, and were now living outside the sphere of control by their parents. However, most interestingly, some of the students I interviewed had only begun smoking since beginning their studies at university. These respondents generally did not begin to smoke *alone* until sometime after they first started, despite the fact that many were in a situation where they were living away from their parents for the first time. Thus, trying to explain this pattern of behavior, the general move toward smoking alone among respondents, in terms of single "causes" (i.e., because they now live alone), would be too simplistic.

in the development of tobacco use, in which the practice has been increasingly outlawed from public places. It is gradually being pushed behind the scenes of public life.

Habituation

Another possible explanation is that of *habituation*. This term is used here to refer to processes of *habitus*[4] *development*. To make this concept clearer, consider the following account:

> *Does smoking help you to concentrate—perhaps to do your homework?*
>
> No way! It gives me a total head rush. No it's like . . . it's like "whoa"!
> How could it help me concentrate? (Mark, 14, student)

The above respondent has only recently started smoking. For him, smoking involves a "head rush." It is clear that, as he understands it, it could in no way be used to help him concentrate. Viewed in bio-pharmacological terms, this can be explained with regard to the respondent's *tolerance* for tobacco. This concept is explained by Krogh (1991: 82):

> The common thread that runs through most theories of withdrawal is that the body seeks *stasis*—it seeks to remain as it is—and accordingly will modify itself to remain the same when chronically pushed in a new direction by a drug. It's rather like a house that is pushed in the direction of cold by the winds of January; the thermostat in the house works against this external influence to keep the home's internal environment the same. The body has, in a sense, a multitude of small thermostats that push in the opposite direction from external drug influences. The pharmacological concept that describes this phenomenon is *tolerance*, normally a good thing in human affairs, but with a slightly different meaning in biology. Pharmacological tolerance means having to take progressively more of a given drug to keep getting the same *effect from it*. The prime example of this is heroin usage: people who are just starting out with it require only a little to get very high; later on they will require a lot to feel the same way; still later they will require even more just to stave off withdrawal. . . . Nicotine has its own forms of tolerance, but, as we might expect, its tolerance is more subtle than that of the opiates. Its most famous tolerance is that kids don't *keep* getting nauseated from smoking once they take it up; there are other ef-

4. The term *habitus* is used here to denote the development of an individual's "second nature." The term refers at once to the biological, psychological, and social dimensions of human beings and, indeed, to the "hinge" between these dimensions: how, for example, the social "imprints" on the biological, from smile lines on our faces, or a propensity for being right-handed, to the impact of war trauma on the structure of a veteran's brain. The concept is further explicated through its application in this section of the book.

fects as well, however. Smokers are unaware of it, but they metabolize nicotine and other drugs faster than do non-smokers. . . . Then, too, there is a kind of short-term tolerance, called tachyphylaxis, that comes with each day's smoking . . . the first few cigarettes of the day quicken the pulse in smokers, while subsequent cigarettes fail to raise it any further. (Krogh 1991: 82; *emphasis added*)

Viewed in this way, it is possible to observe why the above respondent experiences tobacco in the particular way he expresses. It is related to the fact that he has not developed a large degree of *tolerance* for tobacco. Indeed, it would appear that with the extract above, Krogh provides us with a natural model for the various stages of the development of tobacco use at the individual level, and perhaps even more interestingly, at the broader social levels. At one end of the process (if we slightly adapt Krogh's example of heroin addiction), the largely *unhabituated* user experiences a great "rush" from tobacco, and needs only a little to get quite powerful effects. At this stage in the process of *habituation* the effects of tobacco are more to lose control than to maintain it. Perhaps the equivalent in the long-term, broad-scale development of tobacco use would be the use of tobacco by Native American peoples. However, as the smoking process continues, users smoke more frequently—perhaps they inhale more deeply—to get a similar intensity of effects from tobacco. Indeed, this phenomenon seems to correspond with the processes that respondents in my study described. Finally, if we continue to follow the model provided by Krogh, users will eventually smoke simply to "stave off withdrawal." Thus smokers will smoke only to feel normal. Tobacco in this context is used much more to gain control or to stabilize feeling states than to lose control, something which, it has been argued, is characteristic of relatively recent stages of the development of tobacco use in the West. The "smoking to stave off withdrawal" stage would also appear to correspond to relatively advanced stages in the processes identified by smokers, particularly the Addicted Smoking stage. It was at these stages that respondents explicitly stated that the main reason[5] they smoked was *because they were addicted*. Most interestingly, this relatively advanced stage does not seem to apply to Native American tobacco use. As we have seen with the example of the Karuk, tobacco was for the most part *not* used to "get normal." Therefore, in terms of answering why there is a similar direction of change to the development of tobacco use in its long his-

5. As mentioned earlier, some felt that at this stage it was no longer a "reasoned" process; it was almost "automatic."

tory and the development of tobacco use among respondents in their short history, it may be because both involve *diminishing degrees of pharmacological involvement* (in the sense that individual users become more tolerant as their smoking progresses, and thus the pharmacological impact of tobacco becomes less pronounced).

However, where the model becomes less adequate as an explanatory device is in accounting for why, in the long-term development of tobacco use in the West, the dominant preference has been for progressively milder forms of tobacco, a process which, as we have seen, began long before increasing concerns for health in relation to smoking. Indeed, using this model, it is difficult to explain why some Regular Smoker respondents in my study *actively preferred* milder forms of tobacco to stronger ones, largely in terms of the effects that these produced. What the concept of tolerance also does not explain is why there are fundamental differences in *how* nicotine-level *stasis* is achieved. For example, among Karuk Native Americans the typical pattern of consumption was the relatively infrequent smoking of very strong tobacco. In contrast, the dominant present-day Western pattern of consumption is the much more frequent intake of relatively mild tobaccos.

Where the concept of tolerance fails is in assuming that users will smoke progressively more to "feel the same way." While this may be the case for a powerful opiate such as heroin, as we have seen, it is much less so for nicotine. The respondents in my study reported using tobacco for a number of different feelings: for example, they would exercise control over their tachyphylaxis (or short-term withdrawal) by protracting abstinence, and use other techniques in order to get the effects that they actively sought. Some respondents intensely disliked the "head rush" effects, while others actively pursued them. In a similar manner, the Karuk user sought *extremely* strong effects from tobacco, whereas the present-day Western smoker generally prefers (by comparison) a milder experience.[6] To the best of my knowledge, there is currently no "underground" market for strains of highly potent tobacco equivalent to those smoked by the Karuk Indians. I have argued

---

6. It would be interesting to undertake a comparative study with other recreational drugs. It is possible that, for example, alcohol use has followed a line of development very different from that of tobacco. For example, alcohol has, to a large degree, not come to be used as a psychological tool in the same manner as tobacco, i.e., legitimately used for both work and leisure. As we have seen, in seventeenth-century Europe, both alcohol and tobacco were linked to "intoxicated reverie." However, crucially, alcohol is *still* frequently used in this manner. Once again, I would point toward what I have termed as the "malleability" of tobacco: its capacity to be tamed, its relative ambiguity, that has been a significant factor in the development of its unique role in the present-day West.

throughout this book that these differences involve much more than mere contrasts in tastes. Rather, they relate to the fact that habituation is also a *social* process. The Karuk tobacco users went through an extensive process of tobacco habituation. Through various cultivation techniques they developed highly potent strains of tobacco because they *actively sought* effects quite different from those associated with the cigarette smoker in the present-day West. Since their bodies were not infinitely malleable, since the process of *habituation* is not boundless, the Karuk were able to continue receiving these kinds of effects throughout their smoking lives. When Europeans tried to smoke these tobaccos, they found them to be far too strong for their tastes. They transferred only the mildest and (to them) the most palatable forms of tobacco to the West. European users, in relation to the demands of Western societies, sought a different, much milder kind of effect. In turn, as has been discussed extensively, twentieth-century tobacco users sought different kinds of effects from users of the seventeenth century, owing to an increasing social pressure toward self-restraint.

Thus, these demands for different strengths of tobacco and hence different effects were not simply expressions of conscious preferences. They also stemmed from demands that formed an internalized part of the tobacco users' social habituses. Such that, as we have seen, when Europeans first smoked Native American tobacco they became very ill for long periods afterwards. Similarly, women of the nineteenth century may well have not been able to "stomach" the pipe and cigar tobacco smoked by their male counterparts. And yet in the sixteenth century it was not uncommon for women to smoke tobacco that would be considered very strong by now contemporary standards. As Roberta Park illustrates:

> Middle class [Victorian] women fulfilled their own stereotype of the "delicate" females who took to their beds with consistent regularity and thus provided confirmation of the dominant medical account that this should be so. Women "were" manifestly physically and biologically inferior because they actually "did" swoon, "were" unable to eat, suffered continual maladies, and consistently expressed passivity and submissiveness in various forms. The acceptance by women of their "incapacitation" gave both a humane and moral weighting to the established so called "facts." (Park 1985: 14)

Thus in the process of habitus formation, or *habituation*, the social effectively *imprints* upon the biological such that people in different societies do indeed have different "constitutions," "palates," "tastes," and "tolerance thresholds." These social habituses do not simply vary *between* societies, they also vary *within* societies. For example, some respondents to the survey discussed in chapter 4 expressed a taste for stronger, "rougher" forms of tobacco, which, they explicitly stated, was related to the metaphor inherent in their self-image as young, tough, and strong working-class women. In so doing, as Graham (1992) has argued, they paradoxically *reproduce* some of the conditions of their disadvantage: greater material deprivation, higher levels of mortality, and the like. Yet their social habituses are such that they may understand and indeed experience smoking as an individual freedom, a source of strength, an emotional resource, even a means of coping with these circumstances.

Furthermore, these social habituses change within users' lifetimes. Consider some of the changes in habitus users may experience in relation to becoming a smoker. The way they feel, how they may control emotions, their sensations of taste and smell all can change significantly with processes of tobacco habituation. Even how smoke is perceived can become transformed when one becomes a smoker or a nonsmoker. Consider, for example, the following account from an ex-smoker:

> The other day somebody, when I was sitting in a train, walked from the smoking carriage to get some coffee with a cigarette in his hand, and it just sort of went past me, and I really gagged and turned away, and I thought, "How inconsiderate," and then I thought, "My God, I'd never ever have dreamt of that being . . . having such an effect on me when I was a smoker." I could see why he would see that as unreasonable, that nonsmokers would object to him just walking through the carriage with a cigarette in his hand. But you immediately detect it, and now I can't imagine how I didn't notice it. How it affects your clothes, sense of smell and taste, everything. (Rick, 51, senior lecturer)

Thus, the "taste" for tobacco, especially tobacco of particular varieties, and the related pursuit of particular effects from the substance are *socially indexed* ones. Thus what many present-day Western cigarette smokers typically have a taste for, actively pursue, is not so much a "smack" of nicotine poisoning (as with the Karuk, and, more acutely, with the tobacco shamans), but rather the *relief* of the "withdrawal" feelings related to the consumption of relatively mild forms of tobacco. Today, the bulk of smokers seek a variety of mild, ambiguous, unfinished, undramatic effects from tobacco consumed over a small dose range. They do so in relation to their understandings of tobacco use, which, in turn, are related to a wide range of social processes. It is through drawing upon and developing the concept of habitus here, and, it is hoped, through future research, that it is possible to lay the foundations for a more adequate understanding of the dynamic interplay of processes which together constitute the experience of tobacco use in the present-day West.

Implications for Policy

My position in this book is neither anti- nor pro-smoking. I am not concerned with answering the question of whether one should be "free" to be a smoker or a nonsmoker. Rather, a central aim has been to examine how the issues referred to above have come to dominate current debates about smoking. That said, it is possible that the arguments presented in this book have a number of implications for policy, and practical implications for people who wish to stop smoking.

In many ways, my research does not paint an optimistic picture for the success of interventions aimed at reducing levels of smoking. Tobacco use is a deeply ingrained part of the cultures of Western societies. Present-day associations between tobacco use and risk, stress relief, and individuality and debates over addiction, freedom, and control are maintained with inexorable consistency in films, books, advertisements, peer culture, television, and so on—both implicitly and explicitly. Policy interventions aiming to persuade people not to start smoking, or to encourage those who are smokers to stop, it is argued here, need to find some way to counter such associations, which themselves might be rationalizations for starting or continuing the practice. Such campaigns would need to address much more than the advertising and marketing strategies of tobacco corporations; the price of tobacco; and the availability of cigarettes to children. It is a great deal easier to criticize existing campaigns than it is to suggest alternatives. There are, nonetheless, a number of guidelines that I would like, tentatively, to suggest.

First, it would be wrong to assume that smokers start and continue smoking without being aware of the health risks associated with the practice. As I have argued in chapter 3, for young people in particular, the prevailing emphasis on the long-term effects of smoking—the links to diseases such as lung cancer and heart disease—might, paradoxically, *enhance* the illicit appeal of smoking as a risky behavior. For young people, diseases that might not develop until the forties, or even later, stand at a *safe* distance temporally. For this reason, public education campaigns should not, it is recommended, sensationalize the long-term risks of smoking. I remember at secondary school being shown a comparison of the lungs of a smoker next to those of a nonsmoker. I joined my classmates in reveling in the gory detail of this illustration. The use of "scare tactics" might only have limited, short-term effects, and might, however well-intentioned, in the long term reinforce implicit associations with tobacco and risky appeal. The health risks of smoking should instead be presented factually. Similarly, simply putting bigger, more dramatic warnings on packs of cigarettes might also have the unintended consequence of positive risk associations in the manner outlined above. Smokers, embracing an unsubtle irony, will, after all, quite happily purchase Death brand cigarettes with the skull-and-crossbones logo on a black background. The health warning on this packet seems a complementary part of its design.

Based on conclusions drawn from my research, public education campaigns aiming to discourage young people from smoking need to address the more *immediate* motivations for starting smoking as well as disseminate information about the long-term risks. Such a focus might entail a discussion of whether cigarettes are stress relieving, or, perhaps, stress generating. Are they effective as a means of weight control? What more effective means might there be? Campaigns need also to counter smoking as a symbol of independence, adulthood, and psychological rescue. Since defiance of authority might be a motivation to start smoking, campaigns conducted in a "preachy," didactic manner may well be self-defeating. The use of participatory, learner-centered methods might, therefore, enjoy greater levels of success. Perhaps, depending on their age group, young people might be engaged in exercises whereby they are asked to "unpack" the meaning of cigarette advertisements, how cigarettes are portrayed in film, and so on: a process of debunking the myths. It is in these ways, and potentially many others, that the understandings developed in this book might be used positively to inform future policy interventions.

In terms of stopping smoking, this book can be taken as a critique of those methods which address only biological components of tobacco use. Nicotine substitution, it has been argued, is the material manifestation of a tautology: *we use nicotine to treat tobacco.* That is, with nicotine patches, gum, or inhalators, tobacco use is not just *discursively* reduced to essentially a means of nicotine self-administration, it is also *physically* reduced to this. Paradoxically, if we accept this understanding of tobacco use—if we accept its reduction to the consumption of just one pharmacological agent—then the use of nicotine substitutes can be understood to constitute *just another form* of tobacco use, one representing a relatively advanced stage in the *medicalization* of the practice. While the use of substitutes does address a real need of tobacco users who face increasing pressure to remove their smoke from public spaces, this can best be understood as a short-term measure which in no way addresses tobacco use in its entirety. Stopping smoking, it is argued here, involves a great deal more than simply no longer inhaling and exhaling tobacco smoke: for it to be successful, it must involve *becoming* an ex-smoker or a nonsmoker.

In association with nicotine substitutes, received wisdom has it that if we gradually reduce the dose of nicotine, we gradually reduce the desire to smoke. (It is interesting that historical data suggest the opposite: the weaker the strain of tobacco in common use, the more frequently it is consumed.) Such ideas appear to be based on the premise that the desire to smoke is purely a biological one. However, what emerges from the discussion in this book is that so very much more is involved: tobacco use plays a role in identity formation, emotion management, psychological control, among others. The desire to smoke, as we have seen, is compounded by certain perceptions, certain social situations, particular events, and specific understandings and interpretations.

The experience of tobacco withdrawal in the present-day West is profoundly mediated by prevailing understandings of tobacco use. It is an experience that hinges on notions of control: being controlled, taking control, maintaining control, expressing control. It is, characteristically, compounded by those situations in which smokers understand themselves to no longer be free to smoke. For example, a woman is sitting in a bar, having just recently given up smoking. She jealously observes the man at the other end of the room who inhales and exhales the smoke of a cigarette that takes forever to burn. "He is *free* to smoke, and I have denied myself this freedom," she thinks. "I have 'given this up,' I have made this 'sacrifice' for my health. And in every social situation from now until time immemorial I will have to watch jealously as other smokers enjoy themselves." What writers such as Allen Carr, whom I mentioned in the preface, do most effectively is encourage ex-smokers to substitute this very negative *experience* of withdrawal for a much more positive one. In effect, he "inverts" the notions of control embodied in the example above. He would encourage this woman to celebrate the fact that she no longer *has* to smoke: she is now *free* from the necessity of having to smoke not just a cigarette in that moment, but the next cigarette, and the next, and the next.[7] She is in a position to pity the poor smoker across the room who is doomed to the continuous effort of maintaining his addiction.

People have *become* nonsmokers in spite of their consumption of nicotine via substitution devices. Similarly, others have remained smokers despite quite extensive periods of not consuming tobacco. What the arguments pre-

---

7. Again, the importance of viewing the practice processually becomes apparent in this connection.

sented in this book indicate is the importance for smokers who wish to stop, but feel they cannot, of developing understandings of their tobacco-using biographies: of elucidating their motivations to smoke; critically exploring rationalizations such as "I smoke because I'm addicted"; recognizing the active and crucial role that they play in maintaining their compulsion to smoke. People who wish to stop need to develop such strategies for dealing with those situations where the experience of withdrawal is likely to be most readily apparent. The arguments presented in this book also highlight the importance of understanding the *development* of tobacco use at the societal and individual levels. Rationalizations and motivations for smoking would appear to shift in a definite direction in the development of a smoker's career, such that those who wish to stop at the Addicted stage would need to employ strategies different from those at the Continued Smoking stage.

Paradoxically, the fear of losing a major emotional resource might be sustaining the need for that resource. This cycle of interdependence could play a major part in why some smokers keep smoking. It is also evident that an element of Pavlovian-like *conditioning* is involved in processes of habituation. Indeed, some smokers in my research reported that they would engage in substitution activities, such as compensatory eating, in an attempt to restimulate their palate after having not smoked for an extended period. In a sense the "strategies" illustrated above can be viewed as a reconditioning of the self through positive reinforcement.

In summary, then, I have argued that while nicotine-substitution devices may have some benefits for smokers who wish to stop, a great deal more about their tobacco use needs to be systematically addressed. Accordingly, the prevailing understanding of tobacco use, and of the compulsion to use tobacco, needs to be challenged. I have argued that smokers who wish to stop should attempt to break away from understanding themselves as simply "enslaved" to biological processes, and should aim instead to elucidate the broader range of processes sustaining their use of tobacco, including the crucial and active role that they themselves have to play in these processes. I am therefore suggesting that in developing strategies to deal with tobacco "withdrawal," smokers who wish to stop must address both the biopharmacological and social-psychological dimensions of the withdrawal experience. In other words, they need to not just stop smoking but make the much broader transition involved in becoming a nonsmoker.

References

Adams, K. R. 1990. "Prehistoric Reedgrass (Phragmites) 'Cigarettes' with Tobacco (*Nicotiana*) Contents: A Case Study from Red Bow Cliff Dwelling, Arizona." *Journal of Ethnobiology* 10:123–39.

Alexander, F. W. 1930. "Tobacco: Discovery, Origin of Name, Pipes, the Smoking Habit and Its Psychotherapy." *The Medical Press* 181 (30 July 1930): 89–93.

Alford, B. W. E. 1973. *W. D. & H. O. Wills and the Development of the U.K. Tobacco Industry, 1786–1965.* London: Methuen.

Apperson, G. L. 1914. *The Social History of Smoking,* London: Ballantine Press.

Ashton, H., and Stepney, R. 1982. *Smoking Psychology and Pharmacology,* London: Tavistock.

Becker, H. 1963. *Outsiders: Studies in the Sociology of Deviance.* London: Free Press of Glencoe.

Bell, C. 1898. *The Cigarette. Does it Contain Any Ingredient Other Than Tobacco and Paper? Does it Cause Insanity?* New York: n.p. Document obtained from the British Library Shelfwork 7660.g.38.

Bourne, E. G. 1907. "Columbus, Ramon Pane and the Beginnings of American Anthropology." *Proceedings of the American Antiquarian Society,* n.s., 17:310–48.

Brandt, A. M. 1990. "The Cigarette, Risk, and American Culture." *Daedalus* 119 (fall): 155–76.

Brooks, J. E. 1937–53. *Tobacco, Its History Illustrated by the Books, Manuscripts and Engravings in the Collection of George Arents, Jr.* 5 vols. New York: The Rosenbach Company.

———. 1953. *The Mighty Leaf: Tobacco through the Centuries.* London: Alvin Redman.

Bucknell. 1857. *Narcotia: or the Pleasures of Imagination, Memory, and Hope United in the Philosophy of Tobacco.* London: Whittaker and Co.

Bureau for Action on Smoking Prevention (BASP). 1992. *Taxes on Tobacco Products.* Brussels: European Bureau for Action on Smoking Prevention.

———. 1994. *Tobacco and Health in the European Union: An Overview.* Brussels: European Bureau for Action on Smoking Prevention.

C. T. 1615. *An Advice on How to Plant Tobacco in England.* London: Nicholas Okes.

Camporesi, L. 1989. *Bread of Dreams.* Oxford: Polity Press. Page 32 cited in Hale 1993: 546.

Carson, G. 1966. *The Polite Americans.* New York: William Morrow.

Colley, J. R. T., W. W. Holland, and R. T. Corkhill. 1974. "Influence of Passive Smoking and Parental Phlegm on Pneumonia and Bronchitis in Early Childhood." *Lancet* 2:1031–34. Page 1031 cited in Jackson 1994: 431.

Collins English Dictionary. 3d ed. 1991. London: HarperCollins.

Cowan, J. 1870. *The Use of Tobacco vs. Purity Chastity and Sound Health.* New York: Cowan and Company Publishers.

Curtin, M. 1987. *Propriety and Position. A Study of Victorian Manners.* New York: Garland.

Denig, E. T. 1953. *Of the Crow Nation.* Smithsonian Institution, Bureau of American Ethnology Bulletin 151, no. 33. Washington, D.C.: GPO.

Dickens, C. [1842] 1985. *American Notes.* Reprint, London: Granville Publishers.

Dickson, S. A. 1954. *Panacea or Precious Bane: Tobacco in Sixteenth Century Literature.* New York: The New York Public Library.

Diehl, H. S. 1969. *Tobacco and Your Health: The Smoking Controversy.* New York: McGraw-Hill.

Dole, G. 1964. "Shamanism and Political Control among the Kuikuru." In *Beiträge zur Völkerkunde Südamerikas,* Völkekundliche Abhandlungen vol. 1. Hanover: Kommissionsverlag Münstermann—Druck. Pages 57–58 cited in Goodman 1993: 19.

Doll, R., and A. B. Hill. 1952. "A Study of the Etiology of Carcinoma of the Lung." *British Medical Journal* 2:1271–86.

Drake, B. 1996. *The European Experience with Native American Tobacco.* <http://www.tobacco.org/History/history.html>.

Elias, N. 1978. *What Is Sociology?* Translated by Stephen Mennell and Grace Morrissey. 1970. London: Hutchinson. Originally published under the title *Was ist Soziologie* (Munich: Juventa Verlag).

———. 2000. *The Civilizing Process.* Rev. ed. 1939. Oxford: Blackwell. Originally published under the title *Über den Prozess der Zivilisation,* 2 vols. (Basel, Germany: Haus zum Falken).

Elias, N., and E. Dunning. 1986. *Quest for Excitement: Sport and Leisure in the Civilizing Process.* Oxford: Blackwell.

English Mechanic. 1872. *Tobacco and Disease: The Substance of Three Letters.* London: N. Trübner and Co., Paternoster Row.

Erasmus, D. 1985. *De Civilitate Morum Puerilium Libellus.* Translated by Brian McGregor. Toronto: University of Toronto Press.

Eriksen, M. P., C. A. LeMaistre, and G. R. Newell. 1988. "Health Hazards of Passive Smoking." *Annual Review of Public Health* 9:47–70.

Ewen, S. 1976. *Captains of Consciousness: Advertising and the Social Roots of the Consumer Culture.* London: McGraw-Hill.

Fairholt, F. W. 1859. *Tobacco: Its History and Associations.* London: Chapman and Hall.

Foucault, M. 1973. *The Birth of the Clinic: An Archaeology of Medical Perception.* Translated by A. M. Sherridan Smith. 1963. London: Tavistock Publications. Originally published under the title *Naissance de la Clinique* (Paris: Presses Universitaires de France).

———. 1979. *Discipline and Punish. The Birth of the Prison.* Harmondsworth: Penguin.

———. 1980. "Body/Power." In *Michel Foucault: Power/Knowledge,* edited by C. Gordon. Brighton: Harvester.

Freedom Organisation for the Right to Enjoy Smoking (FOREST). 1991. *A Response to Passive Smoking.* Information Sheet no. 1. London: FOREST Publications.

Furst, P. 1976. *Hallucinogens and Culture.* San Francisco: Chandler and Sharp.

Garber, M. 1992. *Vested Interests: Cross-Dressing and Cultural Anxiety.* London: Routledge.

Gernet, A. von. 1992. "Hallucinogens and the Origins of the Iroquoian Pipe/Tobacco/Smoking Complex." In *Proceedings of the 1989 Smoking Pipe Conference,* edited by C. F. Hayes III. Rochester Museum and Science Service, Research Record no. 22. Rochester, N.Y.: Rochester Museum and Science Service.

Gilbert, J. I. 1772. *L'anarchie médicinale.* Neuchâtel: n.p. Page 198 cited in Foucault 1973: 4.

Glantz, A., J. Slade, L. A. Bero, P. Hanauer, and D. E. Barnes. 1996. *The Cigarette Papers.* London: University of California Press.

References

Goodin, R. E. 1989. "The Ethics of Smoking." *Ethics* 99:574–624. Pages 574 and 587 cited in Goodman 1993: 243.

Goodman, J. 1993. *Tobacco in History: The Cultures of Dependence.* London: Routledge.

Goudsblom, J. 1986. "Public Health and the Civilizing Process." *The Milbank Quarterly* 64, no. 2:161–88.

Graham, H. 1992. *When Life's a Drag: Women Smoking and Disadvantage.* London: HMSO.

Greaves, L. 1996. *Smoke Screen. Women's Smoking and Social Control.* London: Scarlet Press.

Gusfield, J. 1993. "The Social Symbolism of Smoking and Health." In *Smoking Policy: Law, Politics, and Culture,* edited by R. Rabin and S. Sugarman. Oxford: Oxford University Press.

Haberman, T. W. 1984. "Evidence for Aboriginal Tobaccos in Eastern North America." *American Antiquity* 49:269–87.

The Habits of Good Society: A handbook of etiquette for ladies and gentlemen. 1868. London: Cassell, Petter, and Galpin, La Belle Sauvage Yard, Ludgate Hill, E. C.

Hackwood, F. 1909. *Inns Ales and Drinking Customs of Old England.* London: T. Fisher Unwin.

Hale, J. 1993. *The Civilization of Europe in the Renaissance.* London: HarperCollins.

Hammond, E. C., and D. Horn. 1958. "Smoking and Death Rates—Report on Forty-Four Months of Follow-Up on 187,783 Men. 1. Total Mortality." *Journal of the American Medical Association* 166, no. 10 (8 March): 1159–72.

Harrington, J. 1932. *Tobacco Smoking among the Karuk Indians of California.* Smithsonian Institution, Bureau of American Ethnology Bulletin 94. Washington, D.C.: GPO.

Harrison, L. 1986. "Tobacco Battered and the Pipes Shattered: A Note on the Fate of the First British Campaign against Tobacco Smoking." *British Journal of Addiction* 81:553–58.

Hart, J. 1633. *KANIKH or the Diet of the Diseased.* London. Page 320 cited in Goodman 1993: 61.

Heywood, J. 1871. *The Tobacco Question. Physiologically, Chemically, Botanically, and Statistically Considered.* London: Simpkin, Marshall and Co.

Higler, M. 1951. *Chippewa Child Life and Its Cultural Background.* Smithsonian Institution, Bureau of American Ethnology Bulletin 146. Washington, D.C.: GPO.

Hirst, F. 1953. *The Conquest of Plague: A Study in the Evolution of Epidemiology.* Oxford: Clarendon Press.

Hughes, J. 1996. "From Panacea to Pandemic: Towards a Process Sociology of Tobacco-Use in the West." Ph.D. diss., University of Leicester.

Jackson, P. 1994. "Passive Smoking and Ill-Health: Practice and Process in the Production of Medical Knowledge." *Sociology of Health and Illness* 16, no. 2:423–47.

Jacobson, B. 1981. *The Ladykillers. Why Smoking Is a Feminist Issue.* London: Pluto Press.

James I. 1954. *A Counterblaste to Tobacco.* 1604. London: Rodale Press.

Johnston, L. 1957. *The Disease of Tobacco Smoking and Its Cure.* London: Christopher Johnson.

Kanner, L. 1931. "Superstitions Connected with Sneezing." *Medical Life* 38:549–75.

Klein, R. 1993. *Cigarettes Are Sublime.* Durham, N.C.: Duke University Press.

Kluger, R. 1996. *Ashes to Ashes: America's Hundred-Year Cigarette War, the Public Health, and the Unabashed Triumph of Philip Morris.* New York: A. A. Knopf.

Koskowski, W. 1955. *The Habit of Tobacco Smoking.* London: Staples Press.

Krogh, D. 1991. *Smoking: The Artificial Passion.* New York: W. H. Freeman and Co.

Labat, J. B. 1742. *Nouveau voyage aux isles de l'Amérique.* Vol. 6 Paris: Delespine. Pages 278–79 cited in Goodman 1993: 79–90.

Lacey, R. 1973. *Sir Walter Raleigh.* London: Cardinal.

Laurence, C. 1996. "Psst! Want to see a video of a fully-dressed woman smoking?" *The London Telegraph,* 2 February 1996, Main News, p. 1.

Leach, E. 1986. "Violence." *London Review of Books,* October.

Leary, D. 1997. *No Cure for Cancer;* transcript of filmed performance. <http://www.endor
.org/leary/index.shtml>.

Lee, P. N. 1976. *Statistics of Smoking in the UK.* 7th ed. London: Tobacco Research Council.

Lohof, B. A. 1969. "The Higher Meaning of Marlboro Cigarettes." *Journal of Popular Culture* 3:441–50.

Mack, P. H. 1965. *The Golden Weed: A History of Tobacco and of the House of Andrew Chalmers 1865–1965.* London: Newman Neame.

Meeler, H. J. 1832. *Nicotiana; or the Smoker's and Snuff Taker's Companion.* London: Effingham Wilson.

Mihill, Christopher. 1997. "Government to Phase Out Sports Sponsorship to Help Discourage 'Trendy Youngsters' from Smoking." *The London Guardian,* 15 July, Health, p. 5.

Mitchell, D. 1992. "Images of Exotic Women in Turn-of-the-Century Tobacco Art." *Feminist Studies* 18, no. 2:327–50.

Monardes, N. 1925. *Joyfull Newes Out of the Newe Founde Worlde.* Translated by John Frampton. London: Constable.

Morgan, L. H. 1901. *League of the HO-DE'-NO-SAU-NEE.* Vol. 1. New York: Burt Franklin.

Mulhall, J. C. 1943. "The Cigarette Habit." *Annals of Otology* 52:714–21.

National Opinion Poll Research Group (NOP). 1993. *Smoking in Public Places.* Report conducted by NOP Social and Political for the [U.K.] Department of the Environment. London: HMSO.

Oberg, K. 1946. *Indian Tribes of Northern Mato Grosso, Brazil.* Smithsonian Institution, Bureau of American Ethnology publication no. 15. Washington, D.C.: GPO.

Old Smoker. 1894. *Tobacco Talk.* Philadelphia: The Nicot Publishing Co.

Park, R. 1985. "Sport, Gender and Society in a Transatlantic Victorian Perspective." *British Journal of Sports History* 2:5–28. Page 14 cited in Shilling 1993:112.

Parker, H. 1722. *The First Part of the Treatise of the Late Dreadful Plague in France Compared with that Terrible Plague in London, in the Year 1665. In Which Died near A Hundred Thousand Persons.* Based on an earlier treatise (London, 1721), "The Late Dreadful Plague at Marseilles Compared with That Terrible Plague in London." London: Printed for the author.

Paulli, S. 1746. *A Treatise on Tobacco, Tea, Coffee and Chocolate.* Translated from the original Latin (London, 1665), *Commentarius de Abusu Tabaci Americanorum Veteri, et Herb.* Printed for J. Hildyard at York, M. Bryson at Newcastle, and J. Lencke at Bath.

Penn, W. A. 1901. *The Soverane Herbe: A History of Tobacco.* London: Grant Richards.

Porter, C. 1972. *Not without a Chaperone. Modes and Manners from 1897 to 1914.* London: New English Library.

Porter, G., and H. C. Livesay. 1971. *Merchants and Manufacturers.* Baltimore: The John Hopkins University Press.

Porter, P. H. 1971. "Advertising in the Early Cigarette Industry: W. Duke, Sons and Company of Durham." *The North Carolina Historical Review* 48:31–43.

Redway, G. 1884. *Tobacco Talk and Smoke Gossip.* London: Printed for the author.

Rosen, G. 1958. *A History of Public Health.* New York: MD Publications.

Russell, M. A. H. 1983. "Smoking, Nicotine Addiction, and Lung Disease." *European Journal of Respiratory Diseases Supplement* 64, no. s126:85–89.

Scharff, R. C. 1995. *Comte after Positivism.* Cambridge: Cambridge University Press.

Scherndorf, J. G., and A. C. Ivy. 1939. "The Effect of Tobacco Smoking on the Alimentary Tract." *Journal of the American Medical Association* 112, no 10:898–903.

Schivelbusch, W. 1992. *A Social History of Spices, Stimulants, and Intoxicants.* New York: Pantheon Books.

Shammas, C. 1990. *The Pre-Industrial Consumer in England and America.* Oxford: Oxford University Press.

Shilling, C. 1993. *The Body and Social Theory.* London: Sage.

References

Steinmetz, A. 1857. *Tobacco: Its History, Cultivation, Manufacture, and Adulterations.* London: Richard Bentley.

Sylvestro, J. 1620. *Tobacco Battered and The Pipes Shattered (about their Ears that idley Idolize so base and barbarous a WEED; OR AT LEAST-WISE OVER-LOVE so loathsome Vanitie).* Pamphlet, n.p. Obtained from Wigston Records Office, Leicester.

Tanner, A. E. 1950. *Tobacco: From the Grower to the Smoker.* 5th ed. 1912. London: Sir Isaac Pitman and Sons, Ltd.

Tate, C. 1999. *Cigarette Wars: The Triumph of the Little White Slaver.* Oxford: Oxford University Press.

Tennant, R. B. 1950. *The American Cigarette Industry.* New Haven, Conn.: Yale University Press.

Thompson, L. 1916. *To the American Indian.* Eureka, Calif.: Printed for the author. Document obtained from the British Library Shelfwork Mic.A.13426.

Tidwell, H. 1912. *The Tobacco Habit: Its History and Pathology.* London: J&A Churchill.

Tooker, E. 1964. *An Ethnography of the Huron Indians, 1615–1649.* Smithsonian Institution, Bureau of American Ethnology Bulletin 190. Washington, D.C.: GPO.

Trübner, N. 1873. *The Phisiological Position of Tobacco.* Reprint from the *Quarterly Journal of Science,* London.

Wafer, L. 1934. *A New Voyage & Description of the Isthmus of America . . . with Wafer's Secret Report (1698) and Davis's Expedition to the Gold Mines (1704).* 1699. Edited, with introduction, notes, and appendices, by L. E. Elliot Joyce. Hakluyt Society, 2d ser., no. 73. Oxford: Hakluyt Society.

Walton, J., ed. 2000. *The Faber Book of Smoking.* London: Faber and Faber.

Welshman, J. 1996. "Images of Youth: The Issue of Juvenile Smoking 1880–1914." *Addiction* 91, no. 9:1379–86.

West, R. 1993. "Beneficial Effects of Nicotine: Fact or Fiction?" *Addiction* 88:589–90.

West, R., and N. E. Grunberg. 1991. "Implications of Tobacco Use As an Addiction." *British Journal of Addiction* 86: 485–88. Page 486 cited in Goodman 1993: 5.

Wilbert, J. 1987. *Tobacco and Shamanism.* New Haven, Conn.: Yale University Press.

Wouters, C. 1976. "Is het civilisatieproces van richting veranderd?" (Is the civilizing process changing direction?) *Amsterdams Sociologish Tijdschrift* 3, no. 3:336–37.

———. 1977. "Informalization and the civilizing process." in *Human Figurations: Essays for Norbert Elias,* edited by P. R. Gleichmann et al., 437–53. Amsterdam: Stichting Amsterdams Sociologisch Tijdschrift.

———. 1986. "Formalization and Informalization: Changing Tension Balances in Civilizing Processes." *Theory, Culture and Society* 3, no. 2:1–18.

———. 1987. "Developments in Behavioural Codes between the Sexes: Formalization of Informalization in the Netherlands, 1930–85." *Theory, Culture and Society,* 4, nos. 2–3:405–27.

Wyckoff, E. 1997. *DRY DRUNK: The Culture of Tobacco in 17th- and 18th-Century Europe.* <http://www.nypl.org/research/chss/spe/art/print/exhibits/drydrunk/intro.htm>. The New York Public Library.

Young Britons League. 1919. *A1 or C3.* London: Young Britons League Against Tobacco.

Index